AMERICAN EXCEPTIONALISM

American Exceptionalism

DEBORAH L. MADSEN

University Press of Mississippi
Jackson

To Stephen A. Fender
mentor and friend

Edinburgh University Press
22 George Square, Edinburgh

Published in the United States of America by
University Press of Mississippi, 1998

Typeset in Monotype Fournier by
Carnegie Publishing, Lancaster, and
printed and bound in Great Britain
by the Cromwell Press Ltd, Trowbridge, Wilts

ISBN 1-57806-108-3

Contents

v

List of Illustrations

Figures

Acknowledgements

This work was funded in part by the award of an Arts Faculty Research Grant by the University of Leicester, for which I am grateful. Much of the research I completed as a Research Associate of the American Antiquarian Society. It is a pleasure to acknowledge the generosity of the Society for making available to me the resources of their library and the expertise of the staff during the period of my research associateship – and after. I wish especially to thank Joanne Chaison and Caroline Sloat for their practical assistance and for their continuing interest in this project. Alan Degutis gave me invaluable computing support, including the construction of bespoke databases, which was certainly above and beyond the call of his duty. Fellow researchers, Neal Salisbury of Smith College, and Barry O'Connell of Amherst College, permitted me unashamedly to pick their brains and in the process enormously enriched my understanding of colonial Indian–White relations. John Krafft of Miami University, Ohio, has been unstinting in his support of my work; Stephen Fender of the University of Sussex, to whom this book is gratefully dedicated, has been my mentor and guide.

Like everything else, this work would not be possible without the help of my husband Mark and our daughters, Selene and Dana.

Introduction

This book provides an accessible yet comprehensive historical account of one of the most important concepts underlying modern theories of American cultural identity – exceptionalism. From the Tudor roots of exceptionalist rhetoric, this book traces the contribution of exceptionalism to the evolution of the United States of America as an ideological and geographical entity. Due attention is paid to the responses of key ethnic groups, specifically native Americans and Chicanos, who engaged with exceptionalist rhetoric in order to challenge and subvert the exceptionalist attack on ethnic cultures. In the twentieth century exceptionalism continues to inform vital aspects of American culture – from the Western, to the post-modern critique of American super-power, representations of the Vietnam conflict, and Toni Morrison's rewriting of the narrative of American history. My intention is to explain the historical context of such contemporary uses of exceptionalism in a form comprehensible to the student, non-specialist scholar and civilian. The thematic scope takes in the cultures of the Puritan and nationalist periods, native American and Chicano cultures, the nineteenth-century American Renaissance, representations of westward expansion in art, films and fiction, aspects of post-modernism (specifically the work of Thomas Pynchon, Toni Morrison and Larry McMurtry) and representations of the Vietnam conflict in fiction and film.

My argument is that American exceptionalism permeates every period of American history and is the single most powerful agent in a series of arguments that have been fought down the centuries concerning the identity of America and Americans. Though the arguments themselves change over time, the basic assumptions and terms of reference do not change, and it is the assumptions that are derived in important ways from the exceptionalist logic taken to the New World by the first Puritan migrants. Exceptionalism describes the perception of Massachusetts Bay colonists that as Puritans they were charged with a special spiritual and political destiny: to create in the New World a church and a society that would provide the model for all the nations of Europe as they struggled to reform themselves (a redeemer nation). In this view, the New World is the last and best chance offered by God to a fallen humanity that has only to look to His exceptional new church for redemption. Thus, America and Americans are special, exceptional, because they are charged with saving the world from itself and, at the same time, America and Americans must sustain a high level of spiritual, political and moral commitment to this exceptional destiny – America must be as 'a city upon a hill' exposed to the eyes of the world. This concept has generated a self-consciousness and degree of introspection that is unique to American culture – and is perhaps exemplified by Hector St John de Crèvecoeur's meditation 'What is an American?', written during the revolutionary period, when issues of national identity were most urgent. Exceptionalism has also generated a significant body of work that counters the mythology of exceptionalism on a variety of grounds: spiritual (Roger Williams and Anne Hutchinson), racial or ethnic (native American and Chicano writers), moral (Nathaniel Hawthorne and Herman Melville), and political (nineteenth-century abolitionists and twentieth-century writers like Toni Morrison and Thomas Pynchon). It is evidence of the power of exceptionalist rhetoric that it has given rise to three centuries of counter-argument. And exceptionalism continues to inform the rhetoric of American politics: Bill Clinton may assert that America is not the world's police, but the ideology of exceptionalism has it otherwise!

The concept of American exceptionalism is used frequently to describe the development of American cultural identity from Puritan origins to the present. Exceptionalism informs the foundational work of such influential theorists of American culture as Perry Miller and Sacvan Bercovitch. I move to an account of exceptionalism in the theoretical writing of Miller and Bercovitch after describing the Tudor inheritance that was exported to Massachusetts and provided a powerful ideological bond between the Old World and the New. But before embarking on the historical dimension, an introduction to the vocabulary of exceptionalism is needed. As will become clear, exceptionalism is above all a way of talking about American history and culture, it is a form of interpretation with its own language and logic. The key terms that will be encountered in the following pages are: 'visible sainthood', 'the saving remnant', 'elect nation' or 'redeemer nation', 'federal covenant', and 'typology' (which also has its own vocabulary).

To take these terms in turn: 'visible sainthood' and 'the saving remnant' are both ways of referring to individuals who have confessed to the experience of grace; they claimed to have been touched by God in such a way that they had been assured of their ultimate salvation. New England Puritans believed, of course, in the doctrine of predestination and so the question of whether each individual belonged to the elect or the preterite consumed much time and attention. The search for signs of God's approval, and ultimate salvation, or signs of God's wrath, and ultimate damnation occupies Puritan diaries, histories and biographies. How to interpret these signs for accurate indications of one's spiritual condition occupies much of Puritan theology. Those who had had a positive experience of God's grace, who could convince the congregation of their authenticity by publicly describing that experience, these individuals were known as 'visible saints' belonging to the 'visible sainthood' of the elect.

The terms 'elect nation' or 'redeemer nation' referred to the collective experience of sainthood or salvation through God's grace. Puritans of the Massachusetts Bay colony believed that God intervened in human history to work the salvation not only of individuals but also entire communities or nations. This is part of the complex Tudor inheritance, discussed in detail below, that these Puritans took with them to New England from the Old World. The colony at Massachusetts Bay they believed had been singled out by God as an entire community of the saved or the elect; within the terms of salvation-history this community had been charged with a special destiny – to establish the conditions of a pure and uncorrupted church that would ensure the salvation of all Christians. The experiment in theocracy in New England, then, was aimed at creating a model church that could be copied by the imperfectly reformed churches of Europe. In the thinking of some Puritan theologians, this idea of ecclesiastical perfection combined with millennial expectations and gave rise to the theory that here in the New World the purified church would create the conditions for Christ's return to earth. The mission that inspired the Massachusetts Bay colonists was then charged with exceptional importance and urgency.

The 'federal covenant' describes the agreement or contract by which the Puritan community could expect collective salvation. Just as a redeemed individual exhibited the signs of sainthood through pious behaviour, serious demeanour, and the keeping of God's laws and those of the magistrates, so a redeemed community expected itself to be pious, well regulated and observant of divine and civil laws. Backsliding, by any member of the community, would place in jeopardy the salvation of the entire group. A sin committed by any one member of the congregation placed in threat the sainthood of all the others. Not surprisingly, this encouraged individuals to watch each other, as they watched themselves, for signs of backsliding or any tendency away from the serious purpose to which they had devoted themselves and to which God had committed them. The ministry encouraged this introspection that was both individual and collective – each person searching their own lives for signs of God's favour and each searching within the collective experience of the community for signs that they would all be saved. The power of the ministry itself was assured under such a system of assumptions. The ministry held the authority to interpret these experiential signs for their divine significance; it lay in the hands of the ministers to measure how far the community had progressed towards its great goal – and how far it had fallen from its great aspirations – just as they judged the spiritual condition of individual members of their congregations.

The favoured method by which the ministers accomplished their work of interpretation was the ancient practice of 'typology'. Since the Puritan intention was to return their church to the pure form of the earliest or 'primitive' church, it made sense for Puritan interpreters to use one of the most important of Christian interpretative methods. Typology was developed early in the Christian era when the writers of the New Testament encountered difficulty explaining the significance of the Old Testament. These writers wanted to keep the Old Testament, for its authority and power as the sacred book of Judaism, but Christ had brought a whole new spiritual dispensation, and so had made the Old Testament obsolete. How to make the Old Testament relevant within a new religion was the problem that the early Christians resolved with their use of typology. They adapted the prestigious Old Testament to the New Testament by arguing that the Old Testament promises the things that are delivered in the New Testament. By viewing both Testaments as the expression of a single God, the early Christians made the Testaments mutually dependent. This relationship between the two sacred books extended the typological view of history, for the Testaments each claimed to be a genuine account of real historical events. So the events that occurred in Old Testament times were seen as foreshadowing or promising the eventual redemption of humanity through Christ. Events and persons represented in the Old Testament retain their own literal and historical truth but take on an extra dimension of spiritual truth when they anticipate episodes and figures of the New Testament. For example, Adam is interpreted typologically as a 'type' (or promise) of Christ who is the 'antitype' (or fulfilment) who fulfils and completes the significance of Adam because through his sacrificial death Christ brings redemption and the expiation of Adam's sin. Similarly, the bread and wine used by the Old Testament prophet Melehizedek foreshadows the Last Supper. Jonah's three days spent in the whale's belly foreshadows the three days Christ spent making his descent into Hell to free the souls imprisoned there. So a complex pattern of promise and fulfilment is created by a typological reading of the two Testaments that make up the Christian Bible.

This use of typology raised a particular problem that proved especially troublesome for Protestants: if the Old Testament foreshadows the New Testament, what does the New Testament foreshadow? Catholicism had answered this question by claiming that Christ's actions in the New Testament foreshadow the work of redemption carried out by the church. But to Protestants, who had during the Reformation violently overthrown a church-dominated theology in favour of a theology focused upon the relationship between God and the individual, this answer was totally unacceptable. Puritans like John Bunyan in *The Pilgrim's Progress* argued that the New Testament fulfils the Old Testament promise of salvation by representing the operation of grace within the individual soul. So the new covenant between man and God which is represented by Christ was interpreted as applying to the faithful soul alone and not to the mediating power of the Church. So long as man will keep the faith he will be saved; this is the covenant promised in the Old Testament and represented by Christ's actions in the New Testament. This kind of reassurance was important to Puritans because, as I mentioned above, a fundamental tenet of their belief was the idea of predestination: the idea that since the Creation it has been decided who will be saved and who will be damned. The difficulty was to discover to which category you belonged and one way to do this was to search your soul for signs of God's grace working within you, and to cultivate your faith while pledging complete faith to God. To the Puritan imagination, God's influence was to be seen not only in the grand sweep of history but also in every detail and episode of life. The entire world is seen as symbolising God's power and design – all earthly things have not only a literal significance but also act as the symbol of divine and timeless things. It is for the faithful believer to discover the spiritual significance of everyday things and to interpret the significance of those things for the truth about his or her own spiritual destiny. A death, a storm, a poor harvest, an Indian attack – all things have a moral, as a test or a warning or a promise. Puritan journals, for instance, record the daily examination of events and their spiritual significances. Examples, such as the following, of this spiritual interrogation of events can be found throughout Governor Winthrop's journal:

> [July 5, 1632] At Watertown there was (in view of divers witnesses), a great combat between a mouse and a snake; and, after a long fight, the mouse prevailed and killed the snake. The pastor of Boston, Mr Wilson, a very sincere, holy man, hearing of it, gave this interpretation: That the snake was the devil; the mouse was a poor contemptible people, which God had brought hither, which should overcome Satan here, and dispossess him of his kingdom. Upon the same occasion, he told the governor, that, before he was resolved to come into this country, he dreamed he was here, and that he saw a church arise out of the earth, which grew up and became a marvelous goodly church.[1]

Reverend Wilson's interpretation extends the typological questioning of everyday events to include not only the progress of the individual soul towards salvation but the salvation of the entire community, under the terms of the federal covenant explained above. New England Puritans used typology as the prime means by which they could measure the success of their mission in the New World. They saw the Great Migration as inevitable, an event already determined by the structure of providential history. Puritan leaders such as John Winthrop were frequently described as fulfilling the promise of Moses, who in the Old Testament led his people out of bondage into the Promised Land. So Winthrop and William Bradford were described as leading their people out of the depravity of the Old World and into the freedom of salvation in the New World. By thus fulfilling the promise of both the Old Testament and the New, the colonists saw their achievement as bringing about the very end of history by establishing the conditions for Christ's return to earth, heralding the apocalypse. These apocalyptic hopes, and the typological method of understanding a divinely-directed history, the New England Puritans inherited from Puritan thinkers in the Old World. In some respects the most important element of the baggage taken by the colonists to Massachusetts was the practice of typology and the sense of being engaged upon a sacred mission which typology served.

Exceptionalism in the Old World and the New

After the reformation of the church in England much effort was devoted to rethinking and reinterpreting the history of the Anglican Church and its relation to the primitive church of the Apostles. Among the prime interpreters of the Tudor period was John Foxe (1517–77), whose *Acts and Monuments of the Church* (1559), known as the 'Book of Martyrs', became a kind of guide book for later attempts to reform the church even further (by those like the Puritan groups that finally removed to the New World).[2] The early impact of this work is indicated by the fact that Elizabethan parish churches were furnished with a Bible and a copy of Foxe's 'Book of Martyrs'. For those who wished to explain and justify the significance of the Settlement, the true origin of the English church was not, in fact, Rome but the East and the origin of the church in England is to be dated with the arrival in England of Joseph of Arimathea. So the English church is best seen as part of the primitive catholic church for which, as Foxe described, 'neither did the east and the west, not distance of place, divide the church', but due to the influence of the Papacy, 'this catholic unity did not long continue' (p. 168). Of course, Foxe uses the term 'catholic' to refer to the diversity of regional churches that gathered under the umbrella of the primitive church. It was the papacy, then, that falsely divided the original church and, by returning leadership of the English Church to England and granting Canterbury independence from Rome, the Settlement returns to that true original church structure. Rome was responsible for dividing the true church and then, exploiting the division, profited from it to become a fantastically wealthy and powerful political power. The self-aggrandisement of the Bishop of Rome and interference in matters of state were issues of repeated concern and offered apologists of the Settlement an opportunity to point out that, within the English church at least, the false separation of spiritual and temporal power had been overcome.

Elizabeth Tudor, the Protestant Empress, was identified as the culminating figure in a historical pattern devoted to setting right the condition of the church. Working through Providence, God had organised the sequence of human history so that Elizabeth reigned over a reformed and purified church. The Elizabethan Settlement is interpreted as the culmination of ecclesiastical history, a plan of history set out in the Bible but encoded in the typological imagery of the Book of Revelation. There, the flight of the woman clothed with the sun into the wilderness for a period of forty-two months before her return is interpreted by Foxe as the flight of the true catholic church which returns as the Church of England. The return of the church and the accession of Elizabeth are brought together in the image of the radiant woman and the identification of Elizabeth *with* the church is inevitable. As Frank Kermode explains, in the view of Puritan commentators,

> Elizabeth is *rarissima Phoenix, ultima Astraea,* the renewer of the Church and faithful true opponent of antichrist. She has undone the work of the wicked popes who usurped the emperor's power and rights; she inherits both Lucius' recognized position as God's vicar, and the imperial power of Constantine and Justinian. Antichrist, the murderous sorcerers of the see of Rome, stands finally exposed. The queen is the defender of the true church in an evil world. In a sense she *is* that Church.[3]

This interpretation of history, both temporal and divine, lends the Church of England antiquity, purity and also gives the Queen a claim to imperial power over the bishops. She rules by divine right and by the authority of divine Providence that placed her at the culminating point of ecclesiastical history. According to Puritan historiography, it is through Providence that God intervenes on behalf of the church of the elect, which also functions as an agent of God's will as He works out in history His objectives of salvation. History is conceived as an epic conflict between Christ and Antichrist or, in Tudor times, between the church of the elect and the Papacy. The true significance of history can be discerned by members of the elect, who read the Bible as an inspired record of salvation-history capable of indicating the extent of God's intervention in past and present history. Of course, the Bible then becomes a guarantee that the historical future will favour the church of the elect. During the Elizabethan period, the belief that England was God's elect nation and Elizabeth His appointed servant to transform the nation into a new Israel was popularly held, in part because of the widespread influence of Foxe's interpretation of the progress of providential history in his time. Thus, Foxe contributed significantly to the apocalyptic nationalism of the seventeenth century, a kind of nationalistic ideology that crucially shaped the belief system of the Puritan theology that was exported to Massachusetts with the Great Migration. New England Puritanism cannot be viewed in isolation and especially not in isolation from the Tudor inheritance that so powerfully bound Old World ideologies to the New. The colonists of the Massachusetts settlements took with them a complex baggage of historical and theological assumptions and from them developed a distinctive and long-lasting narrative of American identity.

Exceptionalism and American Studies

In a series of landmark studies, the historian Perry Miller defined the direction of American Studies for the later twentieth century. *The New England Mind: The Seventeenth Century* (1939), *The New England Mind: From Colony to Province* (1953) and *Errand into the Wilderness* (1964) renewed interest in the Puritan culture of early New England by placing the achievement of the Massachusetts Bay settlers within the context of the history of Christian thought generally and the history of the European Reformation specifically. But what made Miller's work so compelling and so influential was his attempt to describe the unique qualities of American Puritanism and the long-term impact of these qualities upon the developing nation. Miller traced the influence of Puritan styles of expression and modes of thought upon the classic literary work of Emerson, especially, but also Hawthorne, Melville, Whitman – the major writers of the nineteenth-century 'American Renaissance'. And what Miller sought to show in his monumental studies was the prescriptive force of exceptionalism as the ideology that motivated the creation of America as the intellectual entity with which we are now familiar.

In *The New England Mind: The Seventeenth Century*, Miller provides a comprehensive account of all aspects of the theology that was developed in colonial New England in the seventeenth century. He begins with religion and learning, and describes the 'Augustinian strain' of Puritan piety. In this way, he uncovers the deep-rootedness of Puritanism within Christian theology and renders American Puritanism a serious subject for theological study. He goes on to consider how this theology is translated into ecclesiastical practice, into a fully developed cosmology and theory of knowledge, into a distinctive style of rhetorical expression, and into a kind of sociological theory that takes account of the idea of covenants: the covenant of grace between God and the individual soul that supersedes the catholic covenant of works, the social covenant between rulers and their subjects, the covenant of redemption between God and Christ and the church covenant between the ministry and the community. However, it is in the companion volume, *The New England Mind: From Colony to Province*, that Miller focuses upon the rhetoric of Puritan expression and it is this focus that distinguishes his particular approach. By identifying the historical, intellectual, theological and social motivations of the rhetoric, Miller is able to shift the centre of interest away from the purely religious towards a cultural approach to American Puritanism. This is Miller's importance for American Studies: the provision of a methodological approach that allows all aspects of the culture to inform an interpretation of colonial Puritan writings. It is also in this book that Miller turns to the issue of American cultural identity, nascent in Puritan writings but even at such an early stage demonstrating a clear commitment to the ideology of exceptionalism. Miller presents the history of the seventeenth century in Massachusetts within a narrative framework provided by exceptionalism.

The argument begins with the notion of 'declension'. This term is used to refer to a falling away from the high principles and ambitions of the Puritan 'errand'. This term was popularised by Miller's 1952 essay 'Errand into the Wilderness', where he argues that the Puritan colonists did not so much flee persecution in England as they went to Massachusetts in order to work out the complete reformation of the church begun but not completed in England and Europe, for the reason that the reformers had no model as their guide. It was this model that the Puritan colonists intended to provide. So New England would be exemplary, God would bless the new land and the newly perfected church, and the temporary colonials would be free to return to govern the perfectly reformed church in England. According to John Winthrop, the colonists were charged with the responsibility of proving the ways of God to man, no less. They would vindicate the ideals of the European Reformation so that ultimately all the churches of Europe would look to New England for the model of church government. The disappointment and sense of betrayal experienced in New England upon Cromwell's toleration and later the restoration of the monarchy gave rise to tremendous public soul-searching; the 'errand' was reinterpreted as a mission sufficient in itself without the status of a model or guide. But the search for an explanation of the New England colony itself produced a literature of self-condemnation, focused upon the consequences of failing to meet the demands of the errand with which God had charged them. Declension was a powerfully negative term here, and within the context of the federal covenant, for it referred to the failure of the community to live up to the standards required for national salvation. The signs of declension and so of God's wrath would be war, famine, disease, just as the signs of God's grace would be prosperity and plenty. The federal covenant was always at risk from the disobedience of the community: if the community were to become depraved then it could call down upon itself its own destruction at God's hand and, of course, the cancelling of the covenant. Puritans looked to biblical precedent such as the destruction of Sodom and to more contemporary examples of colonial settlements that failed to survive. The risk of catastrophic failure was quite real and ever present. Ministers warned their congregations of the dangers of declension through a developing tradition of fast-day and election-day sermons which were devoted to a consideration of recent afflictions suffered by the community.

The 'jeremiad', as it developed through the second generation, became a conventional form in which the terms, conditions and duties of the covenant were outlined and the success or failure of the community in keeping to the covenant was measured. Frequently an exhortation to renew faith and dedication to the Puritan mission, the jeremiad became increasingly important within a society facing challenges from all sides. The Indian Wars of the later seventeenth century, in particular, were used by ministers like Increase and Cotton Mather to warn the community of the terrible punishments that awaited all those who failed to contribute to realising God's grand plan for New England. The genre of captivity narratives was, in part, engineered by the Mathers to dramatise the horrors of life away from the protection of the settlement and the spiritual protection of the ministry. The expansion of the settlements into areas that had been wilderness was inevitable as the colonial population expanded but the influx of non-Puritans and the expansion of trade and secular pursuits placed the spiritual mission of the Massachusetts Bay colony under particular pressures. Miller identifies the development of the 'Protestant ethic' as symptomatic of these secular pressures and the compromise of the 'Half-Way Covenant' as symptomatic of the ministry's attempts to accommodate change without surrendering the exceptional destiny of their congregation.

The Half-Way Covenant was designed to bolster a declining church membership by allowing the children of church members to be declared themselves members, subject to the future experience of God's grace. These 'half-way' members were not 'visible saints' because they had not the personal experience of God's intervention in their lives but they could reasonably expect that such an experience would be theirs by reason of the piety of their parents. Restrictions were placed upon half-way membership: these members could not participate in the Eucharist, for example, and they would have to profess publicly their assent to the covenant before becoming full members. The Half-Way Covenant was immensely controversial and to some it represented an unacceptable dilution of the intensity of the New England mission. When James II sought to consolidate the colonies against France in 1686, he appointed Sir Edmund Andros as governor of the Dominion of New England. Andros's autocratic style was deeply resented by New Englanders and when news reached Boston that James had been deposed, they were quick to imprison the governor and send him back to England. However, before this 'Glorious Revolution' of 1689 and during the repression of the Andros regime, the New England churches were concerned to preserve what civil liberties they had and to win back the freedoms represented by the old charter. Increased church membership and a vital church culture were of the utmost importance in these terms. The jeremiad offered a way of representing the tyranny of Andros as a punishment for failing to keep the terms of the federal covenant and so the jeremiad was an important strategy for motivating individuals to renew their faith and their dedication to the church, with the hope that the special destiny of New England would still be theirs.

It is in this context that Miller deals with the Salem witchcraft hysteria. In 1692, he claims, witchcraft was peripheral to the real concerns of the colony, which were political and social and were based on the declining base of church membership. In order to survive the effects of the Half-Way Covenant and the new charter, the church needed to produce a generation of pious children, to further the exceptional mission upon which their parents and grandparents had embarked. At the end of the seventeenth century, according to Miller, New England society was fragmented, split apart by the effects of trade, smallpox, anti-ministerial sentiment, war on the frontier. But by the close of the seventeenth century, what had been established was a peculiar way of thinking about the culture of New England as a beacon of hope for the persecuted (but only persecuted fellow-Puritans), as a model society, as God's New Israel or chosen people selected for an exceptional destiny that will be difficult and painful but also glorious and the envy of all other nations.

Sacvan Bercovitch is the prime inheritor of Perry Miller's interpretation of Puritan culture. Bercovitch extends into the modern period Miller's questioning of the significance of Puritan self-images. *The Puritan Origins of the American Self* (1975) begins Bercovitch's inquiry into the cultural mechanisms by which America, as a nation of migrants, produces 'Americans': citizens who think of themselves as belonging to a national mythology, as possessing distinctive national characteristics, and as part of a national unity rather than a collection of isolated individuals. In other words, Bercovitch asks what fires the American melting pot? His answer revolves around the federal covenant described by Miller and the power of historical reinterpretations of that concept at specific historical moments. To this he adds the capacity for self-creation that Puritan theology attributes to believers. Bercovitch describes the imperative under which Puritan believers laboured as they sought to identify themselves and the progress of their souls towards salvation with the promises and models represented in the Bible. In Bercovitch's estimation, the importance of typology for individual believers lay in its power to create identifications across time and so permit individual Puritans to identify with key events in God's providential history. Only after one has assumed the image of the divine can an individual read correctly the significance of scripture, of history, of his or her own life experiences. The exceptional destiny of America is to transform itself into a model nation; the correspondingly exceptional destiny of Americans is also self-transformation. In the chapter entitled 'The Myth of America' Bercovitch discusses how colonial attitudes and methods of interpretation were inherited by the nineteenth century, in ways that are of relevance for the twentieth century.[4] He argues that colonial interpretation obscured the difference between secular and sacred selfhood, confusing the two and fusing them in a spiritualised conception of national identity and what it means to be an American citizen. For a thinker like Ralph Waldo Emerson, who was profoundly influenced by the Puritan legacy, the image of the New World lends the perceiver a splendour that arises from the errand upon which all Americans are engaged; but perceivers must prove themselves by transforming themselves in the image of the New World. America and Americans are thus involved in a complex interplay of national and personal identity-formation. The concept of 'Americanus', from the Mathers to Emerson, is a replacement for rather than an alternative to the actual course of events in American history, according to Bercovitch. Events are transformed in the course of interpretation into the providential signs of nationalism. The history of America is a history of redemption – of individuals as well as of the nation itself – and this commitment to America as an exceptional nation is reflected in the way the lives of public leaders have been written as continuing the spiritual biography of America, as the nation and its people work towards the salvation of all humankind.

The work of Perry Miller and Sacvan Bercovitch perpetuates the exceptionalist mythology of America by promoting the idea that America has a coherent national identity and that a consensus concerning the nature of American national identity does reign. Consequently, Miller and Bercovitch are among the most important theorists of American Studies, the discipline devoted to the understanding of American culture. The object of study is constructed for us, as Americanists, by scholars like Miller and Bercovitch and they are aided by centuries of self-conscious argument and meditation on the part of Americans about the character of the society they are creating. From the colonial period, through the Revolution, again during the upheavals of the Civil War and into the twentieth century, Americans have agonised over what they are and where they are headed. Exceptionalism is the ideology to which such thoughts most frequently return; why this should be is explained in the pages that follow.

Notes

1. John Winthrop, *The Journal of John Winthrop*, in Nina Baym, *et al.* (eds), *The Norton Anthology of American Literature*, 4th edn (New York and London: W.W. Norton & Co., 1994), vol. 1, p. 181.

2. John Foxe, *Acts and Monuments of the Church*, ed. M. H. Seymour (1838). Originally published as *Commentarii Rerum in Ecclesia Gestarum, maximarumque, per totam Europam, persecutionum, a Vuicleui temporibus ad hac usque aetatem descriptio. Liber primus.* Strassburgh, 1554 and expanded as *Rerum in Ecclesia Gestarum quae postremis et periculosis his temporibus euenerunt, maximarumque; per Europam persecutionum, ac Sanctorum Dei Martyrum, caeterarumque; rerumque; rerum si quae insigniorus exempli sint, digesti per Regna et nationes Commentarij. Pars Prima.* Basel, 1559. Translated as *Actes and Monuments of these latter and perillous dayes, touching matters of the Church, wherein ar comprehended and described the great persecutions and horrible troubles … Gathered and collected according to the true copies and wrytinges*

certificatorie, as wel of the parties them selues that suffered, as also out of the Bishops Registers, which wer the doers therof. London, 1563. A second English edition, in two volumes, appeared in London in 1570. See William Haller, 'John Foxe and the Puritan Revolution', in Richard F. Jones (ed.), *The Seventeenth Century: Studies in the History of English Thought and Literature from Bacon to Pope* (Stanford, CA: Stanford University Press, 1951), and V. Norskov Olsen, *John Foxe and the Elizabethan Church* (Berkeley, Los Angeles and London: University of California Press, 1973).

3. Frank Kermode, *Shakespeare, Spenser, Donne: Renaissance Essays* (London: Routledge & Kegan Paul, 1971), p. 41.

4. Sacvan Bercovitch, *The Puritan Origins of the American Self* (New Haven and London: Yale University Press, 1975), pp. 148–78. Other relevant titles are: Sacvan Bercovitch, *The American Jeremiad* (Madison and London: University of Wisconsin Press, 1978), Sacvan Bercovitch (ed.), *The American Puritan Imagination: Essays in Revaluation* (Cambridge: Cambridge University Press, 1974), Sacvan Bercovitch (ed.), *Reconstructing American Literary History*, Harvard English Studies 13 (Cambridge, MA and London: Harvard University Press, 1986), Sacvan Bercovitch (ed.), *Typology and Early American Literature* (Amherst: University of Massachusetts Press, 1972), Sacvan Bercovitch and Myra Jehlen (eds), *Ideology and Classic American Literature* (Cambridge: Cambridge University Press, 1986).

CHAPTER I

Origins: Exceptionalism and American Cultural Identity

In this chapter, the mythology of the redeemer nation is explained with reference to seventeenth-century Puritan sermons, poetry and prose. Key writers here are William Bradford, John Cotton, John Winthrop, Roger Williams, Samuel Danforth, Michael Wigglesworth, Mary Rowlandson and the Mathers. Benjamin Franklin's reinterpretation of the nation's exceptional destiny is used to focus a discussion of the role of exceptionalism in the rhetoric of the revolutionary period.

Immigration

There is a key difference between the Puritan colonies at Boston and at Plymouth in terms of their mission in the New World. Although both colonies were settled by members of the Congregationalist church, John Winthrop and the colonists of the Massachusetts Bay Company were 'non-Separating' Congregationalists whilst William Bradford and the settlers at Plymouth were 'Separating' Congregationalists. What this meant was that the Separatists intended to make a permanent and lasting colony in the New World rather than a temporary refuge from the difficulties and persecutions they had endured in Europe. Bradford had no intention of developing a perfectly reformed church, to be a model to the imperfectly reformed churches of England. And so, when members of the Plymouth church make reference to Old Testament precedent in describing aspects of their experience in the New World, this reference is quite different in tone to that used by the Massachusetts colonists, who represented themselves as necessarily repeating the sacred history of the Israelites. In his history *Of Plymouth Plantation*, Bradford describes their safe arrival at Cape Cod only to be confronted by an all-encompassing wilderness:

16

Neither could they, as it were, go up to the top of Pisgah [the peak from which Moses saw Canaan] to view from this wilderness a more goodly country to feed their hopes; for which way soever they turned their eyes (save upward to the heavens) they could have little solace or content in respect of any outward objects.[1]

Bradford certainly believed that God watched over the Plymouth settlers and that God motivated the migration but he did not present the settlement as a necessary stage in salvation-history, nor did he extrapolate from scripture a future destiny for the colony. Robert Cushman, one of the founders of Plymouth, gives extensive reasons for the fundamental differences between the removal of the Jews, described in the Bible, and seventeenth-century New World migration. First, he argues, the means by which men are called upon to migrate are very different: in biblical times, God summoned men by dreams, visions, predictions to travel from country to country and town to town according to the divine will but now the ordinary examples of scripture, 'reasonable and rightly understood and applied' call and direct the migrants.[2] More significantly from the point of view of exceptionalism, Cushman argues that New England is fundamentally unlike Canaan, the promised land given by God to the Jews. Canaan was

legally holy and appropriated unto a holy people, the seed of Abraham, in which they dwelt securely, and had their days prolonged, it being by an immediate voice said, that he (the Lord) gave it them as a land of rest after their weary travels, and a type of eternal rest in heaven.[3]

So Cushman identifies the fulfilment of the biblical promise represented by the Israelites as the spiritual reward of heavenly rest after death, not as the settlement of New England. Where the non-Separatists identified themselves as latter-day Israelites occupying the New Canaan by divine decree, Separatists argued that the biblical promises of the Old and New Testaments can only, at this stage in the world's history, be fulfilled on a purely spiritual plane; the Bible can no longer be used to predict the future of human history. Cushman specifically denies any likeness between New England and Canaan. He claims that there is no longer any country at all that approaches the nature of Canaan: 'there is no land of that sanctimony, no land so appropriated, none typical; much less any that can be said to be given of God to any nation, as was Canaan'.[4]

The non-Separating Congregationalists of Boston argued that their colony was absolutely typical of Canaan and had been given to them by God, as promised in scripture, for the purpose of constructing a purified church. This purpose is clearly omitted from Cushman's list of reasons that may legitimately lead men to migrate to New England: they may choose to live where they can do good for themselves and others; they may engage in the 'conversion of the heathen'; or they may put to profitable use land that is lying unused. He does not set out an exceptional destiny as the beacon of hope in a world of corruption; he does not envision the New World colonies as 'a city upon a hill' – the famous phrase used by John Winthrop to describe the glorious mission upon which his company set out in 1630.

It was in 'A Modell of Christian Charity', the sermon Winthrop delivered on board the *Arbella*, the flagship of the Winthrop fleet, that he claimed 'wee shall be as a Citty upon a Hill' when describing the special destiny awaiting the community of saints as they voyaged to Massachusetts.[5] Winthrop uses the occasion to exhort his fellow-colonists to knit together into a social unity that will reflect and support their spiritual unity. He argues that social relations are regulated by the law of nature and the law of grace; that is, moral law which regulates nature in its innocent state and the law of the gospel or grace which is given only to those in a regenerate state. According to the law of grace, all true Christians are of one body in Christ so if one member suffers, all suffer and if one is honoured then all rejoice. The concept of mutual dependence was very important to the Massachusetts Bay Puritans, for the federal covenant would work only so long as all members of the community voluntarily kept their faith and helped others to preserve their faith. The mission, the errand into the wilderness, required a degree of unity that was social as well as spiritual, if the collective salvation of the community was to be achieved.

The seriousness of the mission with which they had been charged by God was the counter-argument used by Puritan leaders like Winthrop when they were accused (as they were) of deserting England at the very time when they were needed most urgently. 'Reasons to Be Considered for ... the Intended Plantation in New England' (1629) is Winthrop's consideration, on the very eve of his departure, of the view of the Great Migration as a desertion of the motherland, taking away the best people at a time when they are needed to counter England's severe moral deterioration. Here, Winthrop betrays a sense of guilt which he is carrying to the New World, as evidenced by the effort he took to clear the collective conscience of the immigrants for the impending voyage. In particular, he takes pains to repudiate the notion that God identifies His church with a specific place or nation: those who go 'are likely to do more good there than here, and since Christ's time the church is to be considered as universal, without distinction of countries, so as he who doeth good in any one place, serves the church in all places.'[6] Further, he suggests that their departure will not cause but in fact foreshadows divine judgement and may prompt others to reform themselves in the effort to prevent such a judgement: 'It will be a great wrong to our church to take away the good people and we shall lay it the more open to the judgement feared.'[7] But he does not depart from the conviction that the only way forward for the church in England is to await the construction of a model church, a completely reformed church in New England. In his journal Winthrop repeats the original motivation for migration: 'to advance the kingdom of our Lord Jesus Christ, and to enjoy the liberties of the gospel in purity with peace'.[8] However, he does change his views on the importance of geographical location. In May 1640 Winthrop became aware of reports that English migrants were being diverted from New England to the West Indies and so wrote to the responsible minister in Westminster, Lord Say, about the report 'and therein showed his lordship, how evident it was, that God had chosen this country to plant his people in, and therefore how displeasing it would be to the Lord, and dangerous to himself, to hinder this work'.[9] The very suggestion that New England might be compared with, or surpassed by, other British colonies as the foremost New World destination contradicted the self-image created by the Boston clergy of the Massachusetts Bay colony as 'a special people, an only people – none like thee in all the earth', as Peter Bulkeley put it in his sermon 'The Gospel-Covenant' (circa 1639–40).[10]

In this sermon, Bulkeley sets out Winthrop's ambitions for the colony but in more explicit terms and using the vocabulary of exceptionalism:

> And as for ourselves here, the people of New England, we should in a special manner labor to shine forth in holiness above other people; we have that plenty and abundance of ordinances and means of grace, as few people enjoy the like. We are as a city set upon an hill, in the open view of all the earth; the eyes of the world are upon us because we profess ourselves to be a people in covenant with God, and

therefore not only the Lord our God, with whom we have made
covenant, but heaven and earth, angels and men, that are witnesses
of our profession, will cry shame upon us, if we walk contrary to the
covenant which we have professed and promised to walk in.[11]

Bulkeley expresses here the two sides of the exceptionalist coin: the
glory that will be theirs, if the community of saints keeps to the terms
of the covenant, creates a purified and perfectly reformed church to be
the world's model, and establishes the conditions for the realisation of
millennial hopes. Alternatively, if they should fail then their failure will
be as humiliating as their glory would have been, in equal measure.
The world's eyes are upon them and if they should betray the covenant
then all the world will know and scorn them for their excess of ambition
and pride.

The risks then were very great for those early settlers, who faced
enormous psychological and emotional challenges as well as the physical
challenge of survival and, on top of all this, the challenge to live up to
the hopes of the entire Christian world. In his paean to New England
and the grand enterprise of the Congregationalist settlers there, 'Upon
the First Sight of New England' (1638), Thomas Tillam addresses precisely these challenges:

> Hayle holy-land wherin our holy lord
> Hath planted his most true and holy word
> Hayle happye people who have dispossest
> Your selves of friends, and meanes, to find some rest
> For your poor wearied soules, opprest of late
> For Jesus-sake, with Envye, spight, and hate
> To yow that blessed promise truly's given
> Of sure reward, which you'l receive in heaven
> Methinks I heare the Lambe of God thus speake
> Come my deare little flocke, who for my sake
> Have lefte your Country; free from all anoye
> Heare I'le bee with you, heare you shall Injoye
> My sabbaths, sacraments, my ministrye
> And ordinances in their puritye
> But yet beware of Sathans wylye baites
> Hee lurkes amongs yow, Cunningly hee waites
> To Catch yow from mee; live not then secure
> But fight 'gainst sinne, and let your lives be pure

Prepare to heare your sentence thus expressed
Come yee my servants of my father Blessed.[12]

The assurance that Tillam expresses early in the poem, that salvation
is assured for these the 'visible saints' of New England and the achievement of their model church-society is assured, gives way to a note of
foreboding at the conclusion. Precisely the high ideals and enthusiasm
of the saints attracts the attentions of Satan, who will win a great victory
if he is able to disrupt the work of this exceptional community. Both
God and Satan watch over the progress of the colony and through the
Boston church prepare to engage in battle. This poem was published
shortly after the Antinomian Controversy (1636) and so deliberately
reminds listeners of the seriousness and precariousness of their mission
at a time when the purity of the errand appeared to be under threat
from within.

The Antinomian Controversy

In the mid-1630s the Massachusetts Bay clergy faced two powerful
threats to their authority and prestige, and to the developing ideology
of exceptionalism that lent legitimacy and divine purpose to their leadership. Anne Hutchinson was the leader of a heretical movement that
came to be known as the Antinomians; Roger Williams engaged in
extensive dispute with the Bay clergy over such issues as religious
toleration, the occupation of Indian lands and the exceptionalist mission
of the colonists in New England. Both Hutchinson and Williams were
exiled for their heretical beliefs but not before they had given expression
to a sentiment of dissent that was to characterise the debate over New
England's identity and destiny.

The ideology of exceptionalism relied absolutely upon the interpretative authority wielded by the ministers, whose job it was to interpret
signs of God's favour or wrath. The ministry was charged with measur-
ing the progress made towards establishing the 'Citty upon an hill' that
Winthrop foresaw as the great achievement of the colonised New
World. And if progress was not being made, then the clergy was
required to set the community back on course. In this way, exceptionalism lent the ministry a great deal of power to intervene in all areas of
colonial life. Mrs Hutchinson's great error was to challenge the necessity

of the ministry as an interpretative power and spiritual guide. She argued that Christ would intervene directly in the life of the redeemed individual, communicating directly all that would be necessary for salvation. Mrs Hutchinson claimed to have been touched directly by the Holy Ghost and argued that the interpretations of biblical, natural and historical signs offered by the ministers were superfluous to one such as herself who received knowledge of spiritual matters directly from God. According to her, God did not need to deal in obscure signs and portents when He could through visitations, prophetic dreams and visions communicate directly with the redeemed soul. Anne Hutchinson was not concerned with the future development of the church in New England, nor was she concerned with the millennial expectations of those engaged in purifying the colonial church. Her interest was in the relationship between the redeemed soul and God, and how one might know whether one was in fact redeemed.

This challenge to the power and prestige of the clergy broadly coincided with the attacks made by Roger Williams upon the activities of the Congregationalist clergy in Boston. Both Williams and Hutchinson, separately, accused the Boston clergy of establishing a 'state religion' wherein the ministers had the power to compel belief, to prescribe behaviour and to write the history of the colony in their own terms and to serve their own interests. Both Williams and Hutchinson challenged the connection between the temporal and spiritual orders that was fundamental to exceptionalist ideology and the covenant theology it supported. Both insisted that only Christ, working upon the soul of individuals, not human institutions, had the power to re-create a purified church.

Roger Williams was emphatic in his insistence upon the complete separation of the church and the state, the historical and the eternal realms, the visible church and the invisible church of the elect. Thus, Williams rejected the fundamental tenet of exceptionalist thinking: that God's work of salvation is worked out by, and completely permeates, everyday life. According to Williams, God's will is unknowable; it does not operate through systems of signs and promises and parallelisms. Only through Christ's personal intervention and a second disruption of history could the Kingdom of God be brought to earth. Human efforts through the progressive unfolding of history are not sufficient, though Williams argues strenuously that it is through the salvation of individuals and not through collective or institutional salvation that the work of redemption will be completed. In these opinions, Williams contradicted the fundamental principles of the Massachusetts Bay mission. Where the Bay ministry believed in collective salvation through the federal covenant, Williams insisted that each individual must be redeemed individually; where the ministry was committed to a view of history as leading inexorably towards collective salvation, Williams adhered to an apocalyptic view of salvation history; where the Bay clergy insisted that the errand into the wilderness of New England was foretold or promised in scripture, Williams denied that any earthly or historical significance was to be found in the biblical symbolism and argued instead that only spiritual meanings are to be found in the Bible. If the Bible refers to any future event, it must be an event that occurs in heaven and is purely of a divine nature. The Old Testament promised events that came to pass in the New Testament; the New Testament does not repeat that same foretelling of future historical events but instead refers to events in the purely spiritual realm of heaven. Williams is especially scornful of the colonists' conception of themselves as engaged upon a divinely ordained mission and of Old and New England as the counterparts to nations described in the Bible. Williams argues that Christianity is basically unlike ancient Judaism because it cannot be identified with a particular geographical location. In his response to a letter published by John Cotton, perhaps the prime architect of New England exceptionalism, Williams asks sarcastically which country Mr Cotton would designate as Babylon or Egypt or Sodom – all corrupt biblical nations in which souls are kept in bondage to sin. 'Doth he count the very land of *England* literally *Babel*, and so consequently *Ægypt* and *Sodome*, *Revel.* 11.8 and the land of new England, *Judea*, *Canaan?*' Williams asks.[13] Williams was banished for his heretical views, not only for his powerful attack on the exceptionalist mythology of the Bay colony but also for his commitment to religious toleration and his insistence that the British monarchy had no authority to grant Indian lands to the Massachusetts Bay Company.

It was John Cotton who engaged extensively with Williams, countering his heretical arguments with what became the orthodox interpretation of New England Congregationalism. In 1630 Cotton had preached 'God's Promise to His Plantations', at Southampton, before the Winthrop fleet. He quotes 11 Samuel 7:10, 'Moreover I will appoint a place for my people Israel, and I will plant them, that they may dwell in a place of their own, and move no more' in order to point out the uniqueness of the Bay colony. God provides a place for all nations, Cotton explains, but to His chosen people He gives the land by promise: 'others take the land by his providence, but God's people take the land by promise: and therefore the land of Canaan is called a land of promise. Which they discern, first, by discerning themselves to be in Christ, in whom all the promises are yea, and amen'.[14] In this view, the colonists have identified themselves as a nation within Christ – as the visible sainthood redeemed by Christ – and as a spiritual nation they have been led to found a geographical nation in the New World. Cotton goes on to explain the ways according to which one is to know whether God has appointed one to a particular place and by what right one may remove to that place. Williams's counter-argument was that the Puritan colonists were no more exempt from social constraints and the force of nature than were any other group of people and certainly the divine errand which they claimed did not authorise them to appropriate the lands already occupied by the native inhabitants of New England. For Williams, the Massachusetts claim to an exceptional spiritual destiny was at odds with its claim to a universal purpose: the colonists of the Winthrop fleet could not, in Williams's estimation, pursue a specific typological parallel with the ancient Israelites and also, at the same time, fulfil a universalised purpose of furthering the redemption of all Christianity. According to Williams, the Puritans could not have it both ways. The developing orthodoxy of the Massachusetts Bay colony required that the global significance of the errand be fulfilled even as the colonists struggled towards their divine destiny. What they must achieve had been promised in the typological rhetoric of scripture and, the clergy reminded them, the eyes of the world were upon this exceptional endeavour.

Declension and the Rhetoric of the Jeremiad

Not only the eyes of the world were upon the colonists as they struggled to fulfil their destiny. Much more importantly, God was ever-watchful of His people's successes and failures, which He would reward or punish. This sense of God's watchful presence gave rise to a kind of typological interpretation called 'punitive typology', which sought signs of God's favour or, increasingly throughout the seventeenth century, signs of His anger as His people failed to keep to the high purpose of their errand. Robert Middlekauff notes in his history of the Mather family that the first use of the term 'errand' to describe the peculiarity of New England history was made by the second generation of colonists and not by the original migrants, for whom phrases like 'the saving remnant' and 'the Kingdom of Light' referred to all godly people rather than exclusively describing the New England churches.[15] A similar shift is noted above in relation to John Winthrop, who, in 1629 argued that the geographical location of the church was irrelevant but in 1640 argued strenuously for the uniqueness of the church that had been established (by God's design) in New England. This is not surprising when one recalls that the high degree of motivation experienced by the generation that left their homes in England to travel to the wilderness of Massachusetts was unlikely to be shared by their offspring, who never themselves experienced religious persecution or the trauma of migration. The second and third colonial generations were, then, judged as lacking the conviction and enthusiasm of the founders and correspondingly the rhetoric of exceptionalism grew darker and more threatening.

John Cotton in a sermon of 1641, 'Gods Mercie Mixed with his Justice or His Peoples Deliverance in Times of Danger', points to the ways in which God seeks to deliver His people into salvation.[16] He may knock upon the door of the soul (the heart) with 'the hammer of his word' (Jer. 23:29), or with the effect of His judgements (Acts 16:26), or with the work of the holy spirit upon the conscience. In each case God will seek to awaken the soul to its peril and renew the faith that leads to salvation. Afflictions, then, can function as God's reminder to renew faith and to renew commitment to the covenant. Cotton argues that fellowship with Christ in suffering is an assurance of ultimate deliverance from affliction. God punished His chosen people because they are so special to Him and because they have been entrusted with a unique spiritual destiny. Affliction can then be seen as a sign of God's ultimate favour but also of His immediate wrath; suffering is a sign that changes must be made to renew personal and collective faith in the terms of the covenant. Using the figure of Noah's Ark, Cotton claims: 'All those that are wrapt up in the Covenant of Gods grace and peace, all the waters of affliction doe but lift them up higher, farre above the highest mountaines of the Earth.'[17] This concept, that God's chosen people are subject to particular suffering by virtue of their exceptional destiny, provided a powerful explanation for the many kinds of affliction that befell the colony: famine, disease, Indian attack, and so on, all could be explained as the signs of God's displeasure as He sought to keep His people to the path of righteousness.

The jeremiad, as this rhetoric of divine threat and warning is known, places the individual soul and the community in a passive relationship with God. The power of God is unimaginable but it is comprehensible through biblical types and precedents. Thomas Hooker develops this theme in 'The Application of Redemption' (1640), where he quotes Hosea 2:14–15, '*I will lead her into the wilderness* and break her heart with many bruising miseries, and *then I will speak kindly to her heart, and will give her the Valley of Achor for a door of hope*'.[18] Hooker points out that the children of Israel faced many afflictions and humiliations in the wilderness before they could come into the promised land of prosperity and plenty. So the people of New England must be prepared for the spiritual plenty that is their destiny by enduring their afflictions with humility and contrition. The covenant is their assurance that their afflictions are designed by God as part of His purpose for them. Thomas Shepard, in 'Salvation by Covenant' (1651), represents the covenant as a means by which humankind can live with the reality of God's absolute power and the means by which the intentions of an unknowable God can, to some extent, be known.

> God the Fathers eternall purposes are sealed secrets, not immediately seene, and the full and blessed accomplishments of those purposes are not yet experimentally felt; the Covenant is the midst between both Gods purposes and performances, by which and in which we come to see the one, before the world began, and by a blessed Faith (which makes things absent, present) to enjoy the other, which shall be our glory, when this world shall be burnt up, and all things in it shall have an end.[19]

God's intentions can never be known completely and with entire assurance, for the divine mind is so completely beyond the reach of human intellect, and so the danger of assuming knowledge must always be kept in mind, Shepard warns. However, God's chosen people of New England can take some comfort from the knowledge that the trials they are sent to endure signify God's continuing commitment to their exceptional destiny.

This is the theme of Michael Wigglesworth's poem, the classic jeremiad 'God's Controversy with New England. Written in the Time of a Great Drought Anno 1662', which threatens an end to the years of divine favour that New England has enjoyed. Backsliding and ingratitude among the colonists places in peril the entire colonial mission. And the wrath that will be unleashed upon them will make the drought they are currently enduring seem as nothing. The faithful remnant will, by then, be too few to save the community; only heroic collective efforts by the entire colony, and Wigglesworth includes the whole community not just the community of saints, will forestall disaster. Only the effective renewing of the federal covenant will save New England from catastrophe. Similar sentiments are expressed by Thomas Shepard a decade later in the sermon 'Eye-Salve. Or a Watch-Word from Our Lord Jesus Christ unto His Churches in New England' (1672). Shepard adds, however, the opinion that the very disobedience of the founders' offspring proves them to be the children of Israel. By threatening divine displeasure, this disobedience demonstrates that the covenant extends to the offspring just like that vouchsafed to Abraham and all of his seed. The partial membership extended to the children of church members through the Half-Way Covenant is unnecessary, from this point of view, and Shepard expresses the sentiments of the clergy who objected to the compromise represented by the Half-Way Covenant in favour of greater use by the magistrates of their coercive powers. Shepard's jeremiad then is directed not only at the community but also at the Boston magistracy.

The jeremiad became the favoured style of sermon rhetoric in the later seventeenth century, especially from the time of the restoration of the monarchy when the Puritan errand appeared to have been betrayed. In election-day sermons, particularly, the community was reminded of the dangers of neglecting their great mission. John Norton in the election sermon of 1661, 'Sion the Outcast Healed of Her Wounds', offers comfort to a people fearful of their isolation in the wilderness by naming them outcasts 'sanctified, outcasts healed, outcasts that care for the truth, and then outcasts on which God will bring the blessing of his own people'.[20] From this divine blessing there will follow esteem and acceptance from God and fellow men, Norton assures his congregation.

The relationship between the jeremiad and exceptionalist ideology was made explicit in Samuel Danforth's election sermon 'A Brief Recognition of New England's Errand into the Wilderness' (1670). Danforth reviews the significance of the New England errand and then exhorts the community to reform themselves and recover the fervour of their commitment.

Such as have sometime left their pleasant cities and habitations to enjoy the pure worship of God in a wilderness are apt in time to abate and cool in their affection thereunto; but then the Lord calls upon them seriously and thoroughly to examine themselves, what it was that drew them into the wilderness, and to consider that it was not the expectation of ludicrous levity nor of courtly pomp and delicacy, but the free and clear dispensation of the Gospel and Kingdom of God.[21]

Danforth describes declension as a disease caused by the dimming of the church's glory and the failure of the congregation to believe in God's power and grace. Unbelief is the primary cause of declension but not the only cause: the pursuit of private interests and worldly cares has turned the congregation away from God and away from the spiritual realm. Danforth points out that in the gospels Christ's disciples were most sharply rebuked for expressing worldly concerns. So New England is punished or rebuked with mildew, severe drought, tempests, floods, sweeping rains and God's special mercies and divine favours are withdrawn.

The Half-Way Covenant was blamed by one faction, led by Increase Mather and his son Cotton, for the reduction of the church's power and prestige. Increase Mather argued that the sacraments were the occasion for a gathering of the saving remnant and could only be enjoyed by visible saints. Those, like Solomon Stoddard, who argued against him claimed that the sacraments are a means of salvation available to all. But to Increase Mather, this amounted to equating New England with the other nations of the world. In his view, New England's special destiny required that the church be purified, that it be comprised only of saints, and to allow entry to those who had not been touched by God's grace reduced the New England church to the level of the imperfectly reformed churches of the Old World, with a corresponding plunge in authority. The Mathers produced a very substantial body of jeremiads, many aimed at identifying the decrease in church prestige with the experience of affliction and natural disasters. Flood, drought, famine, pestilence, Indian attack: all were interpreted as signs of God's displeasure with His people, who were failing to sustain the high ideals of the first settlers and were fast failing in their mission.

Even the controversy and argument generated by the Half-Way Covenant itself is interpreted as a sign of God's wrath by Increase

Mather in his sermon 'The Day of Trouble is Near' (1673). Mather argues that the main difference between this world and the next is that in the world to come there will be no troubles, no dissent, no distress:

> When God begins to depart, that's a sign that trouble is near ... Unity, is a sign of the Lord's Presence; live in peace, and the God of Love and Peace shall be with you. Hence breaches and divisions, inasmuch as they are an evidence of the Lords departure from a people, are a sign of miseries at hand.[22]

God's withdrawal is a damning judgement upon His people and a sign that they have been placed upon probation; that they must learn from these afflictions and correct their ways to become a united people, reforming, believing, heavenly and humble. Above all, Mather identifies increasing worldly interest for the backsliding of the community; he laments that the original interest of New England, which was religion ('which did distinguish us from other English Plantations, they were built upon a Worldly design, but we upon a Religious design'), has now been replaced by a new worldly interest and a new God.[23]

Not only sermons but also popular forms such as the captivity narrative were used to disseminate this notion of a punitive typology at work in the lives of the Bay colonists. The signs of divine displeasure were to be interpreted typologically, as the ministers directed, but the intention of the signs was to punish and chastise a backsliding people. Perhaps the most famous captivity narrative in this style is *A Narrative of the Captivity and Restoration of Mrs Mary Rowlandson* (1682), Mary Rowlandson's account of her captivity among the Narrangansett Indians, who attacked her frontier town of Lancaster, Massachusetts, in February 1676.[24] *The Sovereignty and Goodness of God*, the title of the first Boston edition, establishes a rhetorical model for an interpretation of the experience of captivity which agrees with Puritan ideology and which exemplifies the status of New England as an infant 'redeemer nation'. Mary Rowlandson is brought to the gradual awareness of her special destiny as, through suffering and pain and the deprivations of Indian captivity, she renounces her earlier selfish and complacent ways and surrenders herself to the knowledge of God's absolute power and sovereignty. Her physical redemption thus comes to mirror her spiritual redemption and her eventual restoration to the community of visible saints in Boston prefigures, in her representation, the future destiny of her soul among the saints in heaven. Further, Mrs Rowlandson claims for her experience an exemplary significance as an indication of the special destiny reserved for God's chosen people of New England. Mary Rowlandson's liberation from suffering, her rescue from the moral and geographical wilderness prefigures, in her account, the future liberation of the community of saints from the bondage of worldly sin into the freedom of heavenly bliss.

Mary Rowlandson's description of her ordeal is punctuated with lengthy exclamations about the power and mercy of God, demonstrated by His constant renewal of her strength and stamina. When she thinks she must surrender to despair and give up the struggle to survive, God preserves her spirit 'that [she] might see more of His power' (p. 37). Thus, at an early stage in the narrative her ordeal assumes a double significance as both a physical and a spiritual trial. God sustains her spirit or will to survive just as He sustains her spiritual desire for salvation through grace. Mrs Rowlandson's ordeal tests her commitment to both spiritual and physical redemption. The ordeal also proves her commitment as a representative member of an entire community seeking redemption.

The experience of captivity thus takes on a complex additional significance. Mrs Rowlandson's suffering in the wilderness becomes the image of personal uncertainty regarding the ultimate destiny of the soul. Her eventual redemption from the Indians, achieved through the efforts of the magistrates in Boston, signifies the final redemption through the efforts of God of the visible saint. More than this, however, Mrs Rowlandson's experience assumes a communal significance as a typological repetition of the biblical story of the Babylonian captivity. In the same way that her suffering repeats that of the captive Israelites, so her eventual release signifies the glorious future destiny of God's newly chosen people in the New World. Like Mary Rowlandson, if the community of the faithful can keep to their faith despite all the uncertainties and difficulties of human history then, like the redeemed captive, they too will be released from bondage to the physical world into the freedom of spiritual salvation. Mrs Rowlandson certainly is not unaware of the communal interpretation invited by her ordeal and this typological significance motivates her use of biblical imagery and especially the image of the Babylonian captivity.

It is during the journey to King Philip's encampment that Mrs Rowlandson describes how she surrenders her unwillingness to weep before her captors and there by the side of the river she gives herself over to uncontrollable weeping. She creates then a parallel between her experience and the captivity of the Israelites in Babylon: 'now may I say [she writes] as Psal. 137:1, "By the rivers of Babylon there we sat down; yea, we wept when we remembered Zion"' (pp. 46–7). The victory of the heathen over the settlers of New England appears to her as a typological repetition of the sufferings of God's chosen people. Through this typological logic, the narrative offers its contemporary readers the opportunity to experience what Annette Kolodny calls 'their community's spiritual vulnerability through the biblical type, and then, more dramatically, their own individual vulnerability through identification with an actual woman who exemplifies the type'.[25] In other words, Mrs Rowlandson's narrative offers both an example of the parallel between biblical events and contemporary events and also offers a demonstration of the fact that no-one is exempt from the implications (both positive and negative, frightening and reassuring) of this parallel.

Mary Rowlandson develops the parallel between her own destiny and that of the entire Puritan community by creating a pattern of Biblical reference that serves to generalise the significance of her experiences so they become applicable to everyone. When she first catches sight of the Indian town of Wenimesset and sees the large number of Indians gathered there she likens her feelings of dismay to the experience of David: 'I had fainted, unless I had believed' (Psalms 27:13). She finds some comfort in the biblical parallel between the taking of her own children by Indians and Jacob's loss of his sons (Genesis 42:36). When she is forbidden to see her daughter in a nearby Indian village, Mrs Rowlandson prays that God will show her some sign of His good will and will give her reason to hope that her trials will end; shortly after this her son Joseph (whose whereabouts had been unknown to her) unexpectedly appears. She exclaims that 'indeed quickly the Lord answered in some measure my poor prayers' (p. 40). The very next day Mrs Rowlandson acquires a Bible, taken by an Indian in the raid on Medfield, and there she finds a scriptural passage which describes both her experience of despair and the hope of ultimate redemption:

In that melancholy time [she tells us,] it came into my head to read first the 28 chapter if Deut., which I did, and when I had read it, my dark heart wrought on this manner, that there was no mercy for me, that the blessings were gone and the curses come into their room, and that I had lost my opportunity. But the Lord helped me still to

go on reading till I came to chapter 30, the seven first verses, where
I found there was mercy promised again if we would return to him
by repentance, and, though we were scattered from one end of the
earth to the other, yet the Lord would gather us together and turn
all those curses upon our enemies. (p. 41)

Mrs Rowlandson concludes: 'I do not desire to live to forget this scripture and what comfort it was to me' (p. 41). This passage encapsulates
the orthodox interpretation of Puritan experience: that in return for
genuine repentance and a faithful heart, God will show mercy to His
people and redemption will finally be theirs. This dispensation applies
equally to individuals and to the community of saints. Despite any
backsliding that may have occurred among the visible saints of New
England, God remains willing to keep to the terms of the federal covenant. He will show mercy where there is true repentance but where
there is no repentance His power will be made manifest instead through
His wrath.

God's power over all aspects of temporal life is made clear to Mrs
Rowlandson. The Indians are represented as satanic agents through
whom God warns and chastises His people. It is only when she is
prevented by her captivity from observing the Sabbath that she remem-
bers how many Sabbaths she misspent or let pass. This recollection
brings with it the guilty awareness that God could justifiably cast her
from His sight but Mrs Rowlandson is surprised and impressed by the
extent of God's mercy that He does not. This guilty realisation is soon
recognised as a crucial step in her chastisement and repentance; only
now does Mrs Rowlandson see clearly the error of her earlier ways and
resolve to reform her conduct: 'as He wounded me with one hand, so
He healed me with the other' (p. 38). God's chastisement is not only
justified but merciful, she realises. The physical wounds she has suffered
provide the occasion for a spiritual healing, and Mrs Rowlandson continues to interpret her trials in this way: as punishment for her sins and
guidance towards God's true way, from which she has strayed. Captivity
presents her with a powerful image of the wilderness condition that is
the spiritual condition of her community and herself, in the absence of
God's guidance.

If the community of saints in New England is true to the terms of
the federal covenant, Mary Rowlandson suggests, then God would
destroy all its enemies among the heathen. As it is, God must use the

Indians to chastise His people and to lead them back to the way of righteousness. It is in this connection that Mrs Rowlandson justifies her own text, by means of the communal subtext she articulates. As scripture spoke to her at crucial moments in her distress to comfort her with the true significance of her suffering and with hope of redemption, so her narrative is intended 'even as the psalmist says to declare the works of the Lord and His wonderful power in carrying us along, preserving us in the wilderness while under the enemy's hand and returning us in safety again' (p. 46). Mrs Rowlandson intends her story to draw attention to the merciful aspect of the chastisement that all of the colonists have experienced in the varying forms of famine, disease, Indian attack, or the extreme trauma of captivity.

Mrs Rowlandson's narrative is often credited with creating the genre of captivity narratives and in the latter part of the seventeenth century this literary form was very popular, combining as it does adventure and exotic elements with orthodox theology, within a rhetorical package that speaks to the New World audience's need for reassurance that all their deprivations will prove worthwhile. In many ways the real mastermind behind this strategy of combining threat with comfort, adventure with instruction, was Cotton Mather, son of Increase Mather and grandson of John Cotton. Cotton Mather's writing took the style of the jeremiad to a new pitch. He identified the native inhabitants of New England as the satanic agents of God's punitive will: the Indians were to be used by God as a scourge and means of affliction for His people. And to this would be added the interventions of Satan himself, 'often the Executioner of the Wrath of God upon a sinful World', in Cotton Mather's description in the sermon, 'Things for a Distressed People to think upon' (1696).[26] In that same sermon, he warns that 'the *Spirit* of God against whom we had *Rebelled*, permitted the *Devils*, from the *Depths of Hell*, to assault us, with as Prodigious Vexations, as ever befel any People under the whole *Cope of Heaven*'.[27] Only the renewal of the covenant could avert disaster. This warning and this style of rhetoric had a profound influence upon Cotton Mather's thinking as he dealt with the outbreak of witchcraft hysteria in New England.

Increase and Cotton Mather recognised in the declension of the Massachusetts Bay colony, in the neglect of their exceptional destiny, the conditions for a satanic challenge. Satan could hope to win a victory over God's people by taking advantage of their weakened spiritual state. Thus, the reports of witchcraft throughout the latter seventeenth century fitted with their diagnosis of the spiritual malaise which New England was suffering. The Mathers extended Thomas Shepard's claim that the divine will could be approached by means of the signs or providences that record God's interventions in our world by emphasising what could be known rather than the imperfection of what knowledge men can obtain about God's will. The Mathers also extended the range of phenomena that could count as divine providences:

> Divine Judgements, Tempests, Floods, Earth-quakes, Thunders as are unusual, Strange Apparitions, or what ever else shall happen that is Prodigious, Witchcrafts, Diabolical Possessions, Remarkable Judgements upon noted Sinners, eminent Deliverances, and Answers of Prayer, are to be reckoned among Illustrious Providences.[28]

Consequently, witchcraft, seen within the logic of the jeremiad, was another sign that the New England errand was under serious threat, that New England was the pre-eminent battleground between God and Satan, and that the colonists neglected this knowledge at their peril. In his account of the witchcraft trials at Salem, *The Wonders of the Invisible World, Being An Account of the Tryals of Several Witches Lately Executed in New England* (1692), Cotton Mather makes precisely this argument. From the declension of the young and the neglect or postponement of their fathers' errand a whole variety of calamities have followed; but the colonists have failed to make the correct use of the disasters that have befallen them − they have not yet repented. He reminds the colonists that the settlement of New England was originally made in the Devil's territories: 'He has wanted his *Incarnate Legions* to Persecute us, as the People of God have in the other Hemispheres been Persecuted: he has therefore drawn forth his more *Spiritual* ones to make an Attacque upon us.' [29] Mather is also aware of the approaching millennium, that the incidence of satanic possessions, natural disasters and cases of witchcraft is likely to increase as the Devil recognises that his time is short if he is to disrupt millennial expectations: 'Just before our Lords *First Coming*, There were most observable Outrages committed by the Devil upon the Children of Men: And I am suspicious, That there will again be an unusual Range of the Devil amongst us, a little before the *Second Coming* of our Lord.' [30]

Where the other ministers involved in the witchcraft hysteria came to see the errors of their judgement, Cotton Mather never retreated from his firm exceptionalist line of reasoning: that the exceptional destiny of

New England had been under siege by the Devil, operating through his agents, to destroy God's chosen people and their promised land. Well into the eighteenth century, Cotton Mather preached the providential significance of natural phenomena such as storms, earthquakes and the like in pieces such as 'Boanerges: A Short Essay to preserve and strengthen the Good Impressions produced by Earthquakes' (1727). The closing exhortation reads: 'All that the *Oracles* of GOD have mentioned, as Things to be done before it, are Accomplished: I say, All Accomplished! Certainly the *Kingdom of God is at hand*: And in the Introducing of it, The Foundations of the Earth shall shake; The Earth shall be utterly broken down; The Earth shall be clean dissolved; The Earth shall be moved exceedingly.' [31]

Exceptionalism and the Creation of a Nation

The concept of the errand continued to inform public pronouncements about the society and culture of Massachusetts Bay, its history and its destiny, right up to the time of the Revolution. However, the formulation of the errand changed subtly in the course of the eighteenth century. Jonathan Mayhew's 1754 election sermon attributes the authority of government primarily to God but immediately to the 'common consent': 'government is spoken of in Scripture as being both the ordinance of God and the ordinance of man – of God, in reference to his original plan and universal providence, and of man, as it is more immediately the result of human prudence, wisdom, and concert'.[32] The purpose of government Mayhew finds in scripture as divine favour towards God's chosen people, so that they might be delivered out of bondage, 'and that, being brought out of the house of bondage, they might be conducted into a good land, flowing with milk and honey; that they might there possess property, enjoy the blessing of equal laws, and be happy'.[33] So, in 1754, the representation of the errand is beginning to echo the terms of the Declaration of Independence: the possession of private property, equality before the law, and the freedom to pursue happiness. On the eve of the Revolution, in 1775, Samuel Langdon's sermon addressed the issue of the direct appointment of councillors by the King to replace those that had been popularly elected. He interprets this development positively, within the context of a renewed errand: America could take this opportunity to cleanse itself of the corruption of the European courts, just as the first settlers freed themselves of European corruption; good government will now be restored; and Langdon ends with a reminder of the catastrophic destruction that God can call down upon the enemies of His chosen people.[34]

Benjamin Franklin also used the vocabulary of exceptionalism to represent his particular vision of the world and the infant American nation within it. In his *Autobiography*, Franklin uses the concept of Providence to describe the principle that guides and shapes the natural world. Of course, within the terms of Puritan theology, 'Providence' had described God's direct intervention in the human world. Franklin uses the term to describe a rational principle that controls the operation of the world and he is very much of his time in this belief. One of the fundamental tenets of the Enlightenment was the idea that the universe is orderly and understandable through the faculty of reason. Because the world is governed by rational principles it can be improved by maximising the rational government of people and institutions. America, a new nation unhampered by the complexities of European history and unburdened by a sophisticated class system and structure of inheritance, offered an unrivalled opportunity for the establishment of a democratic society based on rational principles. The guiding principle of reason that required re-engineering to produce an improved or in fact exemplary nation Franklin described as 'Providence'. And as the *Autobiography* progresses, Franklin's own work is shown to further the rational and utilitarian work of Providence and to create of his own life a model citizen and a model American.

What Franklin means by 'American' is related to the context of revolutionary unrest in which he wrote. The characteristics that he chooses to highlight coincide with the revolutionary ideals of the new nation. Franklin begins his autobiography with an account of his ancestors who are described as champions of freedom, religious dissenters. From them, Franklin's inheritance is not money or land or title, but a commitment to the ideal of freedom. This theme also arises from Franklin's description of his father – from him he received no inherited privileges but the more valuable virtues of industry, community spirit, practicality and common sense. These, in Franklin's estimation, are the characteristics of the model American. The *Autobiography* represents Franklin's life as enacting the newly formed American myth of individual self-realisation in a land of opportunity. It is in this way that Franklin redefined the mythology exceptionalism, away from its religious origins as an errand into the wilderness where a grand and purified church would be established, peopled by the visible saints chosen by God, and awaiting the glorious end of time. Franklin represents the American errand as the creation of a secular state that is purified of the corruption of European politics and a social structure based on inherited title. It is the secular America that will be a model of democratic government and the envy of all the nations of the earth. Franklin himself embodies this impulse to create oneself anew, to take opportunities when they arise and then to interpret success as the consequence of being American. To be American and to be exemplary become the same thing, in Franklin's view. His life develops from poverty and obscurity to wealth and international fame; he starts life as a colonist but lives to become a citizen of an independent nation. And one of the most important aims of his autobiography is to teach readers how they, too, can become model Americans. The tone is didactic and the didactic intention causes Franklin to shape the story of his life in particular ways: he removes or minimises all elements that are purely personal and not representative of the kind of life he is dramatising. For example, the death of his son is turned into a recommendation of inoculation; he mentions his father's first wife only when describing his parents' tombstone. When he is finally unable to achieve perfection, Franklin argues that perfection itself is imperfect, because it inspires envy and hatred! His life may not be absolutely perfect but it is exemplary; at the outset of his autobiography Franklin claims that he would repeat his life exactly as it was, but since he cannot relive his life he will recollect it instead. The model characteristics of his life Franklin described as belonging to America in his 'Information to Those Who Would Remove to America' (1784). Hard work, industry, thrift, common sense, altruism, moral integrity and fair-mindedness – these are the qualities that will guarantee success in America. Franklin warns against immigrating those who seek an easy life, those who are idle or those who expect to be treated according to some inherited rank: these individuals will never make Americans. Franklin powerfully redefined the Puritan mission: recasting the terms of success, where material prosperity assumed a prominence it had not had before, where the conditions of life for Americans were defined less in spiritual terms than earlier, where the collective salvation of the community was transformed into a form of government that would protect the rights of all citizens. What remained was the perception that America would continue to be judged by the other nations of the world to whom America would remain a model, a guide, a measure. And also a guardian of the inalienable rights of man, so recently enshrined in the Constitution: it is in this aspect that America appears in Philip Freneau's poem, 'On Mr Paine's Rights of Man' (1795).

> So shall our nation, formed on Virtue's plan,
> Remain the guardian of the Rights of Man,
> A vast republic, famed through every clime,
> Without a king, to see the end of time.[35]

Freneau thus represents an important element of the evolving mythology of American exceptionalism: America is to be not only a model nation but also will be the world's guardian, regulating the conduct of other nations, and representing the world's last and best chance at salvation.

Notes

1. William Bradford, 'Of Plymouth Plantation' (1630–50) in Alan Heimert and Andrew Delbanco (eds), *The Puritans in America: A Narrative Anthology* (Cambridge, MA and London: Harvard University Press, 1985), p. 57.
2. 'Robert Cushman's reasons and considerations touching the lawfulness of removing out of England into the parts of America', in Alexander Young (ed.),*Chronicles of the Pilgrim Fathers of the Colony of Plymouth, 1602–1625* (1841 rpt, New York: DaCapo Press, 1971), p. 241.
3. Ibid.
4. Ibid.
5. John Winthrop, 'A Model of Christian Charity' (1630), in *The Winthrop Papers* (Boston: Massachusetts Historical Society, 1931), vol. 2, p. 295.
6. John Winthrop, 'Reasons to Be Considered for ... the Intended Plantation in New England' (1629), *Proceedings of the Massachusetts Historical Society*, vol. 8 (1864–65), pp. 420–5.
7. Ibid.
8. John Winthrop, *Winthrop's Journal: History of New England, 1630–1649*, ed. James Kendall Hosmer. Original Narratives of Early American History (1908, rpt New York: Barnes & Noble, 1959), vol. 2: 1640–1649, p. 100.
9. John Winthrop, ibid., vol. 1: 1630–1640, p. 334.
10. Peter Bulkeley, 'The Gospel-Covenant' (c. 1639–40), in Alan Heimert and Andrew Delbanco (eds), *The Puritans in America: A Narrative Anthology* (Cambridge, MA and London: Harvard University Press, 1985), p. 117.
11. Ibid., p. 120.
12. Thomas Tillam, 'Upon the First Sight of New England' (1638), ed. Harold Jantz, *Proceedings of the American Antiquarian Society*, vol. 53, p. 331.
13. Roger Williams, 'Mr Cotton's Letter Lately Printed, Examined and Answered', *The Complete Writings of Roger Williams*, ed. Perry Miller (New York: Russell & Russell, 1963), p. 360.
14. John Cotton, 'God's Promise to his Plantations,' in Alan Heimert and Andrew

Delbanco (eds), *The Puritans in America: A Narrative Anthology* (Cambridge, MA and London: Harvard University Press, 1985), p. 77.

15. Robert Middlekauff, *The Mathers: Three Generations of Puritan Intellectuals, 1596–1728* (New York: Oxford University Press, 1971), p. 34.

16. John Cotton, *Gods Mercie Mixed with His Justice or His Peoples Deliverance in Times of Danger*, 1641. Facsimile reproduction introduced by Everett H. Emerson (1958, rpt New York: Scholars' Facsimiles and Reprints, 1977).

17. Ibid., pp. 35–6.

18. Thomas Hooker, 'The Application of Redemption by the Effectual Work of the Word and Spirit of Christ for the Bringing Home of Lost Sinners to God' (1640) in Alan Heimert and Andrew Delbanco (eds), *The Puritans in America: A Narrative Anthology* (Cambridge, MA and London: Harvard University Press, 1985), p. 177.

19. Thomas Shepard, 'Salvation by Covenant', preface to Peter Bulkeley, 'The Gospel Covenant', 2nd edn London, 1651 in Richard Reinitz (ed.), *Tensions in American Puritanism* (New York: John Wiley & Sons, 1970), p. 50.

20. John Norton, 'Sion the Outcast Healed of Her Wounds' (1661) in Alan Heimert and Andrew Delbanco (eds), *The Puritans in America: A Narrative Anthology* (Cambridge, MA and London: Harvard University Press, 1985), p. 228.

21. Samuel Danforth, 'A Brief Recognition of New England's Errand into the Wilderness' (1670) in A. W. Plumstead (ed.), *The Wall and the Garden: Selected Massachusetts Election Sermons, 1670–1775* (Minneapolis: University of Minnesota Press, 1968), p. 61.

22. Increase Mather, 'The Day of Trouble is at Hand', *Jeremiads*, ed. Sacvan Bercovitch, A Library of American Puritan Writings, vol. 20 (New York: AMS Press, n.d.), p. 10.

23. Ibid., p. 23.

24. Mary Rowlandson, *A Narrative of the Captivity and Restoration of Mrs Mary Rowlandson* (1682) in Alden T. Vaughn and Edward W. Clark (eds), *Puritans Among the Indians: Accounts of Captivity and Redemption, 1676–1724* (Cambridge, MA and London: The Belknap Press of Harvard University Press, 1981). Future page references are given in the text.

25. Annette Kolodny, *The Land Before Her: Fantasy and Experience of the American Frontiers, 1630–1860* (Chapel Hill and London: University of North Carolina Press, 1984), p. 21. See also the classic studies by Roy Harvey Pearce, *Savagism and Civilization: A Study of the Indian and the American Mind* (1953, rev. edn; Berkeley, Los Angeles and London: University of California Press, 1988), and Richard Slotkin, *Regeneration Through Violence: The Mythology of the American Frontier, 1600–1860* (Middletown, CT: Wesleyan University Press, 1973).

26. Cotton Mather, 'Things for a Distressed people to think upon', *Days of Humiliation: Times of Affliction and Disaster, Nine Sermons for Restoring Favor With An Angry God (1696–1727)*, ed. George Harrison Orians (Gainesville, FL: Scholars' Facsimiles and Reprints, 1970), p. 20.

27. Ibid., p. 26.

28. Increase Mather, 'An Essay for the Recording of Illustrious Providences, wherein an Account is given of many Remarkable and very Memorable Events, which have happened in this last Age; especially in New England' (1684) in George Lincoln Burr (ed.), *Narratives of the Witchcraft Cases, 1648–1706*, Original Narratives of Early American History (1914, rpt New York: Barnes and Noble, 1963), p. 13.

29. Cotton Mather, *The Wonders of the Invisible World, Being An Account of the Tryals*

of Several Witches Lately Executed in New England (1692, rpt London: John Russell, 1862), pp. 13–14.

30. Ibid., p. 61.

31. Cotton Mather, 'Boanerges: A Short Essay to preserve and strengthen the Good Impressions produced by Earthquakes' (1727), *Days of Humiliation: Times of Affliction and Disaster, Nine Sermons for Restoring Favor With An Angry God (1696–1727)*, ed. George Harrison Orians (Gainesville, FL: Scholars' Facsimiles and Reprints, 1970), p. 372.

32. Jonathan Mayhew, 'An Election Sermon' (1754), in A. W. Plumstead (ed.), *The Wall and the Garden: Selected Massachusetts Election Sermons, 1670–1775* (Minneapolis: University of Minnesota Press, 1968), p. 292.

33. Ibid., p. 293.

34. Samuel Langdon, 'A Sermon' (1775), in A. W. Plumstead (ed.), *The Wall and the Garden: Selected Massachusetts Election Sermons, 1670–1775* (Minneapolis: University of Minnesota Press, 1968), pp. 357–73.

35. Philip Freneau, 'On Mr Paine's Rights of Man' (1795), in Nina Baym, *et al.* (eds), *The Norton Anthology of American Literature* (New York: W. W. Norton & Co., 1994), vol. 1, p. 810.

CHAPTER 2

Dispossession: Native American Responses to the Ideology of Exceptionalism

The discussion of the importance of exceptionalism in the formation of the American nation as an ideological entity is balanced with an account of native American writers who sought, in a variety of ways, to contest exceptionalist claims. Key writers here are Samsum Occum, Hendrick Aupaumut, John Wannuaucon Quinney, William Apess, Charles Eastman, Luther Standing Bear, D'Arcy McNickle, Vine Deloria Junior, James Welch, Leslie Marmon Silko and Gerald Vizenor. This chapter reflects the extent of native engagement with the evolving ideology of Anglo-America and also responds to the relative lack of scholarly recognition of the importance of this body of work in this context.

Native Americans and the New World Mission

Native American responses to exceptionalism were generally at several removes: what that means is the values and assumptions of exceptionalism were translated into white policies to control Indian communities, and it was against these policies the Indian tribes responded. Exceptionalism shaped the policies and the tribes responded to the policies and the ideology that informed them. It is important to remember that Indians did not react to exceptionalism in isolation; it was the social, political and economic consequences of exceptionalist ideology that evoked native responses. The rhetoric of exceptionalism, however, was available to native Americans. Some, such as the Cherokee Elias Boudinot, appropriated exceptionalist rhetoric to argue for a place within the Republic for Indians, who could then share the exceptional destiny of the United States. Others, like the Seneca Handsome Lake, gave expression to an entire counter-mythology of the European discovery of the New World and in this way led native resistance to white conquest. Either way, native Americans took advantage of exceptionalism to turn the vocabulary of American idealism into criticism of actual social and economic practices.

European attitudes towards native Americans were shaped, from the earliest times, by the assumption that native peoples would not survive the European onslaught. In a seminal work, *Native American Tribalism: Indian Survivals and Renewals*, D'Arcy McNickle explores the historical consequences of the belief that the native people of the New World would inevitably become extinct. McNickle points to the recovery in native populations in this century, in direct contradiction of the powerful image of the 'vanishing American', and this gives a bitterly ironic perspective to the historical narrative he unfolds.

After the Revolutionary War, the regulation of Indian affairs was the cause of some contention between those who saw this as a state responsibility and those who saw it as a matter of federal jurisdiction. The states resisted taking sole responsibility for, and bearing the cost for, Indian affairs but did not want to relinquish jurisdiction in any matter.[1] Consequently, the Articles of Confederation gave Congress 'the sole and exclusive right and power of ... regulating the trade and managing all affairs with the Indians' but with the constraint that Congress must not infringe on the right of any state. The control of land sales was the focus of governmental interest in Indian affairs, and not only during these years. The policy expressed in the Royal Proclamation of 1763 was adopted by the Continental Congress in 1779 in a resolution that 'No land [shall] be sold or ceded by any of the said Indians, either as individuals or as a nation, unless to the United States of America, or by the consent of Congress', and this policy was made permanent law when the federal Constitution was adopted (p. 49). But in 1787 the Northwest Ordinance, which attempted to control westward migration, was seen as little more than the legalisation of the westward European invasion, from an Indian point of view (p. 51). Pressure upon the executive government, both from the states and from Congress, to ignore tribal land claims and to forcibly remove Indians from their lands was extreme as settlers sought more territory. A powerful argument was proposed, that in winning the war against Britain the United States had become sole owner of the territory that had previously been the North American colonies. Henry Knox, George Washington's Secretary of War, was the first Administrator of Indian Affairs and he adamantly refused to set aside the Indians' claims: 'The Indians, being the prior occupants, possess the right of the soil. It cannot be taken from them unless by their consent, or by rights of conquest in case of a just war. To dispossess them on any other principle would be a great violation of the fundamental laws of nature' (quoted by McNickle, p. 52). Knox believed that the encroachment of white settlers upon traditional hunting grounds would reduce the available sources of food and so coerce the Indians into voluntarily selling their land (p. 52). The mythology of the vanishing American who could not live with the modern democratic civilisation that America was divinely fated to bring to the wilderness of the New World, was invoked to resolve the otherwise irresolvable tension between European claims to the land and the prior claims of the native people. Within the terms of this mythology, which was itself informed by exceptionalist principles, native Americans faced a choice between physical extinction and cultural extinction, assimilation or death. Within the narrative of American exceptionalism there is no role for tribal sovereignty or native separatism. The United States must achieve its glorious destiny by bringing about the triumph of perfected, democratic institutions and this leaves no room for residual tribal governments or indeed any alternative form of social organisation.

The writings of Samson Occum and Hendrick Aupaumut in the later eighteenth century point to the futility of native attempts to escape these brutal alternatives by partial assimilation or by voluntary removal away from white communities. Samson Occum was a Mohegan, born 1723 in New London Connecticut. Between the ages of sixteen and seventeen he was converted by Christian evangelical preachers and, after teaching himself to read, he travelled to New Lebanon Connecticut to study with the Reverend Eleazar Wheelock. Wheelock became Occum's teacher and mentor; after Occum moved back to New London, first, and then to Montauk Long Island, where he married and settled as schoolmaster to the Montauk Indians, the two corresponded regularly. Occum was ordained a minister by the Presbytery of Suffolk in 1759 and in 1765 he travelled to London to help raise funds for Wheelock's Indian Charity School (founded in 1754). He was a very successful public speaker and in the course of his two-year stay in Britain he raised more than twelve thousand pounds. But when he returned to America, he found his family in desperate financial distress and, further, he discovered that the funds he had raised were to be used to move the school from Connecticut to New Hampshire rather than extend and improve it. His suspicion that the Indians would have little benefit from the new school proved correct as Dartmouth College, as it was renamed, ceased to minister to Indian students.

At this low point Occum wrote a ten-page autobiography, which remained unpublished in the Dartmouth archive until 1982. In the 'Narrative' (1768) he describes his continual struggle to feed and support his large family whilst working as schoolmaster and, during the prolonged absences of the regular missionary, as minister as well to the Montauk Indians. After he was licensed to preach, his congregation included the Shencock Indians and Occum tells how: 'I have been obliged to Set out from Home after Sun Set, and Ride 30 Miles in the Night, to Preach to these Indians.' [2] He ran an evening school for those who could not attend during the day, and put much effort into developing novel methods for teaching reading and writing. He writes of the need to raise his own vegetables and livestock, to hunt and fish before or after school, in order to keep his family fed. Throughout the 'Narrative' the financial troubles that dogged his life are always present. So it is not surprising that the 'Narrative' should conclude with a bitter denunciation of the racism that is Occum's only explanation for the discrimination he encounters even within the church bureaucracy. He is especially bitter to learn that a white missionary was given one hundred pounds plus the money to employ an interpreter for only one year's work among the Indians. Occum exclaims:

> You See what difference they made between me and other missionaries; they gave me 180 Pounds for 12 years Service, which they gave for one years Services in another Mission. – In my Service ... I was my own Interpreter. I was both a School master and Minister to the Indians, yea I was their Ear, Eye & Hand, as Well as Mouth. I leave it to the World, as wicked as it is, to Judge, whether I ought not to have had half as much (p. 946).

Occum concludes that the reason why he is treated unjustly is simply his race: 'I *must say*, "I believe it is because I am a poor Indian". I Can't help that God has made me So; I did not make my self so. –' (p. 947). The consciousness of racial discrimination runs through Occum's writing.

What fame he achieved in his lifetime came as a result of the execution sermon Occum was asked to preach at the hanging of Moses Paul, also a Mohegan, who in a drunken rage had killed a respected citizen, Moses

Cook, in Waterbury Connecticut. The *Sermon* ran through nineteen editions, well into the nineteenth century. Occum addresses Moses Paul: 'You are an Indian, a despised creature.'[3] And preaching from this Indian perspective, he goes on to deliver a sermon that draws heavily upon the rhetoric of the jeremiad and the vocabulary of exceptionalism. So he emphasises not salvation for the elect but redemption for all who repent of their sins: 'He that hath no money may come; he that hath no righteousness, no goodness, may come; the call is to poor undone sinners; the call is not to the righteous, but sinners, calling them to repentance' (p. 651). He emphasises the sinfulness of *all* nations, not the especially and symbolically sinful nature of New England: 'As long as Christ is neglected, life is refused, and as long as sin is cherished, death is chosen; and this seems to be the woful [*sic*] case of mankind of all nations, according to their appearance in these days; for it is too plain to be denied, that vice and immorality, and floods of iniquity are abounding every where amongst all nations, and all orders and ranks of men, and in every sect of people' (p. 642). However, in the exhortation specifically addressed to Indians, Occum urges that the particular sin of drunkenness be repented; he emphasises the damage done to person, family, community and soul by the abuse of alcohol that afflicts his fellow-Indians. The condemnation of drunkenness and the complicity it creates in the suffering of native people became a common theme in Indian expression (speeches and writing) since. Throughout the sermon, the stress is upon the advantages for the individual of a godly life. Occum repeats that from the moment of birth we are all dying and that life should then be seen as an extended preparation for death. To die well is the crowning glory of a life lived well and to live well is to live by Christian teachings. But as Occum's account of his own life revealed, the teachings of Christianity could not be reconciled with the unjust and racist practices of actual Christians.

Occum spent his last years among the Christian Indians he had helped remove to the settlement of Brothertown, on the Oneida lands in western New York. After the Revolutionary War the leader of the Stockbridge Indians, Hendrick Aupaumut, also encouraged acceptance of the Oneida's invitation to remove to Oneida Creek, where New Stockbridge was established in the mid-1780s. Aupaumut was moved to this decision by the dwindling numbers of his people, the continual encroachment of white settlement upon tribal land, and the proximity of the vices of the Indians' white neighbours. In time, Aupaumut came to support further removal, further west, further away from whites, but also away from the Oneidas themselves, who opposed the settled agricultural life favoured by the Stockbridges and who attempted to spread the Long-house Religion of Handsome Lake (discussed below) among the Stockbridge Indians. In fact, the period through the first half of the nineteenth century saw the Stockbridges remove repeatedly. The opinions expressed by Aupaumut and his unswerving loyalty to the United States made him an influential figure in relations between Indians and the government of the new Republic.

In 'A Short Narration of my Last Journey to the Western Contry [sic]' (c. 1793) Aupaumut describes his travels among the Delawares, Shawnees, Miamis, Chippewas, Ottawa, Wyandot, Pottawatomi and Kickapoo. In the discussions he reports, he is concerned to clear his reputation of the accusation that he supports the interests of whites against those of his own people. He attempts to refute the declaration by Joseph Brant, leader of the Mohawks and supporter of the British, that George Washington laid claim to all Indian lands (a view that was expressed in Washington: that by winning the war against Britain, America had won sovereignty over all lands previously held by the crown). Further, Aupaumut blames Britain, not the United States, for the injustice suffered by the tribes:

> These white people was governed by one Law, the Law of the great King of England; and by that Law they could hold our lands, in spite of our dissatisfaction; and we were too fond of their liquors. But now they have new Laws of their own, and by these Laws Indians cannot be deceived as usual, &c.[4]

He urges that the tribes negotiate with the 'United Sachems' to resolve grievances caused by lawless frontiersmen or 'Big knifes' who terrorised the tribes and who are likened to outlaws by Aupaumut as he draws a parallel with outlaw tribes (he cites the Cherokee) and lawless individuals within the Indian tribes. He points out that Indian and white communities alike suffer the outrages of lawless individuals, and he is not afraid to identify the complicity of some Indians, those who abuse alcohol, in their own suffering. Aupaumut is, above all, concerned to emphasise the common humanity and the commitment to justice that he believes Indians and whites hold in common. As Aupaumut presents his views he reveals the extent to which the tribes were divided on the issue of white intentions; he represents the arguments for accommodation (not assimilation) to the permanent presence of Europeans.

At the other extreme, the arguments for resistance are represented by Handsome Lake, of the Seneca tribe, who experienced a sequence of visions in 1799; the relation was recorded in 1929 by Arthur C. Parker, also a Seneca who worked closely with Anglo-American ethnographers to preserve fast-disappearing tribal traditions. In these apocalyptic visions, Handsome Lake was instructed to inform his people that unless the traditional tribal ways were reinstated immediately and in full, and the influence of Europeans upon tribal life sincerely repented, then the world would be consumed by fire. Complete separatism was the message of Handsome Lake's visions; in relating the visions he used the vocabulary and iconography of American cultural mythology to reverse the power of the exceptionalist myth. In the vision since known as 'How America Was Discovered' (c. 1799), it is the Devil, not God, who sends European settlers to the New World.[5] In a sacred book, uncovered by a young man in his Queen's possession, he discovers that the Lord has not returned to earth as promised. When he questions his elders about this, they send him to find the Lord. He then has a vision of a castle of gold, set in the midst of a wondrous island, and in the castle he finds a figure that he assumes is the Lord. He is instructed: 'Across the ocean there is a great country of which you have never heard. The people there are virtuous, they have no evil habits or appetites but are honest and single-minded. A great reward is yours if you enter into my plans and carry them out. Here are five things. Carry them to the people across the ocean and never shall you want for wealth, position or power' (p. 183). He confides his vision to Columbus, who takes him across the ocean, carrying with him cards, so the people will gamble away their goods; money to make them dishonest and covetous; a fiddle to make them dance; whiskey to excite their minds to evil; and blood corruption to destroy their physical health. The relation concludes by identifying the man in the gold palace as the Devil who, when he saw the extent of the evil he had unleashed, even he lamented what he had done. Handsome Lake articulates a clear counter-mythology to explain the European invasion; his myth answers the same cultural need as the mythology of American exceptionalism except, of course, Handsome Lake speaks to the need of native Americans for direction and guidance in the face of the threat posed by Europeans to tribal existence.

The early years of the nineteenth century saw the rising power of exceptionalist mythology translated into the concept of Manifest Destiny – the belief that the United States was destined to bring a perfected form of democratic capitalism to the entire North American continent – and a policy of forcible removal of those tribes that would not retreat before the advance of democratic civilisation. These developments within the ideological life of the Republic were counter to the developments within judicial opinion regarding the status of native Americans. In the 1830s the Supreme Court, through Justice Marshall, recognised the self-governing powers of Indian tribes; in 1831 Justice Marshall delivered the opinion:

> It may well be doubted whether those tribes which reside within the acknowledged boundaries of the United States can, with strict accuracy, be denominated foreign nations. They may, more correctly, perhaps, be denominated domestic dependent nations ... They and their country are considered by foreign nations, as well as by ourselves, as being so completely under the sovereignty and dominion of the United States that any attempt to acquire their lands, or to form a political connection with them, would be considered by all as an invasion of our territory (quoted by McNickle, p. 54).

So tribal communities were defined judicially as independent, self-governing nations within the nation. While Marshall's view prevailed in the courts, in government different sentiments were expressed, representative of which were the views of Andrew Jackson who regarded treaties with Indians as an absurdity and native culture as too far removed from European concepts of government to allow meaningful negotiation. The Indian Removal Act was adopted by Congress and approved by the President on 30 May 1830, thus forcing the Eastern tribes of Choctaws, Creeks, Chickasaws, and Cherokees, and the Ohio River and Great Lakes tribes as well, the Ottawas, Pottawatomies, Wyandots, Shawnees, Kickapoos, Winnebagos, Delawares, Peorias, Miamis, the Sauk and the Fox, on to land set aside for them west of the Mississippi (p. 74). The tribes resisted vigorously, as did some members of Congress, this blatant disregard for Indian rights and for the moral obligation expressed in earlier treaties with these tribes. Expressions of outrage were overwhelmed by the power of exceptionalist rhetoric and the image of the vanishing American this rhetoric promoted. One famous witness of the removal, Count Alexis de Toqueville watched a group of Choctaws crossing the Mississippi at mid-winter 1831 and he remarked: 'The Indians have been ruined by a competition which they had not the means of sustaining.'[6]

During the controversy over the removal policy there appeared the first published native autobiography; *A Son of the Forest* (1829, rev. edn 1831) told of the early life of William Apess, a Pequot of mixed ancestry who claimed to be descended of the colonial Wampanoag leader Metacomet, known as King Philip by the English. Apess was largely raised by whites, having been bound out (to a series of masters) at the age of four or five after being severely beaten by his alcoholic grandmother. He was converted to Methodism in 1813 and, when he was forbidden by his master to practise his religion, he ran away to serve in the War of 1812 and only in 1817 was he reunited with his Pequot family. He served as a lay preacher until his ordination as a Methodist minister in 1829, and it is the concept of the equality of all people before God that is powerfully argued in his writing and which galvanised his audiences. In *The Experiences of Five Christian Indians of the Pequod Tribe* (1833), *Indian Nullification of the Unconstitutional Laws of Massachusetts Relative to the Marshpee Tribe; or, The Pretended Riot Explained* (1835) and *Eulogy on King Philip* (1836) Apess repeated his belief that salvation is available to all, regardless of colour, class, gender or nationality; indeed, he liked to point out that Christ himself was not white and, if humanity was created in God's likeness, then God is most certainly not white.[7] And he uses biblical quotation and Christian principles to contrast the professions of religion made by those whites who treat Indians with callous disregard for their rights and their humanity. The savagery of the civilisers is one of Apess's frequent themes, explored at length in his *Eulogy on King Philip, as Pronounced at the Odeon, in Federal Street, Boston*, an address to mark the 160th anniversary of Philip's death. In this speech, Apess gives a detailed account of the early contact between the tribes of New England and Puritan settlers. His historical narrative places in question the divine mission that the colonists claimed as their inspiration and motivation, largely by contrasting what they did with the Christianity they professed and by contrasting the manner of their treatment by Indians and the way they treated the Indians upon whom they depended in the early days. Apess begins by describing Philip's father, the Pokanoket sachem Massasoit, who bore with benevolent resignation a series of outrages: 'injuries upon injuries, and the most daring robberies and barbarous deeds of death that were ever committed by the American Pilgrims, were with patience and resignation borne, in a manner that would do justice to any Christian nation or being in the world' (p. 278). The violence and injustice committed by the settlers were increased in horror, for Apess, by the hypocrisy they revealed: 'O thou pretended hypocritical Christian, whoever thou art, to say it was the design of God that we should murder and slay one another because we have the power' (p. 279). Later, Apess directly takes up the exceptionalist notion that the Indians are a tool used by God to scourge His chosen people, to punish them for backsliding and neglecting their glorious mission; in response Apess argues that if God desired to punish His elect He could as well do it Himself as work through native intermediaries. Apess rejects the typological reading of scripture, history, and the natural world which supported the exceptionalist narrative of conquest and in its place chooses to contrast the teachings of scripture with the practices of the settlers, the colonists' interpretation of their mission with the actual history they have created. And so he reports the murder of Wituwament, a Massachusett sachem, and his companions by Miles Standish; the beheading of the sachem and the public display of his disembodied head upon a pole. Apess comments of these brutal murders: 'We wonder if these same Christians do not think it the command of God that they should lie, steal, get drunk, commit fornication and adultery. The one is as consistent as the other. What say you, judges, is it not so, and was it not according as they did? Indians think it is' (p. 282). Having impugned the Christian righteousness of the colonists, Apess then attacks the divine mission they claim. The idea 'that Indians were made, etc., on purpose for destruction, to be driven out by white Christians, and they to take their places; and that God had decreed it from all eternity' (p. 287) is rejected as absurd, given the destruction, the injustice and prejudice, the vice and iniquity and corruption that is the New World in the wake of European settlement. The rights of native people by virtue of their humanity, their equality before God and their salvation through Christ provide a measure of the extent to which they have been betrayed, exploited and devastated by the exceptionalist mission in the New World and its descendent ideologies in the United States.

Apess was himself an exceptional individual; a social reformer and activist way before his time, a time when the rights of native people were disregarded as never before, when removal and separation rather than equality within democracy seemed inevitable. John Wannuaucon Quinney, a Mohican, represented the view that Indians must, however reluctantly, accommodate the wishes of white America. He was born at New Stockbridge, the settlement led by Hendrick Aupaumut, and he shared the accommodationist views of the older leader. Quinney oversaw the removal of the Stockbridges to Wisconsin and he represented the tribe as they moved away from the traditional model of government to a constitutional form of tribal government, he represented the tribe in the almost constant negotiations with Washington over land issues right up to his death in 1855. Thus, he saw the fate of people subject to the ideology of Manifest Destiny – the idea that the United States was divinely destined to expand and to carry the experiment in democratic government to the entire North American continent – which became so powerful in the mid-nineteenth century. In the year before his death, Quinney was called upon to deliver the Independence Day speech at Reidsville, New York. In his address, he reveals his intense awareness of the irony of the occasion and he takes advantage of this to present the story of the discovery of the New World, and its subsequent history, from the point of view of the Mohican (the Muh-he-con-new Nation in the address). He begins with an uncompromising description of his subject:

> It may appear to those whom I have the honor to address, a singular taste, for me, an Indian, to take an interest in the triumphal days of a people, who occupy by conquest, or have usurped the possession of the territories of my fathers, and have laid and carefully preserved, a train of terrible miseries, to end when my race shall have ceased to exist.[8]

He describes the coming of the Indians to the north-east and the establishment of a great confederacy of tribes, including the Mohicans whose wise men foretold the advent of a strange race, 'who would eventually crowd them from their fair possessions' (p. 1790). Wannuaucon (as Quinney signs this address) uses scriptural references to emphasise the disparity between the reception extended to the first Europeans by the natives and the recompense those natives received. 'They asked for rest and kindness, we gave them both. They were strangers, and we took them in – naked and we clothed them' echoes Matthew 25: 35–36, 'For I was an hungered, and ye gave me meat: I was thirsty, and ye gave me drink: I was a stranger, and ye took me in: Naked an ye clothed me.' But in return, the natives received devastating diseases, smallpox and measles, vice and strong liquor that decimated and divided the tribes so that co-operation to reduce the threat presented by the invaders became impossible, Indians were cheated and duped by laws and legal procedures they could not understand but were subject to 'by right of discovery'. Wannuaucon rejects all arguments, all forms of justice, that defend the white appropriation of Indian lands. Implicitly, he discards the exceptionalist justification for conquest first by presenting the Indians as better Christians than their Christian saviours and, second, by challenging the concept of justice employed by whites: 'Let it not surprise you, my friends, when I say, that the spot on which we stand, has never been purchased or rightly obtained; and that by justice, human and divine, it is the property now of the remnant of that great people from whom I am descended. They left it in the tortures of starvation, and to improve their miserable existence; but a cession was never made, and their title has never been extinguished' (p. 1792). The kind of justice practised by the United States, he points out, is characterised by the destruction of his tribe, of which he is virtually the last.

John Wannuaucon Quinney uses the Christian vocabulary of American exceptionalism to launch a bitter condemnation of the European conquest but some Indians used the power of exceptionalist terminology to promote an image of native Americans working together with white Americans to further the exceptional destiny of the United States. An example of harnessing exceptionalist rhetoric to promote Indian assimilation is found in 'An Address to the Whites' (1826) by the Cherokee Elias Boudinot. At the time Boudinot wrote, extreme pressure was being applied to the Cherokees to remove from their traditional lands in Georgia for land set aside for them in the Indian Territory. Many Cherokees bitterly resisted pressure to move and when, in the winter of 1838–9, soldiers were sent to enforce the 1835 Treaty of Echota, the result was the Trail of Tears. Boudinot was one of the signatories to the Treaty and in 1839 he was murdered, along with several other signatories, in revenge for what was seen as the betrayal of his people. Boudinot believed that removal and, ultimately assimilation, was the only course open to the Cherokees if they were to survive. In his 'Address' he points to the willingness of the Cherokee tribe to become civilised (i.e. Europeanised), the extent to which they had already civilised themselves as they have moved to the settled agricultural life promoted by whites, and he argues that the Cherokee nation will become a faithful ally to the United States both in military matters and in the more intangible accomplishment of the glorious national destiny: 'on [the Cherokee] destiny hangs the destiny of many nations. If she completes her civilization – then may we hope that all our nations will – then, indeed, may true patriots be encouraged in their efforts to make this world of the West, one continuous abode of enlightened, free, and happy people.'[9] The success of the democratic experiment, the progress of the nation's Manifest Destiny, is inextricably bound up with that of the native people, in Boudinot's argument. The United States must take the Indians with it, as it progresses towards its glorious future, if that future is to come into being. Boudinot uses what was at the time an increasingly powerful set of ideological terms to argue for a place for his people in the life and mythology of the Republic.

Through the nineteenth century the tide of westward migration was of such proportions, accelerated by the discovery of gold in California, then Colorado and the Dakotas, that Congress became impatient with the process of making formal treaties with Indian tribes and increasingly the view was expressed that relations should be a matter for legislation not negotiation. Subsequently, the Appropriation Act of 1871 contained a rider: 'Hereafter, no Indian nation or tribe within the territory of the United States shall be acknowledged or recognized as an independent tribe or power with whom the United States may contract by treaty' (quoted by McNickle, p. 77). Existing treaties were still acknowledged and formal agreements in relation to such matters as land were still made but Indians were no longer involved in the process of making the legislation that affected their civil and property rights. Treaties had previously encapsulated and protected traditional tribal attitudes towards land and property ownership: individuals had rights of occupancy and use but land was not merchantable in the European sense, it was commonly owned by the tribe (pp. 77–8). Tribal attitudes and values were no longer to benefit from the sanction lent by treaties.

The growing sense of uncertainty regarding the whole issue of treaty-making and the increasing division among and within tribes about strategies with which to deal with the growing invasion of traditional tribal lands are dramatised in James Welch's recent novel *Fools Crow*.[10] The narrative is set in the 1870s among the Pikuni (Blackfeet) tribe and deals with tribal responses to the increasingly dominant presence of 'Napikwans' or whites. As the narrative progresses, we discover how the eponymous hero earns his name in battle and gains prestige within his band as a man of vision and healer. Initially, his band of Lone Eaters live at a sufficient distance from white settlers that their only contact is with the local trader. Increasingly, however, the impact of white proximity is felt in the disillusionment of the young men, who feel betrayed by the leader who will not act against the white invaders, and by the presence of disease, smallpox, which eventually decimates the whole tribe. The lack of tribal unity is emphasised as members of different bands seek different responses to the white presence: Medicine Chief leads a violent resistance while Heavy Runner seeks to identify himself as an ally and Three Bears seeks a middle way by accommodating the Napikwans' demands but giving away nothing that is not demanded. Although the elders of the tribe do not want to recognise the signs, they are given fewer and fewer alternatives to complete capitulation to white demands. The superior weapons and numbers of the Napikwans lead the Lone Eaters to believe that the supreme spirit, Sun Chief, has abandoned them in favour of the whites, who come from the east where Sun Chief begins his daily journey. And so the band is well aware that in battle they would be wiped out; however, the scarcity of game, as the wildlife is destroyed and the land cleared for the white men's cattle, brings starvation and disease that also threatens the people with extinction.

The narrative builds three main threads that come to a crisis towards the end: the chiefs of the Pikuni are summoned to meet with cavalry officers, from whom they receive an ultimatum. The conditions for averting punitive attacks on the tribes are impossible to meet: the control of renegade Indians who are indiscriminately killing whites, the return of stolen horses, the end of all raids on white property and persons. The chiefs know they cannot deliver the promises they must make, even as they undertake to meet the Napikwans' demands. Smallpox begins to spread through the band, decimating families. And Fools Crow is summoned in a dream by a powerful spirit to make a ritual journey for the good of his people. He is led to the sacred Feather Woman, who reveals to him the future of his people. In her drawings he sees the complete absence of the game upon which the tribe relies for food and clothing; he sees his people starving, their corpses piled up unburied, he sees the people ravaged by disease, and he sees the children standing miserably in a Napikwan schoolground fenced with barbed wire. Fools Crow understands then that the extinction of his people, through starvation, disease and acculturation or deracination, is inevitable. What he is not prepared for is the massacre he encounters, at the end of the novel. Despite negotiations and treaties and agreements, he finds that the women, children and old people of Heavy Runner's band have been massacred by 'seizers' (the cavalry) while the men were off hunting. As he uncovers the charred bodies in the burned ruins of the camp he also finds a few survivors who are so traumatised by the horror of what they have experienced that they no longer want to live in a world where such atrocities occur. But Fools Crow will not allow them to entertain an image of themselves as vanishing Americans. 'Fools Crow thought of the final design on the yellow skin in Feather Woman's lodge. He saw the Napikwan children playing and laughing in a world that they possessed. And he saw the Pikuni children, quiet and huddled together, alone and foreign in their own country. "We must think of our children," he said' (p. 386).

At the time of which Welch is writing, legislation was being devised to accelerate the process of civilising or Europeanising the Indians, transforming them into the American citizens that the nation was divinely destined to create across the continent. The most powerful and the most damaging of these Acts of legislation was the General Allotment Act or Dawes Act of 1887. By this legislative device, Indians could be moved out of the path of westward migration and Indian land holdings could be reduced. These were the effects of the Act, which saw 90 million of 140 million acres held by Indians pass into white hands by the 1930s (McNickle, p. 83). Ironically, proponents of the legislation were officials representing organisations designed to protect and promote the interests of Indians. The possession of one's own land was perceived to be a powerful 'civilising' influence that would bring about the eradication of 'barbaric' ways and hasten the assimilation of Indians to white American society. An agent of one of the Sioux tribes argued that: 'as long as Indians live in villages they will retain many of their old and injurious habits. Frequent feasts, heathen ceremonies and dances, constant visiting – these will continue as long as people live together in close neighborhoods and villages. I trust that before another year is ended they will generally be located upon individual land or farms. From that date will begin their real and permanent progress.' [11] The Act provided that the President would divide tribal lands and assign 160 acres to each family head, 80 acres to single persons over eighteen and orphans under eighteen, and 40 acres each to others under eighteen; each Indian would make his own selection otherwise a government agent would select for him; title to the land was placed in trust for twenty-five years or longer at the President's discretion; citizenship was conferred upon allotees and other Indians who adopted 'the habits of civilized life'; and surplus lands after allotment might be sold to the United States (pp. 82–3). The government purchase of 'surplus' land moved large stretches of land out of Indian hands; and the sale of individual holdings before the expiry of the trust period, but upon production of a 'certificate of competency' issued by the Secretary of the Interior, accelerated the loss of Indian land.

The intended effect of the allotment policy is graphically described by William Fuller in his 1884 painting *Crow Creek Agency, Dakota Territory* (Figure 2.1). There, the assimilation envisioned by philanthropists and government agents is represented by the Indians neatly dressed in European clothes who dominate the foreground; they are the guests of a few Indians in tribal dress, with whom they contrast vividly. The tipis of these uncivilised Indians do not fit the neat geometric arrangement of the houses and buildings, fields and paddocks that are depicted in the background. Roads and white picket fences form geometric lines that criss-cross the painting and are regularly interspersed with the neat square buildings of the government agency, with the church placed symbolically in the middle of the composition. The traditional tribal dwellings violate the neat regularity of the white settlement; tipis are arranged in broadly circular patterns, though some are placed randomly where space permits between rows of fences. The sky dominates the composition which is divided horizontally in half and the chaotic patterns created by the clouds (echoed by the smoke of the tribal campfires and the river steamboats) form a striking contrast to the geometrical regularity with which the landscape of the agency has been divided up. The painting is executed in the naive style, suggesting that the tensions between white and tribal cultures, assimilated and tribal Indians, nature and civilisation are entirely accidental. The contrasts are all the more dramatic for the painter's apparent unconsciousness of them.

The consequences of allotment for traditional Indian culture were devastating: Indians were dispossessed; tribal existence became difficult with members distributed geographically and the tribal identity became weak and debased. The effect of forced assimilation through allotment is the subject of Louise Erdrich's novel *Tracks* (1988), which follows the effect of land sales and dwindling tribal resources upon a band of Chippewas, who find themselves starving, decimated by disease, completely dependent upon government hand-outs, and divided against each other by greed and self-interest. No provision was made for descendants

Figure 2.1 William Fuller, Crow Creek Agency, Dakota Territory, 1884; oil on canvas 24½ × 41¾in. Amon Carter Museum, Fort Worth, Texas; in memory of René d'Harnoncourt, trustee, 1961–8.

of the allotees since the legislators expected that Indians would disappear. The proceeds of land sales were not invested as a tribal resource and often disappeared in administrative costs and the like, anyway. But following a government-authorised study of Indian conditions by Lewis Meriam, in 1926, a change occurred in government policy. Meriam analysed in detail the fate of Indians under the government's trusteeship and he was particularly critical of the allotment policy: 'It almost seemed as if the government assumed that some magic in individual ownership would in itself prove an educational civilizing factor, but unfortunately this policy has for the most part operated in the opposite direction.' [12]

The destruction of tribal communities through the impact of such disastrously destructive policies as allotment gave rise to a number of influential autobiographical works by men such as Luther Standing Bear and Charles Eastman, men who lived through the experience of allotment and produced texts which expressed a nostalgic longing for a lost tribal past. *Land of the Spotted Eagle* (1933) was written upon Luther Standing Bear's return to the Pine Ridge Sioux Reservation after an absence of sixteen years. He was shocked by the condition in which he found his people: demoralised, overcome by disease, cheated of their treaty rights, and their traditional culture fast disappearing. He found his opinion of federal Indian policy confirmed and decided to educate the public about the true nature of traditional Sioux culture and the status of Indian people within American society. *Land of the Spotted Eagle* is more strident in tone than his earlier work, like *My People the Sioux* (1928), especially the final chapters, 'Later Days', where he describes his years at Carlisle Indian school in Pennsylvania and his return to the reservation. [13] The bulk of the book describes the beliefs, rituals, conventions and lifestyle of the Lakota Sioux, told from the perspective of each life-stage: infancy, boyhood, adolescence; then aspects of life such as family arrangements, civil arrangements, social customs, and Indian beliefs and philosophy. Standing Bear describes his subject matter as: 'my life, and that of my ancestors, upon the plains of what are now the States of North and South Dakota; of our freedom, our love for nature, and respect for life, animate and inanimate; our trust and faith in the Supreme Power, Wakan Tanka; and our principles of truth, honesty, bravery, and brotherhood peace which guided our social lives' (p. 226). Standing Bear had a traditional tribal upbringing, despite the growing presence of the American army in the years immediately before his birth. It was in 1868, following the Fort Laramie treaty councils, that the Sioux agreed to reside on a reservation and ultimately their territory became the Rosebud Reservation. When the Dawes Act of 1887 was applied to the Sioux, Luther Standing Bear and his brother Henry took their allotments at Pine Ridge. He worked as assistant teacher, clerk, storekeeper, assistant minister, rancher; in 1902 he became a member of Buffalo Bill's Wild West Show, and later moved to California where he worked as an actor and lecturer.

Standing Bear criticises the first colonists, whom he describes as having 'remained to become usurpers'. 'They did not try to understand us and did not consider the fact that though we were different from them, still we were living our destiny according to the plan of the Supreme Dictator of mankind.' So, the Indian has been misrepresented in all aspects of character and life (p. 227). Standing Bear repeats that theme common to so many Indians writers: the equality of Indians with Europeans and the superior civilisation of the native peoples, who have withstood all manner of savagery and barbarism committed by white settlers. 'Books, paintings, and pictures have all joined in glorifying the pioneer – the hunter, trapper, woodsman, cowboy, and soldiery – in their course of conquest across the country, a conquest that could only have been realized by committing untold offenses against the aboriginal people. But who proclaims that every battle by the American Indian was a holy fight for the protection of wives, little children, and home-land; that every 'massacre' was the frenzied expression of the right to exist?' (p. 228), Standing Bear asks. He expresses outrage that the legacy of so much suffering for native people should be continued discrimination and hardship. He contrasts the actual history experienced by tribal people in the period since conquest with the glorious destiny Americans expect is their divinely appointed destiny:

> It is now nearly four hundred years since 'civilization' was brought to us, and this is the situation: All groups of public opinion and action, the schools, universities, men's and women's clubs, churches, and other organizations are apathetic toward the Indian and his situation. ... Even the law has forsaken him, and the Indian today is not only unheard and unheeded, but robbed, pillaged, denied his heritage, and held in bondage. The greatest hoax ever perpetrated upon him was the supposed citizenship of 1924 when President Coolidge signed a bill that freed the Indian. The signing of that bill changed not in the slightest measure the condition of the Indian. Not one agent was

removed from office, Indian boys and girls are still segregated in school life, and the reservation and reservation rule still exist (p. 229).

But he saves his most bitter condemnation for the reservation system and the apartheid imposed upon native Americans, who henceforth became prisoners in their own land: 'The reservation became a place where people were herded under every possible disadvantage and obstruction to progress until the race should pass out from sheer physical depletion' (p. 244). He points out that the fact that the President declared the Indian a US citizen, on 5 June 1924, actually disclosed the fact that 'a bonded and enslaved people lived in "the land of the free and the home of the brave"', despite the ending of slavery more than a half century earlier (p. 245). He asks how, when the condition of the Indian is so shocking, the United States government can claim the right to guide and supervise native peoples. Poor white families who are destitute because of poor financial management are not placed under the guidance and supervision of the government, Standing Bear points out. It is this claim to right, the right to govern, that Standing Bear disputes and identifies as the root of the negative attitude that has condemned the Indian to a desperate dependency.

In the final chapter, 'What the Indian Means to America', Standing Bear describes the manner in which the Indian has been shaped by the land in which the tribes live. He begins with the observation that the figure of the Indian has come to symbolise America, and that this is appropriate since 'the hand that fashioned the continent also fashioned the man for his surroundings'. This is the message that emerges most clearly from Standing Bear's account of Lakota life, a life lived in close relationship with nature and the values promoted by the natural world: 'a great freedom – an intense and absorbing love for nature; a respect for life; enriching faith in a Supreme Power; and principles of truth, honesty, generosity, equity, and brotherhood as a guide to mundane relations' (p. 247). The land and the man were one, in traditional tribal life. But the white man is alienated from the formative processes of the continent and can no more understand American nature than he can understand American native peoples and this, not anything done or omitted by Indians, has brought about 'the Indian Problem'. European food, clothing, housing, attitudes proved deadly to Indians: Standing Bear reports that of the children who left his tribe with him to travel to Carlisle Indian School, fewer than half were still alive three years later.

The white man excused his presence here by saying that he had been guided by the will of his God; and in so saying absolved himself of all responsibility for his appearance in a land occupied by other men (p. 249).

Standing Bear is bitterly sarcastic when describing the logic of American exceptionalism. He explains how the sacred law of the white man was written in a book, and his actions were foretold in that book, in a manner only European eyes could see: 'And what better proof that his advent into this country and his subsequent acts were the result of divine will! He brought the Word!' (p. 249). Standing Bear is especially bitter because the privilege accorded the word supplanted the primacy of the spoken word in tribal culture. The superior man became the man who could write his name; the tribal wisdom expressed in verbal rituals was lost and those Indians who could not write were branded savages. Standing Bear inverts this value structure and argues that, seen on tribal terms, the Indian is much more civilised than Europeans. On this basis, he questions the authority by which whites presume to 'civilise' native people: 'Who can say that the white man's way is better for the Indian? Where resides the human judgment with the competence to weigh and value Indian ideals and spiritual concepts; or substitute for them other values?' (p. 251).

It was to escape this self-proclaimed right to 'regulate' Indian 'affairs' that Standing Bear left the reservation because he would not be held in bondage to whites any longer. In *The Soul of the Indian* (1911), Charles Alexander Eastman (Ohiyesa) set out to achieve the same kind of record of a disappearing traditional tribal life as Standing Bear. Eastman restricts his attention to the 'inner life' of the Sioux people, before contact with Europeans. This is important because, as he remarks, after contact the original beliefs and philosophy of the tribes underwent rapid transformation. In achieving this aim, however, Eastman is compromised by his own mixed-blood status. He bases his book upon his own childhood recollections, yet his maternal grandmother was married to the western artist, Captain Seth Eastman; their daughter Mary Nancy Eastman married Chief Many Lightnings of the Wahpeton Sioux. So even when Eastman was a child, his tribe had already experienced extensive contact with Europeans, and it is the process of transformation rather than the life that preceded it that is his subject. Eastman's life was very different to that of Luther Standing Bear, though they both attended Carlisle

Indian School. Eastman belonged to the Dakota Sioux, Standing Bear to the Lakota Sioux. Eastman was among the best-educated Indians of his time, receiving a Bachelor of Science degree from Dartmouth College in 1887 and a medical degree from Boston University three years later. In his description of his attitudes during this period, in his autobiography *From the Deep Woods to Civilization* (1916), Eastman reveals the extent to which he had internalised white values and white cultural mythology:

> Throughout my student days in the West, I had learned to reverence New England, and especially its metropolis, as the home of culture and art, of morality and Christianity. At that period that sort of thing got a lodging in my savage mind more readily than the idea of wealth or material power. Somehow I had supposed that Boston must be the home of the nation's elect and not far from the millennium.[14]

In time, Eastman was appointed physician at Pine Ridge Agency, where he witnessed the events leading to the Wounded Knee massacre and the subjection of his people.

Eastman uses his description of tribal spirituality to argue for equity between Indians and Europeans:

> We know that all religious aspiration, all sincere worship, can have but one source and one goal. We know that the God of the lettered and the unlettered, of the Greek and the barbarian, is after all the same God; and, like Peter, we perceive that He is no respecter of persons, but that in every nation he that feareth Him and worketh righteousness is acceptable to Him.[15]

Eastman begins with 'the Great Mystery' and the manner in which this spirit would be worshipped, through fasting, scourging or hardship, the purifying vapour-bath, prayer, offerings, and physical rites, relating these practices to religious rituals found in Christianity and he concludes: 'I believe that Christianity and modern civilization are opposed and irreconcilable, and that the spirit of Christianity and of our ancient religion is essentially the same' (p. 24). In the chapters that follow he describes the family altar, ceremonial and symbolic worship; the moral code; 'the unwritten scriptures' by which Eastman refers to the Sioux creation stories, the history, poetry and prophecy that comprise the native 'Bible'; and finally death, funeral customs, the occult and prophecy. It was only after the great Sioux uprising of 1862 that

Christian missionaries made significant numbers of converts among the Plains Indians and traditional religious practices went into decline. This was at the time when reservation life was enforced, together with government policies designed to eradicate tribal culture and replace it with the culture of white America. Cultural survival through religion, family and community ritual, moral and ethical values are what Eastman and Standing Bear are seeking to preserve by recording their experiences of them. Allotment revealed, above all, the vast distance separating Indian and western worldviews, despite the opinion repeatedly expressed that white and native Americans share a common spirituality and humanity. Humanity the races may share in common but the complex ways in which that humanity is given expression are irreconcilably different, as revealed in texts like D'Arcy McNickle's novel *Wind from an Enemy Sky*.[16]

This novel was published posthumously the year following McNickle's death in 1977. However, he had begun work on it as early as 1938, and continued to work on it until his death. The story is told from the point of view of Antoine, grandson of Bull, the chief of the Little Elk people, who has just returned home from an Indian government school. He finds his grandfather still living in the mountains where he refuses to abandon the traditional ways and adopt a settled farming lifestyle on the government agency as his brother Henry Jim has done. Antoine also finds his people in crisis; a new dam has been built in the mountains that has 'killed the water' by diverting the course of the river into the valley where water is needed by the white farmers who have settled there. The helpless rage experienced by members of the tribe who have seen their land taken from them and their children taken away to boarding school, many never to return, reaches a crescendo with this latest outrage. In the attempt to give expression to this rage, Bull's nephew Pock Face kills the first man he sees superintending the dam; it emerges that this young man is the nephew of the dam's builder, a financier, entrepreneur and philanthropist Adam Pell, who insists that he must discover the reason for his nephew's seemingly senseless murder.

Adam Pell is also the director of the Americana Institute, which holds the sacred Feather Boy bundle which Henry Jim had given away years before in the attempt to redirect his people's spiritual attention away from the old ways and towards Christianity. At the time of the novel's opening, Henry Jim has begun to realise the enormity of his mistake and the error of judgement that has led him to become one of the government's 'model Indians'. He wants Feather Boy back. He has come to believe that only the return of the sacred bundle will empower the Little Elk people and bring to an end the calamities they have suffered. The government agent, Rafferty, is an enlightened 'modern' man with progressive ideas and he tries to locate the sacred bundle. It is only after Adam Pell, who thinks of himself as a friend of the Indians and who, according to his sister, has made a 'hobby' of Indians, has come to understand the sheer rage that caused Pock Face to kill and realises a little of his own complicity in creating the occasion for the crime that any effort is expended to discover what has happened to the sacred bundle. They find that the bundle has been destroyed, eaten away by mould and moths as it lay neglected in the museum's basement. The question then of how best to respond to this loss exposes the profound difference between white and Indian attitudes. Adam Pell is upset by the loss of this artefact that was of such significance to the tribe; he had hoped to assuage his conscience by returning the bundle to the tribe he has wronged by taking their water. He fails completely to understand the significance of the bundle as a deity, as a living spiritual presence that, for the Little Elk, offers the only hope of a future. When Henry Jim gave Feather Boy away he severed all ties with the tribe and his brother refused to speak to him for more than thirty years. It is only his effort to retrieve the bundle that re-establishes those ties of kinship. And when the tribal medicine man, Two Sleeps, dreams his vision of Feather Boy and learns that the bundle is destroyed, he is devastated: he 'returned like a man coming back from the dead. Days would go by before the old one could sit up, he was so torn with pain and weakened by fever, and the people were troubled … as the days passed and the old one stayed behind his closed eyes, the silence began to speak for itself' (p. 199). By dreaming of the death of Feather Boy, Two Sleeps has dreamed the death of the Little Elk people and their God. Adam Pell cannot understand this. He does begin to grasp the extent of the injustice the Little Elk and other tribes have suffered, by the allotment policy and, before that, other means of appropriating Indian lands in the name of progress and the American mission.

This growing intelligence on Adam's part contributes to the final tragedy by emphasising the nobility of the men – Adam, Rafferty and Bull – who are caught up in a web of circumstance that is tangled beyond comprehension because of the separate racial consciousness of the actors in the drama. Because Adam cannot understand what the loss of Feather Boy means to the Little Elk people, he defies advice and insists on admitting his responsibility for the loss of the artefact. As evidence of his failure of understanding, he offers in its place a priceless South American tribal artefact which has meaning to him by virtue of its value and rarity but is meaningless to the Little Elk, who have a desperate need for their own real, living, effective tribal deities. When the reality of their loss becomes apparent, that Adam Pell has taken the water and now has taken their spirit, Bull kills first him and then Rafferty before he is killed himself. The tragedy is the loss of valued individuals who fail crucially to penetrate another's world view. The difference among these men is not one of humanity but of intellectual sympathy and racial or cultural identity.

When McNickle began work on *Wind From an Enemy Sky* conditions for native people and chances for tribal survival had begun to improve. The Roosevelt administration finally accepted that Indians were not in fact becoming extinct and the administration adopted reforms to halt and to reverse in part the damage done by the policy of allotment, to add to the resource base, and to involve Indian organisations in Indian affairs (McNickle, p. 93). The Indian Reorganisation Act of 1934 prohibited any further division of tribal land and allowed the Secretary of the Interior to return to tribal hands lands which had not been taken up by homesteaders; it authorised an annual appropriation for land purchase and a credit fund for economic development; tribes were authorised to govern themselves either in the manner of customary tribal usage or by formal written constitutions. But after World War Two the reform programme came under heavy attack by those who wanted to see an end to United States' responsibility for Indian affairs. Senator Arthur V. Watkins of Utah led the movement to bring to an end or 'terminate' the trusteeship by which the United States took moral and legal responsibility for the effect of legislative decisions upon the Indian peoples. Senator Watkins argued that the idea of Indians living separate from the mainstream of American life was neither possible nor desirable; rather, Indians should be freed of government interference in their lives and in their property. The policy of termination, adopted by the Eisenhower administration, transferred jurisdiction over criminal and civil law from the tribes to the states; further, the end of federal supervision was envisioned as the Secretary of the Interior was directed to review all laws and treaties and recommend what amendments or nullifications were required to release the United States from its responsibilities. The policy was applied initially to two tribes, the Klamath and Menominee, both of which were destroyed as a result; restrictions on the sale of allotment land were lifted and again land passed out of Indian ownership at a disastrous rate. The further implementation of the policy was halted pending Congressional review, during which time public opinion turned towards the Indian and the policy was not pursued (see McNickle, pp. 104–12).

The Kennedy–Johnson administration undertook the reform of Indian affairs as part of the campaign against poverty, through the agency of the Office of Economic Opportunity rather than the paternalistic Bureau of Indian Affairs. Community action programmes, the Head Start programme for early education within the home, the Upward Bound programme to encourage completion of high school and college entry, all returned responsibility to Indian tribes whilst providing the necessary federal resources (see McNickle, pp. 118–19). Presidents Johnson, in 1968, and Nixon, in 1970, in presidential addresses criticised previous Indian policy and gave support to the policy of democratic pluralism, endorsing the concept of partnership not paternalism. This was a radical departure from the idea that controlled attitudes towards Indians since the seventeenth century: that to civilise the native population meant to Europeanise them, that improvement and progress must be measured by approximation to a western lifestyle and culture. Vine Deloria Jr, in his manifesto *Custer Died for Your Sins* observes, 'while Nixon may have failed in spectacular fashion in other aspects of his presidency, in retrospect his administration must be granted very high marks for its Indian policy. In responsiveness to Indian aspirations, it will probably be seen as the best administration in American history, and in terms of its accomplishments it should be ranked close to the New Deal, which radically turned the tide in favor of Indians. In comparison to recent administrations, the Nixon years are exceedingly bright and filled with accomplishments.' [17]

In recent native American writing the policies of allotment and termination and the desire to force assimilation upon native people produce a discourse that resonates with apocalyptic imagery of genocide and terminal violence. Leslie Marmon Silko's *Almanac of the Dead* and Gerald Vizenor's *Bearheart: The Heirship Chronicles* are both powerfully evocative of the destructive force unleashed by white racism and American imperialism in this century. Silko creates a nightmare world of terrorism, torture, random violence, addiction, vice, greed and corruption, where everyone has forgotten even the prospect of a future but instead they are consumed with self-interest and with staying alive. The Americas have become a police state, each separate only in name, the corrupt dictators who rule by fear and physical threat, and the corrupt financiers who keep them in power, exert power that is almost total. They are 'the Destroyers', those about whom the Indian Tacho tells when questioned by his master about the power of blood:

> Were there human sacrifices anymore? [Menardo asked] Not by the Indians, Tacho said, but the human sacrificers had not just been the Mexican tribes. The Europeans who came had been human sacrificers too. Human sacrificers were part of the worldwide network of Destroyers who fed off energy released by destruction.[18]

The human landscape of Gerald Vizenor's *Bearheart: The Heirship Chronicles* is also consumed by the destructive energies unleashed by a corrupt Europeanised civilisation. Proude Cedarfair, the tribal keeper and protector of the sacred cedar forest, and his wife Rosina are forced to abandon the woodland home they have never left and make what becomes a ritual journey through the blasted land that is a postapocalyptic America that has run out of fuel. They escape the crazed and drunken violence of the elected tribal leader whose violent hatred of tribal people, customs and culture far surpasses the hostility of federal agents, but they encounter as well as the agents of destruction themselves also a succession of victims of violence. These victims have internalised the destructive energies they encounter in the world: Bishop Omax Parasimo thinks in terms of popular Hollywood definitions of Indians, Belladonna Darwin-Winter Catcher defines herself as Indian in romantic clichés, Matchi Makwa chants 'Our women were poisoned half white' (p. 59). The master of destruction, the Evil Gambler known as Sir Cecil, personifies all that is evil, selfish and destructive in his world, as he freely admits:

> Killing is just too easy now. Look at what has happened to the values of people and the corruption in government ... That thin plastic film known as social control hanging over the savage urge to kill was dissolved when the government failed and the economic world collapsed. What reason was there not to kill when money no longer worked? The government and private business, the businesses bigger

than government, started this indifference toward death with their pollution and industrial poisons ...The government tortured people and sanctioned killing.[19]

The genocidal energies directed towards tribal people through policies such as allotment and termination, but also through the invasion and appropriation of tribal land, through starvation and disease are, in texts like these by Silko and Vizenor, turned against the aggressors at last. Once the tribal people have been destroyed or subjugated those forces of destruction do not simply go away; they remain, and like a cancer they corrupt and destroy those who once directed them. Precisely this was the warning articulated by William Apess, who foresaw a time when the injustices, the destructiveness, the racial hostility, the lack of humanity evinced by those colonists who claimed to be God's elect would become the historical legacy inherited by the future generations. What Silko and Vizenor do in novels such as these is project into an imaginable American future the unimaginable horrors of the native American past. Their indictment of the ideology of Manifest Destiny and the exceptionalist mythology that informs it takes shape within the dramatisation of what has manifestly become America's destiny. The apocalyptic culmination of American history envisioned by the Puritan colonists who attempted to create a perfect church-society becomes in the native American imagination of Silko and Vizenor a punitive apocalypse where the arrogance, self-congratulation and self-interest that were the sins of the Founding Fathers are now visited upon the sons.

Notes

1. D'Arcy McNickle, *Native American Tribalism: Indian Survivals and Renewals* (New York, Oxford and London: Oxford University Press for the Institute for Race Relations, 1973), p. 50. Future page references are given in the text.
2. Samsum Occum, 'A Short Narrative of My Life' (1768), in Paul Lauter, *et al.* (eds), *The Heath Anthology of American Literature*, 2nd edn (Lexington MA and Toronto: D. W. Heath & Co., 1994), vol. 1, p. 944. Future page references are given in the text.
3. Samson Occum, 'Sermon Preached at the Execution of Moses Paul' (1772) in Nina Baym, *et al.* (eds), *The Norton Anthology of American Literature*, 4th edn (New York and London: W. W. Norton, 1994), p. 650. Future page references are given in the text.
4. Henderick Aupaumut, 'A Short Narration of my Last Journey to the Western Contry [*sic*]' (*c.* 1793), in Lauter, *et al.* (eds), *The Heath Anthology of American Literature*, p. 1144. Future page references are given in the text. The manuscript

was undiscovered until 1827, when it was published in *Memoirs of the Pennsylvania Historical Society*.

5. Handsome Lake, 'How America was Discovered', in Lauter *et al*. (eds), ibid., vol. 1, pp. 182–4. Future page references are given in the text.

6. Alexis de Toqueville, *Democracy in America* (1898), quoted by McNickle, *Native American Tribalism*, p. 3.

7. William Apess, *On Our Own Ground: The Complete Writings of William Apess, A Pequot*, ed. with introduction by Barry O'Connell (Amherst, MA: University of Massachusetts Press, 1992). Future page references are given in the text. It is in the essay, 'An Indian's Looking-Glass for the White Man', included in the first edition of *Five Christian Indians*, that Apess observes 'If black or red skins or any other skin of color is disgraceful to God, it appears that he has disgraced himself a great deal – for he has made fifteen colored people to one white and placed them here upon this earth' (p. 157).

8. John Wannuaucon Quinney, 'Quinney's Speech' (1854), in Lauter, *et al*. (eds), *The Heath Anthology of American Literature*, vol. 1, p. 1789. Future page references are given in the text.

9. Elias Boudinot, 'An Address to the Whites' (1826), in Lauter, *et al*. (eds), ibid., vol. 1, p. 1800.

10. James Welch, *Fools Crow* (New York: Viking Penguin, 1986). Future page references are given in the text.

11. D. S. Otis, 'History of the Allotment Policy', *Hearings Before the Committee on Indian Affairs*, House of Representatives, 73rd Congress, 2nd session, 1934. Quoted by McNickle, *Native American Tribalism*, p. 81.

12. Lewis Meriam, *et al*., *The Problem of Indian Administration* (Washington, DC: Brookings Institution, 1928). Quoted by McNickle, ibid., p. 92. See also Vine Deloria, Jr, *Custer Died for Your Sins: An Indian Manifesto* (1969, rpt Norman, OK: University of Oklahoma Press, 1988), 'The Disastrous Policy of Termination', pp. 54–77.

13. Luther Standing Bear, *Land of the Spotted Eagle*, foreword by Richard N. Ellis (1933, rpt Lincoln and London: University of Nebraska Press, 1978). Future page references are given in the text. Luther Standing Bear, *My People the Sioux*, ed. E. A. Brininstool, introduction by Richard N. Ellis (1928, rpt Lincoln and London: University of Nebraska Press, 1975).

14. Charles Alexander Eastman (Ohiyesa), *From the Deep Woods to Civilization*, introduction by Raymond Wilson (1916, rpt Lincoln and London: University of Nebraska Press, 1977), p. 70. Future page references are given in the text.

15. Charles Alexander Eastman, *The Soul of the Indian: An Interpretation* (1911, rpt Lincoln and London: University of Nebraska Press, 1980), foreword, pp. xiii–xiv. Future page references are given in the text.

16. D'Arcy McNickle, *Wind From an Enemy Sky* (1978, rpt Albuquerque: University of New Mexico Press, 1995). Future page references are given in the text.

17. Vine Deloria Jr, *Custer Died for Your Sins*, p. viii.

18. Leslie Marmon Silko, *Almanac of the Dead* (New York: Viking Penguin, 1991), p. 336. Future page references are given in the text.

19. Gerald Vizenor, *Bearheart: The Heirship Chronicles* (1978, rpt Minneapolis: University of Minnesota Press, 1990), p. 127.

CHAPTER 3

Exceptionalism in the
Nineteenth Century

This chapter returns to the uses of exceptionalism to explain and justify the expansion of the United States. Emerson's use of the concept to characterise the unique qualities of America and the American is attacked by Hawthorne and Melville as part of a spiritual and moral critique of their contemporary America. Anti-slavery writers used the rhetoric of exceptionalism to attack the 'peculiar institution' as an integral part of American culture as it had developed. Despite these arguments, exceptionalism became a key element, represented powerfully in the visual art of the period, in the ideology of 'Manifest Destiny' that attempted to justify the annexation of the Hispanic south-west and the continuing subjugation of native Americans.

Exceptionalism and the American Renaissance

The term 'American Renaissance' was coined by the critic F. O. Matthiessen as the title of his book, *American Renaissance: Art and Expression in the Age of Emerson and Whitman* (1941). Matthiessen used the phrase to describe the achievement represented by a group of texts published between 1850 and 1855: Emerson's *Representative Men*, Hawthorne's *The Scarlet Letter* and *The House of the Seven Gables*, Melville's *Moby Dick* and *Pierre*, Thoreau's *Walden* and Whitman's *Leaves of Grass*. In Matthiessen's estimation, the publication of these texts marks the moment of America's cultural independence, as opposed to political independence; the moment when America emerged as a distinctive culture, equal to but different from the culture of Europe. The thematic link among these writers is their common objection to the materialism and commercialism dominating American national life and the extent to which this worldly concern presented an obstacle to the realisation of America's exceptional destiny. In the works of these 'Renaissance' writers, Matthiessen found a return to the rhetoric of the Puritan founders. In imaginative literature, these writers were exploring the same issues and using a style of rhetoric derived from the founders of the nation. So Matthiessen identifies the relationship between the material world and an ideal 'other' world – 'another world yet one to which we feel the tie' – as the common ground uniting his Renaissance writers to each other and binding them to an American tradition that reaches back to the colonial roots of the nation. Where America is heading, and how the national values must be reformed in order to realise the glorious destiny that will be America's: these are the themes upon which Matthiessen focuses.

> They [Emerson, Hawthorne, Thoreau, Whitman, and Melville] all wrote literature for democracy ... They felt that it was incumbent upon their generation to give fulfilment to the potentialities freed by the Revolution, to provide a culture commensurate with America's political opportunity. Their tones were sometimes optimistic, sometimes blatantly, even dangerously expansive, sometimes disillusioned, even despairing, but what emerges from the total pattern of their achievement – if we will make the effort to repossess it – is literature for our democracy. In reading the lyric, heroic, and tragic expression of our first great age, we can feel the challenge of our still undiminished resources.[1]

Where their Puritan (intellectual) ancestors had anticipated an exceptional destiny based upon the perfection of ecclesiastical institutions, nineteenth-century intellectuals anticipated the perfection of political, specifically democratic, institutions. The substance of the rhetoric had changed in the course of the eighteenth century, moving inexorably from religion to politics, but the nature of exceptionalist rhetoric remained essentially the same. America will now be the global champion of democracy and privileged guardian of political values.

An indication of the importance of American democracy to the writers Matthiessen identifies can be found in 'Democratic Vistas' (1871), Walt Whitman's prose critique of American destiny, which he describes in openly exceptionalist terms:

> To-day, ahead, though dimly yet, we see, in vistas a copious, sane, gigantic offspring. For our New World I consider far less important for what it has done, or what it is, than for results to come. Sole

among nationalities, these States have assumed the task to put in forms of lasting power and practicality, on areas of amplitude rivaling the operations of the physical kosmos, the moral political speculations of ages, long, long deferr'd, the democratic republican principle, and the theory of development and perfection by voluntary standards, and self-reliance. Who else, indeed, except the United States, in history, so far, have accepted in unwitting faith, and, as we now see, stand, act upon, and go security for, these things? [2]

Later in the same essay, Whitman claims that the words America and democracy are convertible, interchangeable, and he predicts that America will become a global force to dominate the world in political, commercial and cultural terms (p. 461).

These sympathies informed Whitman's entire literary career. In his work, Walt Whitman took it upon himself to represent all of American society and to dramatise his empathy with all Americans, even the meanest. This, in Whitman's estimation, was the characteristic of American genius, closely related to Emerson's concept of the poet who enjoys a special relationship with the natural world and is, as a result, the privileged interpreter of the correspondences revealed in nature and the arbiter of relations among the self, nature and society. In his epic of America, 'Song of Myself', Whitman's form and content are completely fused into one as the poet gathers to himself all that comprises the nation and gives expression to this assimilation in the poem. For example, section 15 is a catalogue of character types, culminating in the lines:

> And these tend inward to me, and I tend outward to them
> And such as it is to be of these more or less I am,
> And of these one and all I weave the song of myself.[3]

The autobiography of the poet unites the poetic form and the themes, creating a perfect unity that parallels Emerson's claim that for the American poet 'history is biography': Whitman's poetic counter-claim, in 'Song of Myself', is that the poet *is* America. In section 5 he confesses:

> And I know that the hand of God is the promise of my own,
> And I know that the spirit of God is the brother of my own,
> And that all the men ever born are also my brothers, and the
>   women my sisters and lovers,
> And that a kelson of the creation is love
> And limitless are leaves stiff or drooping in the fields (p. 27).

The image of leaves is taken up at the beginning of the following section in the image of grass, which is both singular and plural, a collective unity powerfully suggestive of the limitless nation, from the soil of which it grows. The grass is the American dead from whose graves it arises, the grass is symbolic of the immortality Americans find in their nation, which, in its unity and collective life, also defeats death. And all, absorbed by the poet, is transmuted by him into the immortality of art. Section 24 Whitman introduces himself by name, 'Walt Whitman, a kosmos', and goes on to explain that description of himself by celebrating the mysterious union of individual and society, the secular spirit within the land and the people that is expressed through the poet.

> I speak the pass-word primeval, I give the sign of democracy,
> By God! I will accept nothing which all cannot have their
>   counterpart of on the same terms.

> Through me many long dumb voices,
> Voices of the interminable generations of prisoners and slaves,
> Voices of the diseas'd and despairing and of thieves and dwarfs,
> Voices of cycles of preparation and accretion,
> And of the threads that connect the stars, and of wombs and of
>   the father-stuff,
> And of the rights of them the others are down upon,
> Of the deform'd, trivial, flat, foolish, despised,
> Fog in the air, beetles rolling balls of dung (p. 43).

In this catalogue, Whitman relates his commitment to American democracy to his poetic function of giving voice to the sublime. Subsequently, section 33 offers a panoramic catalogue of sights: America's geographical expansiveness, beauty and abundance. Whitman's message throughout his epic celebration of America's potential is that the American poet is like a priest or prophet bringing egalitarian salvation; Whitman's primary revelation to the masses is that they are the source of national value and the agents of the nation's glorious democratic destiny.

Perhaps Whitman's greatest inspiration came from Ralph Waldo Emerson's work, where the mythology of American exceptionalism combined with the ideals of the Romantic movement that was sweeping Europe, to supplant the rational ideals of the eighteenth-century Enlightenment. This meant that a number of reversals took place in terms of cultural values: emotion now took precedence over reason, intuition over logic, nature over civilisation, the individual over society, spirituality over commerce, and so on. America was seen by many to respond very positively to this new evaluation of experience. Where America lacked a sophisticated social structure and extensive history of civilisation, it possessed an abundance of natural splendour and wilderness where the individual was responsible for his or her own destiny and where the immersion in nature might give rise to feelings and a kind of understanding that surpasses rational logic. In the untouched innocence of the American wilderness the national destiny could be redefined as the transcendence of European corruption and sophistication and the realisation of a unique alternative destiny. Emerson was not ignorant of the growing commercialism of America in the early nineteenth century but he was optimistic that the new emphasis upon essential truth rather than superficial appearances would transform the image of America from one of debased materialism to one of spiritual advantage. In America, unlike the corrupted societies of Europe, one can see clearly beyond the vagaries of historical appearance to the timeless truths embodied by nature and the original or primitive organisation of society, to which America must return in fulfilment of her exceptional destiny.

The essay 'Nature' has become the most familiar of Emerson's works, the essay in which he sets out the fundamental ideas that inform his thinking. In this essay, Emerson describes nature as the medium for establishing an 'original relation to the universe'. What he means by this is that through nature we can see God face to face. According to Emerson, nature is comprised half of physical matter and half of soul. The human soul needs nature in order to become whole and this reconciliation of self and nature must be made anew by each generation and by each new society. Only nature can truly provide for the health of the individual self and of the community. What Emerson is proposing is a new interpretation of the covenant; where individual Americans and America collectively must covenant themselves to nature in order to fulfil the national destiny. Knowledge of nature can be achieved only in isolation, in the wilderness, and so America offers unrivalled opportunities for an exceptional relationship with nature. What this relationship brings is the discovery of true spiritual identity in nature. This 'true identity' reveals the individual self as a 'particle of God', a medium of the 'Universal Being'. The image Emerson uses is that of a 'transparent eyeball' which, being nothing, sees all. The self in this way becomes part of the harmony between the human and the natural that is the primitive state America is destined to achieve as a nation. This experience is what Emerson refers to as the living out of truths before apprehending them as truths – an experience that exemplifies the superiority of intuition and feeling over abstract logic.

It is in 'The American Scholar' that Emerson turns explicitly to the issue of America as a nation and the direction in which American society is progressing. He begins by contrasting love of letters and the intellectual life with the pervasive love of materialism that he finds around him. He looks, optimistically, to a future American culture that is self-reliant and complete in itself rather than unbalanced, as at present. The fate of society is bound up with the fate of individuals. Present society inhibits the individual with social divisions and specialisations (the professions) that limit individual potential. The self is then incapable of harmonious existence in the present society, which values only literal, material things and achievements. Nature and not society in its present form will, in the future, provide the true measure of personal value and achievement. Emerson is confident that nature would come to be the dominating force in American life, as the nation approaches its prescribed destiny. In America, citizens cannot escape the self-knowledge that comes from nature and works as a liberating force upon human thought because it reveals the web of correspondences that unites all of the creation together into a seamless whole. Consequently, American nature must become the model for an ideal American society.

The connection between 'Americanness' and the American landscape that Emerson celebrates had been explored extensively, only a few years before the decade of the American Renaissance, in James Fenimore Cooper's Leatherstocking Tales, which were published between 1823 and 1841. This series of five novels appeared at a time when American settlement was expanding rapidly westward, transforming the wilderness into tamed frontier. The struggle between the wilderness and encroaching civilisation is examined through the figure of Natty Bumpo, who is represented through the novels at various stages in his life – from youth to old age – in the course of which he becomes an archetypal American character, in the mould of Daniel Boone and other frontier heroes. Natty's instinctive honesty, courage and generosity define him as a mythical figure of American frontier life; his conception draws upon no European literary model yet he represents an American incarnation of the noble savage, the natural aristocrat who learns from and responds directly to the natural world, in which he is at home. The conflict between simplicity and sophistication that is so important to Romantic thought is given an American interpretation in Natty's opposition to the direction of American progress. His natural values and primitive virtues oppose the increasing materialism of a nation more concerned with commercial trade than with spiritual commerce.

In the second of the Leatherstocking novels, *The Last of the Mohicans* (1826), Cooper describes the power of nature to teach men how to live as being like that of God:

> I have heard it said, that there are men who read in books, to convince themselves there is a God! I know not but man may so deform his works in the settlements, as to leave that which is so clear in the wilderness, a matter of doubt among traders and priests. If any such there be, and he will follow me from sun to sun, through the windings of the forest, he shall see enough to teach him that he is a fool, and that the greatest of his folly lies in striving to rise to the level of one he can never equal, be it in goodness, or be it in power.[4]

Leatherstocking's Christian respondent, David Gamut, soon drops his own sermonising from the Bible in the face of the scout's natural wisdom and the truth of his accusation that the settlement of the wilderness has obscured the source of instinctive wisdom. At the beginning of the following chapter, Hawk-eye describes the setting sun as 'the signal given to man to seek his food and natural rest, ... better and wiser would it be, if he could understand the signs of nature, and take a lesson from the fowls of the air, and the beasts of the field!' (p. 124). In Hawk-eye's estimation, and Cooper's narrator appears to concur with it, it is the wise man who is able to read the signs of nature, but that is because nature itself is his tutor and source of understanding. This close and sympathetic relationship is represented by Cooper as the measure for civilised corruption; a close relationship with nature is normal, the alienation of humanity from nature such as occurs in the towns and settlements is unnatural and corrupt. As the scout with his Mohican companions, Uncas and Chingachook, guide the Munro sisters across the frontier wilderness, human qualities are shown to be reflected in their relationship with the beauty of the land: this is particularly the case when the sisters encounter the sublimity of Glenn Falls (in Chapter 5). The attitude towards the American landscape revealed to them exposes different values held by the various characters: whether they consider the wilderness as darkly mysterious, or as a place to hide, or as a source of wisdom and a resource – each choice reflects a different kind of personality by which the exceptional nature of Hawk-eye is measured.

The first novel of the Leatherstocking series, *The Pioneers* (1823), relates this sympathetic view of nature to the issue of how society should be regulated and governed, how individuals should relate to each other and, most importantly, how society should progress in its destined direction. In *The Pioneers*, each character represents a different attitude towards the question of government: young Oliver upholds family rights and the right of inheritance; Judge Temple holds democratic values and supports the right of individual initiative; Indian John upholds the right of inheritance but through a moral imperative not the right of birth; and the Leatherstocking upholds the right of use. This issue is urgent in *The Pioneers* because in the timescale of the novel the American landscape is changing its status and becoming an asset rather than a communal holding. Nature is being violated and nature's laws are being replaced with petty legal systems that condone exploitation when they should promote conservation. The wilderness is vanishing and with it the values that distinguished America from the corrupt societies of the Old World; the opportunities for spiritual renewal offered by the wilderness are shrinking. The exceptional destiny of America is precisely to resist this kind of corruption but, where the original colonists believed that they had purified their society and their church, Cooper represents this as a struggle that is still as urgent in the nineteenth century as it had been two centuries earlier. What is at stake in this struggle is the national character and the future of the American nation. The American wilderness has produced characters like Leatherstocking or Hawk-eye, who represent all the virtues of the New World, but who are under threat like the land itself, as the game is trapped out and the frontier shifts ever-westward.

As Elizabeth Temple, returning from years away at school, surveys the precincts of her home she is struck by the difference those few years have made. The town of Templeton is established, the wilderness has receded, the frontier has been civilised – so many of the trees are gone. Cooper is savagely critical of the fashion in which scarce and non-renewable resources like trees, pigeons, fish are thoughtlessly wasted in this process of civilising the wilderness. Cooper describes the settlers shooting pigeons with cannon, fishing with massive nets and killing the

trees to extrude maple syrup. This thoughtless waste is related to the
rise of conspicuous consumption in place of a subsistence economy.
Earlier, Natty could live alone and hunt for his food but the development
of extensive and often specialist markets has meant providing for a mass
of people, which creates the opportunity for greed, for the pursuit of
self-interest, and for exploitation of resources. Both Natty and the Judge
agree that 'wasty ways' must end, but they disagree profoundly on the
principle by which this should be achieved: the Judge is in favour of
moderation through commercialisation, rationalising and governing the
operation of market sectors, such as sugar production.[5] Natty cannot
agree with this, and protests that their condemnation of such wasteful-
ness does not indicate any like-mindedness.

> No, no; we are not much of one mind, Judge, or you'd never turn
> good hunting grounds into stumpy pastures. And you hunt and fish
> out of rule; but, to me, the flesh is sweeter where the creater has
> some chance for its life: for that reason, I always use a single ball,
> even if it be at a bird or a squirrel (p. 254).

The historical romance that Cooper is writing in this and the other
Leatherstocking Tales engages historical forces of progress and of
reaction, struggling for prominence.[6] In *The Pioneers*, Natty represents
the forces of reaction and the story engages him in a struggle with the
forces of progress, exploitation and legalism that comprise the very civilisation that he, working as a frontier scout for the trappers and military
forces that precede civilisation, has helped to bring to the wilderness. In
these novels, the nature of American civilisation and how this progress
may further the exceptional destiny of the new nation is what is at issue.
Cooper's dramatic representation of the transformation of wilderness
into private property suggests a pessimistic vision of America's ability
to realise the great democratic promise it possesses. The struggle for
national destiny has not yet been won, in Cooper's fiction.

The optimism expressed by Emerson and Whitman was sharply
contradicted by the pessimism of Cooper's historical view, which, in
turn, was overshadowed at mid-century by the work of Nathaniel
Hawthorne, who, with his friend and fellow Herman Melville, savagely
criticised optimistic predictions for America. Though they shared Emerson's distaste for the commercialism of the nation, they were less
prepared than Emerson to allow for the possibility of dramatic cultural
reformation. In the story prefatory to Hawthorne's *The Scarlet Letter*

(1850), 'The Custom-House', he presents a scathing view of the Republic. This is a semi-autobiographical sketch; Hawthorne's tenure at the Salem custom-house was a political appointment, and when the government changed Hawthorne found himself out of a job. This experience contributes to the bitter tone of 'The Custom-House' but does not explain passages like the following description of the custom-house itself:

> Over the entrance hovers an enormous specimen of the American eagle, with outspread wings, a shield before her breast, and, if I recollect aright, a bunch of intermingled thunderbolts and barbed arrows in each claw. With the customary infirmity of temper that characterizes this unhappy fowl, she appears, by the fierceness of her beak and eye and the general truculence of her attitude, to threaten mischief to the inoffensive community; and especially to warn all citizens, careful of their safety, against intruding on the premises which she overshadows with her wings. Nevertheless, vixenly as she looks, many people are seeking, at this very moment, to shelter themselves under the wing of the federal eagle; imagining, I presume, that her bosom has all the softness and snugness of an eiderdown pillow. But she has no great tenderness, even in her best of moods, and, sooner or later, – oftener sooner than late, – is apt to fling off her nestlings with a scratch of her claw, a dab of her beak, or a rankling wound from her barbed arrows.[7]

Hawthorne's sarcastic delineation of a federal government that is actively hostile towards its citizens, which offers insult and injury to those it should protect, gives a good indication of Hawthorne's view of the nation's capacity to realise in practice the democratic ideals of its rhetoric. In the narrative that follows this sketch, *The Scarlet Letter*, Hawthorne represents the Puritan inheritance that informs his contemporary America. The style of Puritanism that Hawthorne presents is drab and gloomy, preoccupied with judgement and punishment, unrelenting and dogmatic. It is not surprising that Hawthorne then shows the nineteenth-century descendants of these Puritans as the victims of an unchanging and decaying culture.

Throughout his work, Hawthorne expresses a recurrent scepticism about the possibility of individual and collective change or transformation; in particular he is doubtful whether it is possible to shrug off the past and in all of his 'romances' (as Hawthorne termed his extended prose narratives) characters are haunted by elements of their personal or historical pasts. According to Hawthorne, it is not possible to achieve a complete self-reformation, to re-make oneself anew, and begin over again in time. Hawthorne did not believe that America could achieve the kind of reformation necessary for a great democratic future; nor did he believe that individuals could achieve in their own personal lives the same kind of reformation. Even more than their different historical perspectives, it was Hawthorne's attack on Emerson's view of the individual, the poet, the privileged interpreter of the natural world, that set the two men apart most radically. *The Scarlet Letter* explores the relationship of the individual in society ironically by focusing upon characters who are isolated from the human community, either by circumstance or by choice. Hester Prynne is an outcast because of her sin of adultery; her estranged husband, Chillingworth, places himself beyond the pale of humanity by discovering Reverend Dimmesdale's secret (that he is the father of Hester's child) and using that secret knowledge to persecute him to death. In this way, Chillingworth transforms himself into the likeness of the Devil or 'the Black Man', as Hester calls him (p. 60). The narrator later describes the change in his features and reports the orthodox Puritan interpretation of the conflict between Chillingworth and the sainted Dimmesdale as a repetition of the biblical paradigm:

> It grew to be a widely diffused opinion, that the Reverend Arthur Dimmesdale, like many other personages of especial sanctity, in all ages of the Christian world, was haunted either by Satan himself, or Satan's emissary, in the guise of old Roger Chillingworth. This diabolical agent had the Divine permission, for a season, to burrow into the clergyman's intimacy, and plot against his soul (pp. 94–5).

Dimmesdale himself sees his suffering in these terms, as a test of his spiritual strength and of his authority as one of God's elect. For Chillingworth, this is a simple act of revenge which he enjoys all the more because the need for secrecy calls upon his reserves of knowledge and cunning. Chillingworth resembles, more than some satanic agent, the model interpreter described by Emerson's poet. Chillingworth enjoys a special relationship with nature, he is able to grasp nature's secrets and read there the powerful medicinal cures that make him such an important member of the Puritan community, he is able to penetrate to the souls of his fellows and understand their experience and emotions. But where Emerson's poet always uses this knowledge for good purposes and is disposed only to do good, Hawthorne's character is motivated by pure evil. Chillingworth commits what Hawthorne termed the unpardonable sin: violating the sanctity of the human heart through hypocrisy, egotism, and the will to domination. Chillingworth's human emotions are overcome by the force of his manipulative intellect and this leads to the death of the heart. When Hester encounters him gathering herbs, she is shocked by his diabolical transformation and wonders whether the nature with which he has such sympathy now shrinks from his step: 'Would he not suddenly sink into the earth, leaving a barren and blasted spot, where, in due course of time, would be seen deadly nightshade, dogwood, henbane, and whatever else of vegetable wickedness the climate could produce, all flourishing with hideous luxuriance?' (p. 126).

Hawthorne was intensely sceptical about the likelihood that America would achieve the glorious destiny set down by exceptionalist mythology. In *The Scarlet Letter* he cast doubt upon the motivation of the Puritan rhetoric out of which exceptionalism emerged. But that did not mean that he could not foresee any historical change at all – for Hawthorne, historical change meant a falling away from not a movement towards the conditions of perfection. Herman Melville shared his friend Hawthorne's sense of scepticism towards America's destiny and the emergence of an American personality that would bring the national destiny closer.

In the novels that F. O. Matthiessen cites as among the masterpieces of the American Renaissance – *Moby Dick* and *Pierre* – Melville dramatises through the characters of his heroes precisely the inability of an isolated consciousness, no matter how privileged, to reveal anything beyond its own egotism. Both Ahab and Pierre are possessed of an exceptional inability to live conventionally; they challenge nature and God as they seek a superior access to knowledge. In a letter to Hawthorne, Melville expressed his concern about the implications of too great a reliance upon the authority of personal judgement:

> We incline to think that God cannot explain His own secrets, and that He would like a little information upon certain points Himself. We mortals astonish Him as much as He us. ... [But] as soon as you say *Me*, a *God*, a *Nature*, so soon you jump off from your stool and hang from the beam. Yes, that word is a hangman. Take God out of the dictionary, and you would have Him in the street.[8]

By setting up their own selves as an absolute measure of truth, they play a dangerous and ultimately deathly game: *Pierre* ends in suicide and *Moby Dick* in the destruction of Captain Ahab's ship and all hands but one, the narrator Ishmael. Ahab, in his single-minded pursuit of the white whale, seeks to pierce the 'paste-board masks', as he calls them, of everyday appearances, to some metaphysical truth within. This increasingly mad obsession endangers the entire crew and leads to the passionate exchange between Ahab and Starbuck, where the latter speaks openly at last about the potential blasphemy of Ahab's pursuit of the white whale. Ahab responds:

> He tasks me; he heaps me; I see in him outrageous strength, with an inscrutable malice sinewing it. That inscrutable thing is chiefly what I hate; and be the white whale agent, or be the white whale principal, I will wreak that hate upon him. Talk not to me of blasphemy, man; I'd strike the sun if it insulted me.[9]

Starbuck's common sense is defeated by Ahab's personal strength, courage and mystery: the monomaniacal authority of the rhetoric of the self. The refusal of the natural world to reveal some transcendent truth defies Ahab's confidence in his own ability to perceive it. And so his ultimate defeat by the whale suggests that greater strength and mystery reside in an unredeemed natural world that is without benevolence towards the world of humanity. Of course, Emerson always assumed that nature was benevolent towards humanity; the very concept that nature might be hostile or indifferent to human destiny would contradict the entire set of Romantic assumptions upon which Emerson's thinking was based, as it would upset the inherited Puritan assumptions about the divine subtext communicated by American nature to God's chosen people. In Emerson's view, a view which Melville and Hawthorne found deeply disturbing and problematical, the destiny of America depended unquestionably upon the readability of the American landscape and the benevolent message to be found there: a message that would describe the glorious destiny awaiting the new nation. However, it was not only in the natural world but in the particulars of nineteenth-century American history (the institution of slavery, overwhelmingly) that critics of exceptionalism found signs of a very different national destiny.

Exceptionalism and the Rhetoric of Abolition

The idealism of America and the conception of a divine destiny awaiting the historical progress of the nation was brutally contradicted by the continuing practice of slave-holding. The 'peculiar institution' of slavery offered a damning vision of a society given over to the corruption it claimed, in its public mythology, to have overcome. Consequently, the rhetorical style exploited by ex-slaves, in writing of their lives in bondage, was that of exceptionalism. It was important for these writers that they maintained a predominantly realistic style, for the pro-slavery response to these narratives was to deny their truth and accuracy. Slave writers, then, found it necessary to vouch for the authenticity of their stories in various ways: by appending letters by prominent public figures like William Lloyd Garrison in the case of Frederick Douglass and Lydia Maria Child in Harriet Jacobs's case. Exceptionalism therefore appears as a powerful sub-text and imagistic motif that contributes an ideological critique of America's self-image in conflict with actual historical practices. This critique lends power and substance to the slaves' recollections of shocking violence, brutality and institutionalised abuse.

Harriet Jacobs (who wrote under the pseudonym of Linda Brent) published her autobiographical narrative of captivity and escape, *Incidents in the Life of a Slave Girl, Written by Herself*, in 1861.[10] In this narrative, she uses the rhetoric of exceptionalism initially to describe her own exclusion from America's myth of national destiny and then to enact a condemnation of the brand of Christianity that supports both slavery and exceptionalism and, by that very combination, undermines its own claim to exemplary moral and spiritual status. In the place of exceptionalist ideology, Jacobs presents her allegiance to an alternative vision of America's potential. She concludes with the prayer, 'May the blessing of God rest on this imperfect effort in behalf of my persecuted people!' (p. 2). This exclamation takes on an additional dimension of meaning when read in the context of exceptionalism and especially the earlier captivity narratives that deployed exceptionalist rhetoric so powerfully. Jacobs hopes through her writing to free her enslaved people, as did the Puritan writers like Mary Rowlandson, who wrote to warn her community of their enslavement to sin. But where Mrs Rowlandson was justly chastised (in her penitent view) as part of God's redemptive plan for New England, Linda Brent is unjustly chastised by the redeemer nation itself and its racialised interpretation of national destiny. Where Mrs Rowlandson is carried into the howling wilderness of the godless interior, Harriet Jacobs writes her story in order to expose the howling moral wilderness that exists at the very heart of American civilisation. Throughout her narrative, Jacobs uses biblical images of captivity to expose the moral wilderness within. She uses the biblical authority of exceptionalism to sanction her own condemnation of slave-holding culture. At the centre of the divinely sanctioned institutions of Anglo-American culture – the home, the church and the state – she finds savagery and chaos. Jacobs's narrative exposes the darkest and most brutal aspects of southern society, which she likens to the whited sepulchre of Matthew 23:27, 'full of dead men's bones and all unclean-ness' (p. 36).

Incidents abounds with instances where the Bible offers a source of comprehension for Linda's various ordeals. Often she finds a vocabu-lary with which to describe the incidents of her life in the paradigmatic scriptural accounts of apparently causeless suffering. Where Linda likens the spiritual condition of her oppressors to that of the followers of Satan, she finds a parallel to her ordeal under slavery in the bondage of the Israelites, that same image so favoured in exceptionalist writing. At the end of a lengthy description of the brutalising effect of slavery upon the masters and slaves alike, she claims 'You may believe what I say; for I write only that whereof I know. I was twenty-one years in that cage of obscene birds' (p. 52). Here, she creates a parallel between her own enslavement and the captivity of the Israelites in Babylon: 'And he cried mightily with a strong voice, saying Babylon the great is fallen, is fallen, and is become the habitation of devils, and the hold of every foul spirit, and a cage of every unclean and hateful bird' (Revelation 18:2).

Linda places her own ordeals within the interpretative framework of merciful chastisement and wonders, 'for what wise purpose God was leading me through such thorny paths and whether still darker days were in store for me' (p. 20). Unlike Puritan captives such as Mary Rowlandson, Linda Brent never does reach a conclusion about the specific sins that are punished by her enslavement. The absence of causation or individual responsibility is one of the most powerful indict-ments of American racial ideology represented through the use of exceptionalist rhetoric. Linda's resistance of the sexual harassment she experiences at the hands of her master, Dr Flint, she describes as 'the war of my life' (p. 19). She likens her master to the Devil, a 'hoary-headed miscreant' (p. 34), and the conflict in which they are engaged as the struggle between vice and virtue, Satan and Christ, for possession of her soul. The spiritual forces fighting for her soul are represented within the narrative by the fiendish Dr Flint and the exemplar of genuine Christian values, Linda's grandmother. This becomes apparent when Linda describes how her master attempts to corrupt the Christian virtues and the teachings of forbearance and patient suffering instilled by her grandmother. 'He peopled my young mind with unclean images, such as only a vile monster could think of' (p. 27). Her saintly grandmother stands as the only protection Linda has from the 'fiends who bear the shape of men' (p. 27). Rather than visible saints, Linda finds that the manifest spiritual condition of those around her is that of the damned. She is surrounded by the visibly lost; only her grandmother approaches the condition of the saved. Not surprisingly, Linda refuses the passive acceptance of suffering that is recommended by exceptionalist rhetoric. Instead she tells how God encourages her to resist the suffering that is imposed by her fellow humans, and assists in her unlawful escape from bondage. Linda now prays for God's assistance and guidance and finds her prayers answered in the form of a white benefactress who hides Linda after she has run away. This woman remains anonymous, identified in the narrative only as a special Providence from God. God's assistance of Linda's escape is one example of divine Providence operating to help those who would escape slavery: the escape of Linda's brother to the North is also interpreted as the work of the divine will. In this way, Harriet Jacobs shows how the providential structure of divine history works not to further but to subvert the proclaimed national destiny of America. Providence aids those marginalised and silenced by mainstream American culture. Yet the operations of Providence are articulated by an exceptionalist style of expression.

Trust in God becomes a meaningful experience after Linda has learned to distinguish the God of the slave-holders from the God who assists her flight. Once she has acknowledged that the mythology of American exceptionalism and the God who directs it pose the most serious threat to her autonomy and freedom, Linda is able to take control of her own destiny. Then she chooses to trust in God and is rewarded. This distinction between the exceptionalist model that oppresses and the biblical parallel that illuminates and inspires is repeated throughout the rest of the narrative. Even in the final chapter, at the end, when her freedom is in sight and yet she is still pursued by members of the Flint family who would return her to slavery, Linda emphasises the extent to which American culture departs from the religious paradigm that supplies the national mythology. Her freedom is guaranteed only after she has been purchased by her benefactress, Mrs Bruce, and the fact that she has been bought and sold is bitter to her: 'The bill of sale is on record, and future generations will learn from it that women were articles of traffic in New York, late in the nineteenth century of the Christian religion' (p. 200). In a letter dated 30 October 1859, Amy Post recalls that soon after her emancipation Harriet Jacobs wrote to her that 'the freedom I had before the money was paid was dearer to me. God gave me *that* freedom; but man put God's image in the scales with the paltry sum of three hundred dollars. I served for my liberty as faithfully as Jacob served for Rachel'.[11] Jacobs focuses her bitterness and outrage upon the crucial distinction between the public mythology and actual practices of American culture. In her America, the logic of biblical parallel simply does not work; Jacobs may serve for her freedom, like Jacob for Rachel, but in a deeply corrupted society the parallel falters and fails. Money rules in a nation that claims for itself an exceptional divine guidance that is denied all the other nations of earth.

The analysis of socio-economic forces is an integral part of the slave narrative form, as the ex-slave struggles to perceive her- or himself as a product of those forces. The slave autobiography, then, offers an analysis of American racism by exposing the difference between authentic identity and the false identity imposed by racism. This sense of living with two identities, this 'double consciousness' as W. E. B. Du Bois called it, has a parallel in the discovery of two 'Americas'. This theme of national identity is represented in Frederick Douglass's autobiography by the journey North; the physical journey symbolises the spiritual movement towards a society where the 'slave' will be accepted as a legitimate citizen. So the journey embodies the flight from a repressive and corrupt society and a false sense of self towards an alternative purified society and the realisation of a true self. *Narrative of the life of Frederick Douglass, An American Slave* (1845) contrasts American slavery with American Christianity, much as Harriet Jacobs does in her autobiography.[12] And in the same way as Jacobs, Douglass comes to recognise the America of the South as the arch-enemy of his freedom and integrity, while America's biblically-inspired national rhetoric assists him in explaining the stages of his liberation.

At the outset of his narrative, Douglass points to the unique character of American slavery: that with the cessation of importing slaves from Africa, the increase in the slave population came from breeding within the domestic population:

> It is ... plain that a very different-looking class of people are springing up at the south, and are now held in slavery, from those originally brought to this country from Africa; and if their increase will do no other good, it will do away with the force of the argument, that God cursed Ham, and therefore American slavery is right (p. 491).

Douglass exposes the absurdity of the biblical justification of slavery just as he shows how the rhetoric of American democracy and American Christianity is made absurd by the reality of slavery. He uses America's beliefs to condemn American practices. Douglass proposes a connection between American Christianity and cruelty, when he describes how his owner Captain Auld, a cruel but cowardly man, overcame his cowardice once he was converted at a Methodist camp-meeting. 'Prior to his conversion, he relied upon his own depravity to shield and sustain him in his savage barbarity; but after his conversion, he found religious sanction and support for his slaveholding cruelty' (p. 525). For Christians such as Auld, the Bible provided justification, if not a divine imperative, for acts of brutality like the merciless beating of a lame woman, which, Douglass reports, their master explained by quoting scripture: 'He that knoweth his master's will, and doeth not, shall be beaten with many stripes' (p. 526). Douglass describes this man, with bitter irony, as 'one of the many pious slaveholders who hold slaves for the very charitable purpose of taking care of them' (p. 526). The experiences that follow cause Douglass to generalise this observation so that he comes to regard a religious slave-holder as the greatest calamity, besides enslavement itself, that can befall a slave. He characterises them as 'the meanest and basest, the most cruel and cowardly' of masters. And the religion they profess, he claims, 'is a mere covering for the most appalling barbarity – a sanctifier of the most hateful frauds – and a dark shelter under which the darkest, foulest, grossest, and most infernal deeds of slaveholders find the strongest protection' (p. 541). Christianity in the South, then, has reversed the terms of Christian values and become its own diabolical opposite. The American South has damned itself by such an emphatic rejection of the religion that supports an exceptional American destiny, and sounded a warning for the nation.

The autobiography as a literary form allows Douglass to re-enact his struggle for freedom but within a larger framework of analysis and historical understanding. It is the mature Douglass, American citizen, who tells in retrospect the story of his younger self and by dramatising the major struggles of his past, Douglass is able to re-affirm the value of that struggle at a time when he discovers that racism takes the place of slavery in the North. Telling the story of his enslavement enables him to see his suffering within the context of the slavery system, and self-respect arises from knowing that the system is responsible for his inferior position and not he himself. In fact, this self is affirmed as worth suffering and struggling for. The autobiography is then a means of coming to terms with an authentic self; it offers a way of exorcising the past, of escaping bondage to the past. By telling his story, Douglass can identify personal inferiority as a key element of the slavery system, a way of manipulating slaves so that they actually repress themselves by perceiving themselves as inferior and worthless. By analysing the mechanisms of slavery in his autobiography, Douglass comes to understand the sense of black inferiority as a kind of psychological collaboration with the ideological system of slavery. The slave-holders enslave black minds to better enslave black bodies. Douglass explains how slaves are required to suppress their self-assertiveness in order to survive; they have to kill the spirit to preserve the flesh because the system demands hypocrisy of them. The power of self-transformation or self-improvement, so central to the mythology of American exceptionalism, is appropriated by Douglass to demonstrate the greater relevance of this mythology to the condition of American slaves than to the lives of American citizens. It is in the appendix to his narrative that Douglass draws together these thematic threads to create a critical distinction between genuine Christianity and the religion practised in slave-holding America.

> To be the friend of one [Christianity proper], is of necessity to be the enemy of the other [American Christianity]. I love the pure, peaceable, and impartial Christianity of Christ: I therefore hate the corrupt, slaveholding, women-whipping, cradle-plundering, partial and hypocritical Christianity of this land (p. 569).

Douglass quotes the Bible to sustain a parallel between American Christians and the Pharisees, Pilate and Herod: the enslavers and persecutors not the liberators, prophets and saints that exceptionalist rhetoric identifies with Americans and the practice of Christianity in America. In the poem that concludes the appendix, Douglass acknowledges the continuing importance to American cultural identity of the notion of God's chosen people, God's elect, the visible sainthood, when he asks:

> We wonder how such saints can sing,
> Or praise the Lord upon the wing,
> Who roar, and scold, and whip, and sting,
> And to their slaves and mammon cling,
> In guilty conscience union (p. 573).

Representing the West: The Visual Arts and Manifest Destiny

Slavery created an unprecedented fracturing of American national life but the opening up of the West to increasing Anglo-American settlement created problems that have proven to be just as long-lasting. In important respects slavery and expansion are aspects of the same issue: the question of whether the new territories of the West should be slave states brought to the fore debates about the national character of the United States that eventually erupted in civil war. American expansion in the nineteenth century was, according to official ideology, the prescribed action of a nation destined to occupy the continent from east to west, creating an empire of middle-class farming people: a democratic 'manifest destiny'. The term was first used by John L. O'Sullivan in the *Democratic Review* in 1845, where he described: 'our manifest destiny to overspread the continent allotted by Providence for the free development of our yearly multiplying millions'. The acquisition of more land, then, was necessary to keep the American experiment in democracy going. This was the visible or 'manifest' destiny of the United States, and the displacement of peoples living beyond the Western frontier may be regrettable but it was equally inevitable, according to the logic of Manifest Destiny. The United States purchased the province of Louisiana from France in 1803 and this sudden and massive increase in land gave the nation both a claim to Oregon and also the self-image of becoming a sea-to-sea nation (see Map 3.1). In the years 1823 to 1824, the fur-trapper Jedediah Smith discovered the South Pass crossing through the Rockies to California and Oregon; other routes were opened

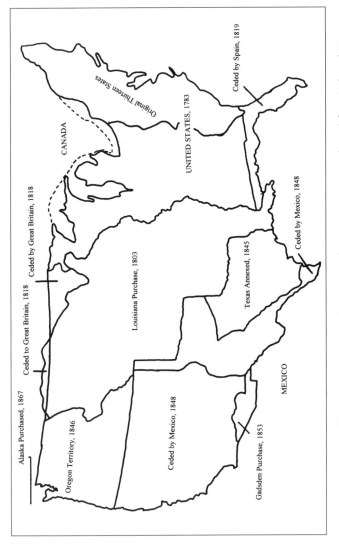
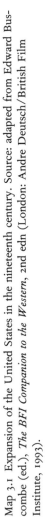

Map 3.1 Expansion of the United States in the nineteenth century. Source: adapted from Edward Buscombe (ed.), *The BFI Companion to the Western*, 2nd edn (London: Andre Deutsch/British Film Institute, 1993).

up through the 1820s and 1830s. Transcontinental settlement at last became possible. Paintings of this newly-opened territory by Karl Bodmer, George Catlin and Alfred Jacob Miller followed, as did written accounts by Washington Irving (such as *A Tour of the Prairies*) and James Fenimore Cooper.[13] For the majority of Americans who lived in the East, the only access they had to knowledge about the West came from the images supplied by the painters and illustrators who sought to satisfy this new market for exotic images of Western life.

The types of painters working in the West were various. Illustrators accompanied such surveys as the 1803 Lewis and Clarke expedition and were funded either publicly or privately. Folk painters chose subjects like Buffalo Bill, who was painted by Rawson Smith and Henry Lewis. Genre painters were popular during the 1840s and 1850s; characteristically they chose as their subjects the people of the West such as fur traders and trappers. Among the painters of the indigenous people of the West, George Catlin is perhaps the best known. He produced retrospective and elegiac images of Indians at the time of the Indian Removal. His work amounted to more than six hundred paintings and his 'Gallery of Indians' exhibition toured until 1870. Noah Webster attempted to purchase this collection for the nation in 1852 but he was defeated by Southern interests who wanted to extend slavery into the new territories of the West and feared the effect of public sympathy for the Indians. After Catlin's death in 1879 the paintings went to the Smithsonian Institution. Despite the power and popular appeal of Catlin's work, the authenticity of his paintings is questionable: often he conflated several tribes into one painting, his subjects were often taken from sketches; in short, Catlin was an artist rather than an anthropologist and so he was interested more in art and achieving artistic effect than in creating authentic representations of Indians. In this way the West was commodified: sold to the East and to Europe, though the motives claimed to be educational and scientific, and in the process an image was constructed of the West to fit that region to the national self-image.

Two distinct perceptions of the West in relation to the nation are revealed in nineteenth-century American painting: the West as a blank space waiting to be made continuous with the East, and the West as discontinuous with the East and offering an escape from the East with its overly sophisticated society. George Caleb Bingham's image of Daniel Boone leading a group of pioneers through the wilderness, *The Emigration of Daniel Boone* (1852), uses a neo-classical style to compensate for America's perceived lack of history and cultural mythology (see Figure 3.1). The family grouping of the pioneers alludes to the flight of the holy family into Egypt: especially allusive is the image of the modest, Madonna-like woman seated on the horse led by Daniel Boone. The three main figures – Boone, the woman, and her husband who walks beside the scout – look directly ahead to meet the viewer's gaze. There is little dynamism in their presentation; the characters are objectively presented, they have no sense of motivation beyond the powerful religious context provided by the iconography. They are posed to look at the viewer. The stylised characterisation of these figures, their neat and fashionable dress, the ideological momentum lent their journey by the Christian symbolism, contrasts sharply with the barren and rocky landscape in which they are pictured. America here is a wilderness, an empty space, to be civilised by pioneers like these whose Manifest Destiny it was to appropriate and cultivate the West. In the background of the painting there appears in outline a green and cultivated landscape which the pioneers have left behind. The central group is followed by figures bringing cattle and farm implements, suggesting that the wilderness will soon be brought to submit to cultivation. Light is used by Bingham to emphasise this suggestion. The rocky cleft in which the figures are posed is dark, shadowy and threatening; the pioneers themselves are bathed in light and the civilised scene depicted in the background is also light. The suggestion is, then, that the light of Christian civilisation, represented by these pioneers, will banish the dark unknown of the untamed wilderness. Of course, the ideology of Manifest Destiny legitimated (or indeed demanded) the destruction of the wilderness as an obstacle to civilisation and with it dependent populations such as the bison but also including Indians. Exceptionalism, in the form of Manifest Destiny, legitimated the destruction of everything that stood in the way of expanding the institutions and culture of American democracy.

In contrast with this view of the West as a *tabula rasa*, awaiting civilisation, was the vision of the West as fundamentally continuous with the civilisation of the East. Landscape painters like Albert Bierstadt, Thomas Moran and W. H. Jackson used the Romantic styling imported from Europe and so influential in America through the work of Ralph Waldo Emerson. In this view, the West was represented as the land of the noble savage; where Bingham emphasised humanity in social terms through the representation of the family, Romantic painting emphasised natural rather than social man. Further, nature was represented as an

Figure 3.1
Claude Regnier after
George Caleb Bingham,
*The Emigration of Daniel
Boone* (1852); lithograph,
18¼ × 23¾ in. Missouri
Historical Society, Saint
Louis.

end in itself rather than just a setting for some human scene. In paintings like Thomas Cole's *Scene from The Last of the Mohicans*, c. 1827, and William Mason Brown's *Landscape with Two Indians*, c. 1850, the human elements are overshadowed by the awesome grandeur of the natural scene. In Alfred Jacob Miller's *Chimney Rock*, 1858–60 (see Figure 3.2), the architectural quality of the natural features of the landscape tower over the minuscule human figures that are completely dominated by the awesome quality of the American wilderness. The mounted Indian figures blend inconspicuously into the natural scene, like the scrubby outcroppings in the foreground. The human figures are dwarfed by their surroundings, which are not structured in reference to the figures but deliberately remain in an unstructured wilderness state. In paintings like these, nature assumes a mystical or spiritual dimension. The American wilderness is represented as possessed of the power to address the soul. American nature can do this by virtue of its superiority over European landscapes, a superiority obtained because America offers so much wilderness, untouched by humankind. Nature in America contains both a spiritual power and a moral significance that are celebrated in Cole's paintings of the Hudson and Catskills (1825–6), which made authentic American landscapes available to art. It was in 1857 that the first painting of Yosemite (by Thomas Ayres) was exhibited in the East and many painters followed him, intending to capture accurately the grandeur of the far West. The influence of these paintings was far-reaching: Thomas Moran's watercolours were used to lobby opinion in favour of the first national parks and the Yellowstone Act of 1872 created the beginning of the extensive national park service. While artists were working to represent the place of the West within the United States and the contribution of the West to American national identity, artists of the Wild West like Frederick Remington and Charles M. Russell were depicting a nostalgic, even elegiac, image of frontier life. Focusing upon places like Montana, in the latter nineteenth century, they produced an image of the West as passing out of existence as the East spreads. It is an ironic vision of the distinctive nature of the West as the prime victim of the nation's Manifest Destiny. America defined by the civilisation of the eastern Atlantic seaboard versus the America of the West is interpreted as a struggle that the West cannot win; like the wilderness, the West itself becomes an inevitable sacrifice to the nation's predestined future.

In the period after the Revolution, right through the nineteenth century, a national iconography developed that incorporated many of

Figure 3.2
Alfred Jacob Miller,
Chimney Rock (1858–60),
watercolour on paper,
$10^{1/4} \times 14^{1/4}$ in. Walters
Art Gallery, Baltimore.

the elements discussed above: the uniqueness of the American landscape and fauna, the historic mission to bring democratic rule to the entire North American continent, the taming of the wilderness and the conversion of the heathen. These elements are all represented in the lithograph *Peace* (1861) by an unidentified artist (see Figure 3.3). At the centre of the picture is a portrait of George Washington, surrounded by smaller portraits of the presidents that succeeded him, and these portraits are ringed by the state shields. Above this circular composition is the shield of the Union, flanked by two cannon, and embellished with bayonets from which fly the flag of the Union. Above that, with its wings outstretched is the American bald eagle: chosen as a symbol of national unity and power because of associations with Zeus (the eagle was the ancient personification of Zeus) and with fauna peculiar to the New World.[14] In early representations of this icon, artists included a lovely young woman offering a cup of nourishment to the eagle. This figure, often named as Columbia, became closely associated with America; with the addition of a plumed helmet she became Minerva, goddess of wisdom, symbolising the Enlightenment view of liberty as the product of rationality and law.[15] In this 1861 representation, the eagle is encompassed by a banner, 'Peace', held aloft by five angelic feminine figures. The figure of Columbia is represented at the bottom of the picture, where she stands upon a pedestal, 'The American Union', bearing the national shield and flag. The central section of the picture, then, represents images of American federal power and might, a vision of national unity achieved through divinely sanctioned force. On each side of this central panel are depicted scenes from American history which represent a pictorial narrative of the nation's exceptional destiny. At the lower right, the arrival of European ships is depicted amid a scenes of agricultural plenty (harvesting wheat and cotton) but factories and steam ships are also included in this vision of American commercial success. To the left side of the central panel, a panoramic view of the national capital is juxtaposed with a scene of rural labour. These historical scenes are surmounted, to the right, by an image inspired by Bingham's painting of Daniel Boone leading the pioneers. Again, to the Christian iconography of the main feminine figure seated on a horse led by the scout is added the elements of civilisation represented by the dress of the other figures and the weapons they carry. To the left of the main panel is a scene of native life. The Indian warrior sits by his primitive shield and bow, behind him a tipi provides the focus for a

Figure 3.3 Unidentified artist, *Peace* (1861); lithograph 23½ × 18½ in. Library of Congress.

domestic scene that is illuminated with light and two figures stand facing the source of light which is outside the frame of the picture. The Christian connotation of these figures suggests that conversion and assimilation is the only route available to native Americans. The doomed nature of the Indians is represented at first by the contrast between their weapons and those carried by the pioneers and then by the cannon and bayonets that dominate the central panel. The entire composition emphasises a historical movement from the past to the present that is a movement towards civilisation, democracy and national unity. This history is the history of exceptionalist ideology, translated into the domestic vocabulary of Manifest Destiny.

Notes

1. F. O. Matthiessen, *American Renaissance: Art and Expression in the Age of Emerson and Whitman* (1941, rpt London, Oxford and New York: Oxford University Press, 1968), p. xv.
2. Walt Whitman, 'Democratic Vistas', *Leaves of Grass and Selected Prose*, ed. John A. Kouwenhoven (New York: Modern Library, 1950), p. 460. Future page references are given in the text.
3. Walt Whitman, 'Song of Myself', ibid., p. 37. Future page references are given in the text.
4. James Fenimore Cooper, *The Last of the Mohicans*, ed. John McWilliams (Oxford and New York: Oxford University Press, 1990), p. 117. Future page references are given in the text.
5. James Fenimore Cooper, *The Pioneers* (New York: Signet, 1980), see pp. 212–18. Future page references are given in the text.
6. See George Dekker, *The American Historical Romance* (Cambridge: Cambridge University Press, 1987).
7. Nathaniel Hawthorne, 'The Custom-House', *The Scarlet Letter*, Sculley Bradley, *et al.* (eds) (New York: W. W. Norton & Co., 1978), p. 8. Future page references are given in the text.
8. Herman Melville, letter to Nathaniel Hawthorne, 16 April 1851, *The Letters of Herman Melville*, Merrell R. Davis and William H. Gilman (eds) (1960, rpt New Haven and London: Yale University Press, 1965), p. 124.
9. Herman Melville, *Moby-Dick; or The Whale*, Harold Beaver (ed.) (1851, rpt Harmondsworth: Penguin, 1982), p. 262.
10. Harriet Jacobs, *Incidents in the Life of a Slave Girl, Written by Herself*, Jean Fagin Yellin (ed.) (1861, rpt Cambridge, MA and London: Harvard University Press, 1987). Future page references are given in the text.
11. Ibid., Appendix, p. 202.
12. Frederick Douglass, *Narrative of the Life of Frederick Douglass, An American Slave*, Christopher Bigsby (ed.) (1845, rpt London: J. M. Dent, 1992). Future page references are given in the text.
13. See Howard R. Lamar, 'An Overview of Westward Expansion', in *The West as America: Reinterpreting Images of the Frontier, 1829–1920*, William H. Truettner

(ed.) (Washington and London: Smithsonian Institution Press for the National Museum of American Art, 1991), pp. 1–26.

14. Joshua C. Taylor with a contribution by John G. Cawelti, *America as Art* (Washington, DC: Smithsonian Institution Press for the National Collection of Fine Arts, 1976), pp. 9–10.

15. Ibid., p. 11.

CHAPTER 4

Annexation: Chicano Responses to the Ideology of Exceptionalism

The native experience of invasion is compared, in this chapter, with the Chicano experience of annexation. Key writers here are María Amparo Ruiz de Burton, Tomás Rivera, Rudolfo Anaya, Rolando Hinojosa-Smith, Angela de Hoyos, Bernice Zamora, Gloria Anzaldúa, Cherríe Moraga, Ana Castillo. Also, important Hispanic writers like the Cuban radical José Martí are included here in order to place the discourse of exceptionalism within the debate over United States imperialism in the Americas.

Exceptionalism, Expansion and the War with Mexico

The doctrine of Manifest Destiny, by which exceptionalist assumptions were expressed in nineteenth-century America, found full expression in contemporary US–Mexican relations. American exceptionalism held that the United States was possessed of a sacred mission to bring the Protestant, democratic institutions and the system of free capitalism to all of the regions of North America, and beyond. Standing in the path of the transcontinental expansion of the United States were the vast territories held by Spain and, later, Mexico. In 1819 John Quincy Adams negotiated the Transcontinental Treaty with Spain, by which the United States acquired Florida and a boundary was established between Spanish and American possessions from Louisiana to Oregon. In 1821 Moses Austin was granted a large expanse of land with which to found a colony in Texas. He died before setting out so his son Stephen took over the role of coloniser and negotiated further, with officials of the new independent Republic of Mexico, the Colonisation Law of 1823. Original Anglo-American settlers from the Mississippi Valley and lower South, together with the adventurers that flooded to Texas, soon outnumbered Mexican Texans. Trouble escalated in 1829 when the Mexican government sent General Luis Mier y Terán to investigate, only to discover that Americans in Texas refused to become Catholic, as required by the Colonisation Law, they kept slaves despite Mexico's abolition of slavery, they refused to obey the Mexican justice system and they refused to pay customs duties.

A local uprising in Galveston in 1832 heightened tensions, so Austin travelled to Mexico City for talks where he was arrested and held in detention. The move for political autonomy in Texas grew until open rebellion broke out in 1835. In February 1836 the garrison at the Alamo in San Antonio was attacked by General Antonio López de Santa Anna and all the defenders were killed. A volunteer force, organised under Sam Houston, defeated Santa Anna at the Battle of San Jacinto in April 1836 and Texas was declared an independent republic under the presidency of Houston. The inclusion of Texas into the Union was problematic because the slave-holding practices of Texans was anathema to the growing abolitionist movement in the United States. For ten years Texas was an independent state until President Polk pledged the annexation of Texas and the reannexation of Oregon; finally Texas became a state in February 1846.

This history ran counter to the ideology of Manifest Destiny. The annexation of Texas proceeded by violence and bloodshed rather than by purchase; rather than bring freedom to an oppressed people, Americans denied freedom to Texan Americans and continued to support slavery in the new state; rather than further unite the nation the controversy over Texas's entry into the Union exacerbated existing divisions and conflicts.[1] Land grants in New Mexico and the trade routes linking Missouri with Santa Fe and Chihuahua increased American interest in and knowledge of the South-west which gave the lie to the image of the West as a vast uninhabited region awaiting the arrival of the pioneers. Here were sizeable populations of Hispanic peoples and Indian tribes such as the village-dwelling Pueblo and the nomadic Apache and Navaho.

The Mexican War was ostensibly fought because Mexico refused to accept the annexation of Texas and President Polk clearly named Mexico, not the United States, as the aggressor. General Zachary Taylor won victories at Palo Alto and Buena Vista but became stuck in northern Mexico, some 1500 miles from the capital. The President reluctantly authorised General Winfield Scott to land a force at Vera Cruz and follow Cortes's route to take Mexico City. Meanwhile, General Stephen

W. Kearney occupied New Mexico and set out across Arizona to conquer California. Colonel Alexander Doniphan took El Paso and Chihuahua City before retiring home to Missouri. John Charles Frémont, exploring the West in 1845, travelled first to California where he and his large armed band received a cold welcome from suspicious Mexican authorities and then to Oregon. However, hearing rumours that war with Mexico was imminent, he returned with his forces to northern California and joined up with a band of rebels under the 'Bear Flag'. They seized northern California while Commodores John D. Sloat and Robert F. Stockton captured the coastal towns. The Americans were shortly thereafter driven from Los Angeles and only when Stockton's marines were joined by General Kearney's weary force from Arizona could America claim victory in the war for California. The gold rush of 1849 brought 90,000 people in that year alone and 200,000 more over the next decade, and effectively overwhelmed the Hispanic and native communities that had preceded them. By the defeat of Mexico

Map 4.1 New Spain in the late eighteenth century. Source: adapted from Michael C. Meyer and William L. Sherman, *The Course of Mexican History* (New York: Oxford University Press, 1979).

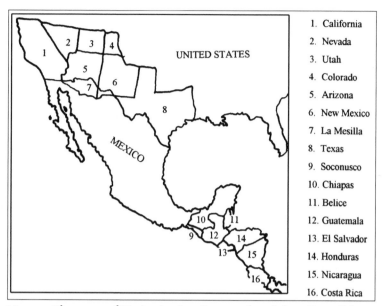

1. California
2. Nevada
3. Utah
4. Colorado
5. Arizona
6. New Mexico
7. La Mesilla
8. Texas
9. Soconusco
10. Chiapas
11. Belice
12. Guatemala
13. El Salvador
14. Honduras
15. Nicaragua
16. Costa Rica

Map 4.2 The extent of Mexico in 1822. Source: adapted from Peter Calvert, *Mexico* (London: Ernest Benn Limited, 1973).

and the 1848 Treaty of Guadalupe Hidalgo, the United States acquired Arizona, California, Nevada, New Mexico, Utah, parts of Colorado and Texas (see Maps 4.1 and 4.2). The crisis over the status of the new possessions, whether they be slave or free, produced the Compromise of 1850: California was admitted to the Union as a free state, New Mexico and Utah were organised as territories with no real reference to slavery, Texas land claims and debts were settled, and a powerful Fugitive Slave Law was enacted. This Compromise, together with the bitter sectional row, just four years later, over whether Kansas and Nebraska should be organised as slave or free territories, is seen by many historians as the prelude to the Civil War.

Senator John C. Calhoun of South Carolina was at the forefront of advocates of slavery but he opposed the incorporation of Mexican territory into the United States primary on the grounds of the racial intermixing that will occur. In an address to Congress (4 January 1848) he compares the situation with Mexico to the attitude of the United States towards the conquered Indian tribes. He argues that the idea of incorporating these native American populations was never entertained:

'we never thought of holding them in subjection – never of incorporating them into our Union. They have either been left as an independent people amongst us, or been driven into the forests.'[2] Calhoun goes on to identify the mixing of 'colored races' with the white race as the cause of trouble for the Spanish and the Portuguese in Hispanic America; he claims that 'free popular government' is not to be found among the 'colored races', although the majority of humanity are coloured. This observation only reinforces Calhoun's belief that white America constitutes an elite, an elite that must be maintained in its racial purity and its purity of purpose. He argues:

> I know further, sir [addressing the President], that we have never dreamt of incorporating into our Union any but the Caucasian race – the free white race. To incorporate Mexico, would be the very first instance of the kind of incorporating an Indian race; for more than half of the Mexicans are Indians, and the other is composed chiefly of mixed tribes. I protest against such a union as that! Ours, sir, is the Government of a white race ... Are we to associate with ourselves as equals, companions, and fellow-citizens, the Indians and mixed race of Mexico? Sir, I should consider such a thing as fatal to our institutions. (pp. 160–1).

For such as Calhoun, the racial constitution of the United States was of supreme importance; the maintenance of the political, social and economic structures that characterise United States culture was the primary issue in relations with Mexico, even superseding the dictates of Manifest Destiny. Calhoun claims that not all peoples are capable of enjoying the free government brought to America by European civilisation and to force free government upon an unwilling population is a grave error; only those who have achieved 'a very high state of moral and intellectual improvement' can maintain free government and only an elite portion of such a purified people 'have had the good fortune of forming a constitution capable of endurance' (p. 162). For Calhoun, America has a racial mission that is of greater significance than the sacred mission articulated by the ideology of exceptionalism: 'I see that it has been urged in a very respectable quarter, [he argues] that it is the mission of this country to spread civil and religious liberty over all the world, and especially over this continent. It is a great mistake' (p. 162). Calhoun was answered by Senator John A. Dix of New York on this issue of the annexation of Mexican territories. Dix argues that the course of American empire is inevitable. Though he has no more desire of incorporating a population of Mexicans, his desire to claim the land outweighs consideration of the Mexicans occupying it.

John Dix points to the expansion westward of the United States' population and claims that no-one can doubt that this population 'is destined to spread itself across the American continent, filling up, with more or less completeness, according to the attractions of soil and climate, the space that intervenes between the Atlantic and Pacific oceans.'[3] So he uses not the theory of Manifest Destiny but the *fact* of a manifest and obvious westward expansion of the population to prove that the incorporation of Mexico must happen in order to open up the additional territory needed to satisfy the appetite of the United States for increased land for settlement. As for the existing population of this territory, he proposes that settlement is exceedingly sparse (about two inhabitants to three square miles in the more than a million square miles of Mexican lands north of the twenty-sixth parallel) and consequently,

[T]he aboriginal races, which occupy and overrun a portion of California and New Mexico, must there, as everywhere else, give way before the advancing wave of civilization, either to be overwhelmed by it, or to be driven upon perpetually contracting areas, where, from a diminution of their accustomed sources of subsistence, they must ultimately become extinct by force of an invincible law. We see the operation of this law in every portion of this continent. We have no power to control it, if we would. It is the behest of Providence that idleness, and ignorance, and barbarism, shall give way to industry, and knowledge, and civilization (p. 163).

Thus, Dix makes an implicit parallel between the situation of Mexicans in the south-west and the Indian tribes that have already encountered the United States' insatiable appetite for land. But it is not to the government of the United States that Dix attributes the invasion, appropriation and annexation of Western lands; rather, it is the operation of Manifest Destiny, directed by divine Providence, that is the agent of political change in this regard. So Dix argues, simply, that the United States refrain from interfering in the inevitable westward progress of American 'civilisation' and that the westward course of empire be allowed to take its course. He concludes: 'I desire to see the inevitable political change which is to be wrought in the condition of [Mexico's] northern departments, brought about without any improper interference on our part' (p. 163). The brutal alternatives for the Mexican population of the south-west envisioned by John Dix – assimilation or extinction – were not among the conditions set down in the Treaty of Guadalupe-Hidalgo, by which Mexico ceded her northern territories to the United States. Indeed, the Treaty provided that full United States citizenship would be bestowed upon all those who chose to remain resident in the ceded areas and that the full rights of property ownership would remain vested in them. These people were given the option of removing south of the new US–Mexico border, where they would remain Mexican citizens. The extent to which this treaty was honoured is revealed by the experiences recorded in autobiography and memoir by those who found themselves subject to the radical cultural trauma of being transformed virtually overnight from citizens of a Catholic, Spanish-speaking, newly-independent nation to citizens of the Protestant, English-speaking and imperialistic United States.

Mariano Guadalupe Vallejo's *Recuerdos históricos y personales tocante a la alta California* (1875) is one of many personal memoirs collected by the scholar Hubert Howe Bancroft for his monumental *History of California* (1884–90). The testaments of the native Californians present a vivid contrast between an idyllic life before the invasion and a life after of disenfranchisement, dispossession, and political, cultural and social displacement. Vallejo belonged to the landholding elite of northern California; he initially supported American annexation but found himself a victim of the Bear Flag insurrection (1846), led by Captain John Frémont; he later lost the bulk of his lands and was reduced to near-penury. He describes the reversal of his fortunes as exemplary of the loss of power, prestige and rights of all *Californios* in what is no longer their home but a part of the expanding American empire.

> The language now spoken in our country, the laws which govern us, the faces which we encounter daily, are those of the masters of the land, and, of course, antagonistic to our interests and rights, but what does that matter to the conqueror? He wishes his own well-being and not ours! – a thing that I consider only natural in individuals, but which I condemn in a government which has promised to respect and make respected our rights, and to treat us as its own sons. But what does it avail us to complain. The thing has happened and there is no remedy.[4]

It was experience of this kind coupled with the perception that justice was not available for the subject people of the south-west that produced those individuals who generated the popular figure of the Mexican bandit.

The outlaw legend was enshrined in legend and expressed in folk songs and tales, novels, biographies and, later, motion pictures. Perhaps the most famous of these Mexican outlaws was Joaquin Murrieta. In keeping with the romantic outlaw stereotype, he was characterised as a social idealist, kind, good humoured and clever, and extremely individualistic. Overwhelmingly the received view of him is nostalgic.[5] Joaquin Murrieta is representative of the Mexicans who experienced gold rush California at a time when the Spanish and Mexicans were dispossessed by newly arrived 'Yankees'. The indigenous population was left unemployed, dispossessed, and made second-class citizens within the expanded United States; they were even defined as 'aliens' under their new government. Outlawry or a concerted vendetta against Anglo-Americans seemed justifiable in a situation where justice was unavailable because the law was in the hands of the oppressors. Outlawry, in these terms, meant murder, robbery and horsestealing. The hero of Giacomo Puccini's opera La Fanciulla del West (The Girl of the Golden West) is a reluctant outlaw of this type. Minnie (the 'girl'), runs a miners' tavern and into her tavern comes Dick Johnson, who is in reality the Mexican bandit Ramerrez, sought by Minnie's suitor the sheriff Jack Rance. The love triangle that develops among these characters is heightened by the fact that we, and then Rance, know Johnson's true identity before he can reveal himself to Minnie. When Rance accuses him of coming to the tavern as a highwayman, in order to steal the miners' gold, Johnson must explain to Minnie how he came to live the life he leads:

> I'm not excusing myself: I'm a bad lot!
> Don't I know it! But I wouldn't have robbed you.
> I am Ramerrez: I was born an outlaw:
> my name has been thief
> from the very day I was born.
> But while my father
> still lived, I never knew it.
> It's six months now
> since he died.
> The only means he left me
> of providing for my mother

and my brothers and sisters was
a gang of highwaymen as patrimony!
I accepted it.
Such was my destiny![6]

In the new California of the United States, Ramerrez finds himself and
his family destitute, deprived of the opportunity to make an honest
living, and forced into a life of crime. The natural grace and nobility
of Ramerrez is apparent to Minnie, who sees him with eyes that are
open to the goodness in all men; the opera is punctuated with Minnie's
declarations of the capacity of all men for redemption. In the conclusion
she saves Ramerrez from the posse that would hang him by reminding
each individual of her own acts of kindness to him and by reminding
them all: 'there's not a sinner ... in the whole world to whom the way ...
of redemption is closed' (p. 94). She is not blinkered by racial prejudice,
unlike those who chant 'Hang the Spaniard', or by the notion that she
belongs to an elite to whom redemption belongs exclusively.

A meeting of music and poetry is found in the folk ballads, known
as corridos, that were popular in the south-west in the late nineteenth
century. These narrative ballads often expressed the cultural conflict
between Mexican-American and Anglo-American cultures that characterised the region. 'Kiansis' concerns the rivalry between vaqueros and
cowboys, and the appropriation of ranching and the cattle drive as a
cultural expression by Anglo-Americans.

> We got to the Salado River, and we swam our horses across;
> an American was saying, 'Those men are as good as drowned.'
>
> I wonder what that man thought, that we came to learn, perhaps;
> Why we're from the Rio Grande, where the good swimmers are
>   from.[7]

The narrator emphasises the danger of the cattle drive and the peril in
which the vaqueros will find themselves; indeed, one of the vaqueros
is killed, 'all he left was his leather jacket hanging on the rails of the
corral'/'en las trancas del corral/nomás la cuera dejó' (pp. 831/830).
The weather is threatening, the trail is long, some of the cattle are
vicious – the life of the vaquero is a hard one. This is the lifestyle that
Anglo-Americans are appropriating, along with the land, and they are
creating a mythology and iconography of the Western cowboy to accompany and legitimise this taking-over of what was once Mexican.

The injustice experienced by the native communities of the south-west is expressed through the concept of outlawry; where true justice is denied and frontier justice is resisted by heroic individuals like the eponymous heroes of the corridos 'Gregorio Cortez' and 'Jacinto Trevino', which deal with violent conflict between Mexicans and the Texas Rangers. In the former ballad, Gregorio Cortez is pursued for the murder of a sheriff and he is wanted dead or alive:

> Then said Gregorio Cortez, with his pistol in his hand,
> 'I don't regret having killed him; what I regret is my brother's death.'
>
> Then said Gregorio Cortez, with his soul aflame,
> 'I don't regret having killed him; self-defense is permitted'
> (p. 835).[8]

But self-defence is not a permitted defence for a Mexican who has been branded an outlaw and bandit, and who is notoriously difficult to capture. He kills several more of the sheriffs who pursue him before he learns that his people are suffering, many of his people have been killed in retribution, and so he surrenders, offering himself up in sacrifice for his people. Thus, Cortez is represented as a victim of the lawlessness experienced by Mexican-Americans at the hands of Anglos and he is victimised by the absence of justice that comes about when justice is administered by the oppressors.

One of the lengthiest indictments of Anglo-American injustice in the wake of the Mexican annexation was María Amparo Ruiz de Burton's novel, *Who Would Have Thought It?* (1872). The story concerns an established New England family, the Norvals, which is disrupted when Dr James Norval returns from a geological expedition to the south-west accompanied by a dark-skinned young girl, María Dolores (Lola) Medina. He also brings boxes of supposed geological specimens. The reception Lola receives from the abolitionist women of the Norval household is devastating. She is sent to eat with the servants, she has nowhere to sleep and she is ostracised from the family. Jemima Norval is incensed that her husband would sully the racial purity of his children's home by bringing into it a girl that she insists is Negro despite the contradiction by her husband that Lola is of noble Spanish descent. In this novel, Ruiz de Burton sustains a complex relationship between public and private spheres, where the private world of family and the institution of marriage echoes the public arena of American nationhood and the institutions formalised by the Constitution.[9] So the hypocrisy, cruelty and prejudice of Mrs Norval reflects critically upon the moral pretensions of the nation she represents. Dr Norval tells his wife Lola's story, that she is the daughter of a Spanish noblewoman, Doña Teresa Almenara de Medina, who was kidnapped by Apache Indians and held captive by them. They were forced to dye their skin to pass for Indians and reduce the chance of escape but the experience of captivity and the shame it will have brought her family are such that Doña Teresa no longer wishes to live. She begs that Dr Norval take Lola with the expedition and raise her in his house but as a Roman Catholic until her father and remaining family can be found. To pay for Lola's support and to recompense Norval for his assistance, she guides the party to a ravine where she has been collecting great nuggets of gold and precious gems against just such an opportunity, and then the dying woman aids their escape from the Apaches. Mrs Norval's hostility towards Lola is heightened upon learning she is a Catholic, which to her is 'abominable idolatry' (p. 24) but she is very taken with the idea of Lola's wealth. Of course, she considers that Lola, a heathen and savage, can have no just claim to this wealth and, when her husband departs on a self-imposed exile (during which he is reported dead), her attempts to possess this wealth by plotting and intrigue know no bounds. In this way, Mrs Norval's appropriation of the Hispanic girl's inheritance functions as an allegory of the American annexation of Mexico's land and mineral wealth. Lola's wealth and her racial profile together produce the complications of the plot as Ruiz de Burton sets out a damning critique of American imperialism.

Mrs Norval fashions herself as a Yankee in the Puritan mould, governed by principles of order, restraint and self-discipline. But in the face of extreme wealth, all of these principles are discarded with unseemly haste. When the treasure chest is first opened before her

> Her soul was floating over those yellow, shining lumps of cold, unfeeling metal. ... she knelt by the chest, and with childlike simplicity began to take pieces of gold and examine them attentively and toss them up playfully. ... The sedate, severe, sober, serious lady of forty was a playful, laughing child again (p. 25).

Continually prompted to greater prodigality by the hypocritical minister Reverend Hackwell, Mrs Norval spends Lola's money lavishly on houses and clothes and entertaining on a grand scale. She uses the money to climb the social ladder and seek suitable matches for her daughters; Lola, meanwhile, is abandoned at the Catholic boarding school chosen for her by Dr Norval. Lola herself is portrayed as possessing a natural nobility: she is beautiful, intelligent, gentle, patient, faithful and incorruptible. The whitening of her skin as the dyes applied by the Indians fades is symbolic of the revelation of her noble character throughout the narrative. She is victimised by those schemers who are after her money: Jemima Norval, initially, but increasingly Hackwell, who leaves the clergy to serve in the Union army and also woos the 'widowed' Mrs Norval so that he might share her sudden wealth. As Lola matures and increases in personal beauty Hackwell devises a plan which would satisfy his lust for Lola's person as well as her inheritance by tricking her into marriage and, when this plan goes wrong, by abducting her. His only rival is Jemima's son, Julian Norval, who is loved by Lola and who loves her for her own noble character. Hackwell schemes to marry off his sister to Julian, using threats, Jemima's pleading, and whatever tricks he can muster. Julian's outrage over Lola's treatment by the women in his family accentuates Ruiz de Burton's criticism of Yankee racism, greed and hypocrisy. When his mother accuses Lola of ensnaring Julian into a promise of marriage, exclaiming 'She is a good Mexican, surely, and knows how to put the dagger to the throat', Julian retorts that in Lola's case it is them, the Yankees, who are the purse-stealers, the usurpers who have left Lola homeless (p. 180). Only the unexpected return of Dr Norval puts an end to the corrupt scheming of his wife and her associates. Dr Norval and his son are pointedly the only exceptions to the generalisation dramatised in this novel, that self-deception, hypocrisy and deliberate misrepresentation are ingrained in the American national character. Coupled with and exaggerating these racial characteristics is a tendency to a selective ignorance that supports the prejudice and self-deception that serve the national interest: Mrs Norval's neighbour, Mrs Cackle (whose family rise to political prominence in the course of the narrative), proclaims, 'To me they are all alike – Indians, Mexicans, or Californians – they are all horrid' (p. 11). The doctrine of Manifest Destiny is then seen to feed on ignorance, hypocrisy, self-deception, but above all on greed, rather than the noble motives of spreading democratic civilisation and devotion to a divine imperative; the sacred mission enshrined in exceptionalist dogma is exposed as a sham in texts like *Who Would Have Thought It?*.

Exceptionalism and Annexation in the Twentieth-Century

In the mid-twentieth century, Chicano resistance to the injustices of the past and the ongoing discrimination against Hispanic peoples, organised initially under the auspices of the United Farm Workers led by César Chávez. The manifesto of Chicano civil rights, 'El Plan Espiritual de Aztlán' (reprinted as Appendix 1 at the end of this book), was written at the First Chicano National Conference in Denver, Colorado in 1969 and provides the ideological and political framework for the Chicano movement. It begins:

> In the spirit of a new people that is conscious not only of its proud historical heritage but also of the brutal 'gringo' invasion of our territories, *we*, the Chicano inhabitants and civilisers of the northern land of Aztlán from whence came our forefathers, reclaiming the land of their birth and consecrating the determination of our people of the sun, *declare* that the call of our blood is our power, our responsibility, and our inevitable destiny.[10]

Aztlán of course signifies those territories annexed by the United States, the homeland claimed by Mexican-Americans, the Chicano/as who trace their cultural roots in the New World to the Aztec, Inca and Toltec peoples, who occupied the land prior to the European invasion of 1492 and who describe themselves as of mixed Indian, Spanish and, later, Anglo bloodlines. For these people, the post-Columbian past is experienced as a legacy of genocide, dispossession and deracination. Rudolfo Anaya and Francisco Lomelí explain: 'During the decade from 1965–1975, Chicanos not only demonstrated in the streets to increase their opportunities and status, they also struggled to define a sense of a mythic past and history in order to recapture what official history had omitted. Aztlán became a collective symbol by which to recover the past that had been wrestled away from the inhabitants of Aztlán through the multiple conquests of the area'.[11] Gloria Anzaldúa, who describes herself as 'a Chicana *tejana* lesbian-feminist poet and fiction writer', gives powerful expression to the experience of the *mestiza*, the mixed-blood, who occupies a cultural, historical and psychological border territory.[12] In 'The Homeland, Aztlán/*El otro México*' she describes the violence of annexation, and the redrawn US–Mexican border, as a '1,950 mile-long wound/dividing a *pueblo*, a

ANNEXATION: CHICANO RESPONSES

culture,/running down the length of my body,/staking fence rods in my flesh' (p. 2).

The image of the border as an artificial division imposed upon and doing violence to a seamless earth is found throughout Chicana/o writing. Bernice Zamora's poem 'On Living in Aztlán' expresses this sense of a people divided:

> We come and we go
> But within limits
> Fixed by a law
> Which is not ours;
>
> We have in common
> The experience of love [13]

The division is artificial, imposed, and unrelated to the common feeling of the people, who retain a culture despite the imposition of Anglo barriers and borders. Anzaldúa concludes her poem: 'This land was Mexican once,/was Indian always/and is./And will be again' (p. 3). But this hope, founded on nostalgia, is balanced by Anzaldúa's account of what life is like now for the descendants of the Mexicans annexed along with the land in 1848. She describes them as the citizens of a borderland: 'a borderland is a vague and undetermined place created by the emotional residue of an unnatural boundary' (p. 3). But this border separates and also brings together the First World and the Third World; it defines the powerful and the powerless, the legitimate inhabitants and the trespassers, the 'normal' and the alien. The essay concludes with a diagnosis of the current malaise affecting the people of the south-western borderland: the brutal choice 'to stay in Mexico and starve or move north and live. [Noting that] ... North Americans call this return to the homeland the silent invasion' (p. 10) but she begins with the pseudo-colonisation of Mexico by the United States: '*Los gringos* had not stopped at the border ... The Mexican government and wealthy growers are in partnership with such American conglomerates as American Motors, IT&T and Du Pont which own factories called *maquiladoras*. One fourth of all Mexicans work at *maquiladoras*' (p. 10).

The economic entrapment of Mexican Americans in a bleak cycle of poverty and discrimination that arises from their dispossession provided the main focus for the Chicano movement of the 1960s and 1970s. The key texts of this period are Tomás Rivera's ... *y no se lo tragó la tierra*

(... *And the Earth did not Devour Him*) (1971) [14] and Rudolfo Anaya's *Bless Me, Ultima* (1972). [15] Rivera was the son of migrant farm workers and himself worked as a migrant farm labourer before going on to a career as an educator and university administrator: he was Chancellor of the University of California, Riverside, at the time of his death. ...*y no se lo tragó la tierra* (... *And the Earth did not Devour Him*) gives expression to the experience of migrant agriculture workers through a young boy whose consciousness organises the twelve sections of the novel. His experience of social and economic injustice, the physical suffering of his parents, siblings and extended family, and the psychological cost of the oppression they suffer produces a crisis that resolves itself in a dawning self-awareness and political identification with *la raza* (the people). It is ironic that the image used to convey the stultifying oppression of these dispossessed people, who move from farm to farm, harvest to harvest, under the most difficult of conditions, is the image of being buried alive. Seething with rage at the sight of his father and little brother delirious with sunstroke because the boss will allow the worker the time to take only one drink a day, the unnamed narrator asks his mother:

> Why? Why you? Why Dad? Why my uncle? Why my aunt? Why their kids? Tell me, Mother, why? Why us, burrowed in the dirt like animals with no hope for anything? ... Why Dad and then my little brother? He's only nine years old. Why? He has to work like a mule buried in the earth (pp. 109, 111).

When his mother replies that the poor are rewarded in heaven, his anger explodes as he curses God despite the dire warnings he has heard that to abandon God, to blame God for worldly suffering, will cause the earth to open and devour him. He curses God and the earth does not swallow him up; instead he experiences the beginning of a political consciousness that offers at least the hope of change. In the absence of empty religious comforts he discovers the beginning of the end of his spiritual alienation and the dawning knowledge that his economic, political and social dispossession are all linked inextricably to the psychological and spiritual dispossession he and those around him have suffered.

Rudolfo Anaya's young hero, Antonio Marez, resolves the contradictions of his life as he becomes aware of the discrete traditions of his people – the sedate farming life of his mother's family opposed to the vaquero traditions of his father's family – by discovering the power of literary expression to record and preserve all of the traditions that compose the culture of the rural Mexican south-west, but especially the culture of the Llano, where the novel is set. It is the arrival of the aged Ultima, the revered *curandera* or folk healer, who sets him upon a course that can satisfy both his mother's ambition that he become a priest and his father's desire that he live the fiercely independent life of the vaquero. In the course of the narrative Anaya uncovers a rich culture with long-established historical traditions deeply rooted in the landscape that, according to Anglo-American mythology, was scarcely inhabited at the time of the United States' westward expansion. The conflict between Anglo-American and Mexican–American versions of the history of the south-west is the concern of Rolando Hinojosa-Smith in his series of novels set in Texas-Mexican border country. The struggle to dominate the narration of regional history, to control the historical record, generates both narrative conflict and prescribes the narrative style in stories like 'Sometimes It Just Happens That Way; That's All'.[16] The story consists of a sequence of documents – legal records, testimonies, newspaper clippings – that present conflicting and often blatantly contradictory interpretations of a single incident: the fatal stabbing of Arnesto Tamez in a bar by Baldemar Cordero. The conflict between the native inhabitants of Texas and the newspapers, legal system and complicit individuals who support and promote the economic domination of Anglo-Texans is dramatically revealed as newspaper articles ignore oral testimony and present a version of events favourable to the town's existing power structure. The Anglo domination of the borderland is seen as a continuing process of deception and programme of deliberate misinformation, which has not ceased since the annexation.

One of the foremost Chicana voices of the *movimiento* is Angela de Hoyos, who, in collections like *Arise, Chicano, and Other Poems* (1975) and *Chicano Poems: For the Barrio* (1975), gave expression to the cultural nationalism that accompanied the growing political awareness that the desperate social status of Mexican Americans was not the product of any inherent racial inferiority but had clear historical and economic motives. The ability to express both the reasons for Chicano oppression and the equality of Chicano culture with all world cultures has become a common theme in Chicano/a writing, attested by the number of Hispanic *kunstlerroman* (autobiographical texts describing the early years of an artist of writer) published in the period since the 1970s. In the poem 'Arise, Chicano!' Angela de Hoyos writes of exactly this problem of discovering a language that is adequate to express Chicano consciousness. For the impoverished farmworker, living in inhuman conditions, the infant's lullaby turns to a dirge, in the fields 'the mocking whip of slavehood/confiscates your reverie', 'rude songs of rebellion' and the 'hymn of hope' can be imagined only in the safety of dreams, and the poem concludes:

> ... wherever you turn for solace
> there is an embargo.
> How to express your anguish
> when not even your burning words
> are yours, they are borrowed
> from the festering barrios of poverty.[17]

In the introduction to the reissue of her collection of poetry, *My Father was a Toltec*, Ana Castillo addresses the anxiety of the mestiza, who is neither Anglo nor Spanish, that she has no legitimate claim to the language of either culture. Experiencing an absence or sense of loss in relation to her own Chicana culture, the mestiza must blaze her own trail through a cultural wilderness: Castillo confesses:

> As for the *writing* of poetry, having no models that spoke to my experience and in my languages, I decided that I would never ever take – and never have taken – a workshop or a writing class at any time anywhere. I was afraid that I would be told that I had no right to poetry ... and that I didn't write English or Spanish well enough to write. So, while I was intent on being a good poet, I had to carve out for myself the definition of 'good'.[18]

The necessity for creating a national identity that will redefine values such as 'good' in a dominant culture that makes 'Mexican' synonymous. with 'bad', even while resisting the tendency to create a monolithic and hence inauthentic national solidarity, is reflected in Castillo's writing, in her poetry that expresses the consciousness of a Mexican American who is also a woman, a Chicana: 'A white woman inherits/her father's library,/her brother's friends. Privilege/gives language that escapes me', she writes in the poem 'A Christmas Gift for the President of the United States, Chicano poets, and a Marxist or Two I've known in My Time'.[19] The urgency of this work, the imperative under which writers like Castillo work to reclaim the dignity, the pride, the minds and souls

of their people, is emphasised by the need to argue back, to contradict
the persistent ideological pressure of Manifest Destiny and to proclaim:

> We are left
> with one final resolution
> in our own predestined way,
> we are going forward.
> There is no going back.[20]

Not only Anglo-Americans enjoy a predestined future such as that set
out by the doctrines of Manifest Destiny and American exceptionalism:
those who have been dispossessed, whose land has been lost, will not
quietly retreat beyond the borders of a shrunken and subject Mexico
but must remain on the land in which their traditions and culture are
rooted, the territory which is still home even if they are aliens in the
nation to which that territory now belongs.

Exceptionalism and Imperialism in the Americas

José Martí, a Cuban radical who embarked upon a voluntary exile to
New York as a result of his activities in support of Cuban independence
of Spain. Martí arrived in the United States in 1880; he wrote extensively,
producing both literary works and documentary accounts of the social
and political affairs of North America for a Spanish-speaking audience
but he also wrote of developments in Latin America. The journal he
founded, *America*, gave expression to his vision of a unified greater
America, comprising all the emergent nations of Central and South
America. Martí sought to unify the factions of the Cuban Revolutionary
Party with his vision of a Cuba that is free of the imperialistic ambitions
of both Spain and the United States and which would be the starting
point for constructing what he called 'Our America': a federation of
societies organised upon the principle of racial and social equality. The
Cuban independence struggle resumed in 1895 and claimed Martí's life
on the battlefield. His essay, 'Our America' describes the object for
which he fought and died: a single America, unique in its native American roots and distant from the foreign influences of Europe, a union of
North and South based on mutual respect and peaceful coexistence. He
asks, rhetorically, who are the real sons of 'Mother America'? 'These
sons of Our America, which will be saved by its Indians and is growing

better; [or] these deserters who take up arms in the armies of a North America that drowns its Indians in blood and is growing worse!'[21] The United States was seen by Martí as potentially a greater danger to his vision of a single America than Spain. He was well aware that throughout the nineteenth century, the United States has expressed interest in buying Cuba (as Alaska had been bought from Russia) or in acquiring Cuba from Spain. The cultural, economic and political domination of Spanish America was a logical next step in the expansion of United States institutions first westward and then south, in keeping with the doctrine of Manifest Destiny.[22] The prospect that the United States may engulf the emergent republics of Latin America, subsuming them within its own imperialistic expansion, was among the most urgent dangers Martí saw to his own pan-American vision.

Very much the same issues as those so passionately expressed by Martí are just as passionately questioned from a late twentieth-century perspective by the Chicana writer Cherríe Moraga, whose essay 'Art in America con Acento' deals with the implications of United States imperialism in Latin America for the Latina/os living within '*las entrañas del monstruo*'.[23] The essay was written one week after what she calls 'the death of the Nicaraguan Revolution' by cause of the US-financed Contra War and economic embargo. She goes on:

> Once again an emerging sovereign nation is brought to its knees. A nation on the brink of declaring to the entire world that revolution is the people's choice betrays its own dead. Imperialism makes traitors of us all, makes us weak and tired and hungry.
>
> I don't blame the people of Nicaragua. I blame the US government. I blame my complicity as a citizen in a country that, short of an invasion, stole the Nicaraguan revolution that *el pueblo* forged with their own blood and bones. After hearing the outcome of the elections, I wanted to flee the United States in shame and despair (p. 300).

Moraga questions not only the impact of North American imperialism upon the nations of Latin America but, more importantly, she questions the ways in which imperialism promotes complicity, making imperialists of all citizens. She describes the rapturous reception of President George Bush by Latinos who celebrated the defeat of the revolution in Nicaragua and wonders how monolithic is the vision of the United States and the global relevance of US interests? And she herself, daughter of an Anglo father and a Mexican mother, 'a testimony to the failure of the United

States to wholly anglicize its *mestizo* citizens' (p. 301), is consumed by the fact of US domination and control in the Americas coupled with the consciousness of a very different kind of America, an America that resists the artificial divisions imposed by imperialistic ideologies:

> We stand on land that was once the country of México. And before any conquistadors staked out political boundaries, this was Indian land and in the deepest sense remains just that: a land *sin fronteras* ... Chicanos are a multiracial, multilingual people, who since 1848, have been displaced from our ancestral lands or remain upon them as indentured servants to Anglo-American invaders (p. 301).

In Moraga's view, it is this consciousness, this historical condition, coupled with the fact that Chicanos are not a monolithic group, and nor are the other dispossessed groups victimised by North American imperialism, that poses a threat to the coherence, the power, of the ideologies and cultural mythologies like exceptionalism and Manifest Destiny that fuel America's imperialistic ambitions. 'Ironically, the United States' gradual consumption of Latin America and the Caribbean is bringing the people of the Americas together. What was once largely a Chicano/Mexican population in California is now *guatemalteco, salvadoreño, nicaragüense* ... Every place the United States has been involved militarily has brought its offspring, its orphans, its homeless, and its casualties to this country: Vietnam, Guatemala, Cambodia, the Philippines' ... (pp. 301–2). Thus, the Third World comes to the First World – but this is only a vision, a hope for the future that American exceptionalism may, by its own contradiction, fracture and disintegrate. Right now, Moraga writes, 'we witness a fractured and disintegrating América, where the Northern half functions as the absented landlord of the Southern half and the economic disparity between the First and Third Worlds drives a bitter wedge between a people' (p. 306). The transformation of consciousness from the 'Americas' to 'Our America', envisioned and hoped for – a century apart – by both Cherríe Moraga and José Martí, requires the transformation of a resilient and powerful cultural ideology; it requires that we go beyond the mythology of American exceptionalism.

Notes

1. See Howard R. Lamar, 'Westward Expansion: An Overview', in William H. Truettner (ed.), *The West as America: Reinterpreting Images of the Frontier, 1820–1920* (Washington and London: Smithsonian Institution Press for the National Museum of American Art, 1991), pp. 9–14.

2. Senator John C. Calhoun, from *The Congressional Globe*, 30th Congress, 1st session, 4 January 1848, rpt Clyde A. Milner, II, Anne M. Butler and David Rich Lewis (eds), *Major Problems in the History of the American West*, 2nd edn (Boston and New York: Houghton Mifflin Co., 1997), p. 160. Future page references are given in the text.

3. Senator John A. Dix, from *The Congressional Globe*, 26 January 1848, rpt, Clyde A. Milner, II, *et al.* (eds), *Major Problems in the History of the American West*, p. 162. Future page references are given in the text.

4. Mariano Guadalupe Vallejo, *Recuerdos históricos y personales tocante a la alta California* (1875), in Paul Lauter, *et al.* (eds), *The Heath Anthology of American Literature*, 2nd edn (Lexington, MA and Toronto: D. W. Heath & Co., 1994), vol. 1, p. 2012.

5. Kent Ladd Steckmesser, *Western Outlaws: The 'Good Badman' in Fact, Film, and Folklore* (Claremont, CA: Regina Books, n.d.), p. i.

6. Giacomo Puccini, *La Fanciulla del West* (1910; London: Decca, 1989), p. 57.

7. 'Kiansis I' in Paul Lauter *et al.* (eds), *The Heath Anthology*, vol. 2, p. 831. Future page references are given in the text.

> Llegamos al Río Salado
> y nos tiramos a nado,
> decía un americano:
> Esos hombres ya se ahogaron. –
>
> Pues qué pensaría ese hombre
> que venimos a esp'rimentar,
> si somos del Río Grande,
> de los buenos pa'nadar (p. 830).

8. 'Gregorio Cortez', in Lauter, *et al.* (eds), ibid., p. 835.

> Decía Gregorio Cortez
> con su pistola en la mano:
> - No siento haberlo matado,
> lo que siento es a mi hermano. –
>
> Decía Gregorio Cortez
> con su alma muy encendida:
> – No siento haberlo matado,
> la defensa es permitida. – (p. 832).

9. María Amparo Ruiz de Burton, *Who Would Have Thought It?*, Rosaura Sánchez and Beatrice Pita (eds). Recovering the US Hispanic Literary Heritage Project (1872, rpt Houston: Arte Público Press, 1995), 'Introduction', pp. ix–xiv. Future page references are given in the text.

10. 'El Plan Espiritual de Aztlán', reprinted in Rudolfo Anaya and Francisco Lomelí (eds), *Aztlán: Essays on the Chicano Homeland* (Albuquerque: University of New Mexico Press, 1989), pp. 1–5. Future page references are given in the text.

11. Rudolfo Anaya and Francisco Lomelí (eds), 'Introduction', *Aztlán: Essays on the Chicano Homeland*, p. ii.

12. Gloria Anzaldúa, *Borderlands/La Frontera: The New Mestiza* (San Francisco: Aunt

Lute, 1987), biographical description, p. 205. Future page references are given in the text.

13. Bernice Zamora, 'Living in Aztlán', *Releasing Serpents* (Tempe, AZ: Bilingual Press/Editorial Bilingüe, 1994), p. 25.

14. Tomás Rivera, ... *y no se lo tragó la tierra/* ... *And the Earth Did Not Devour Him*, trans. Evangelina Vigil-Piñón (1987, rpt Houston: Arte Público, 1992).

15. Rudolfo Anaya, *Bless Me, Ultima* (Berkeley: Tonatiuh-Quinto Sol Publications, 1972).

16. Rolando Hinojosa-Smith, 'Sometimes It Just Happens That Way; That's All', in Paul Lauter, *et al.* (eds), *The Heath Anthology*, vol. 2, pp. 2574–82.

17. Angela de Hoyos, 'Arise, Chicano!', in Roberta Fernández (ed.), *In Other Words: Literature by Latinas of the United States* (Houston, TX: Arte Público, 1994), p. 69.

18. Ana Castillo, *My Father was a Toltec and Selected Poems, 1973–1988* (New York and London: W. W. Norton, 1995), pp. xvii–xviii; see also *Massacre of the Dreamers: Essays on Xicanisma* (New York: Plume, 1995).

19. Ibid., p. 63.

20. Ibid., 'We Would Like You to Know', p. 83.

21. José Martí, *Our America: Writings on Latin America and the Cuban Struggle for Independence*, trans. Elinor Randall with Juan de Onis and Roslyn Held Foner, ed. Philip S. Foner (New York and London: Monthly Review Press, 1977), p. 85. Future page references are given in the text.

22. See the brief introduction to José Martí by Enrique Sacerio-Garí in Paul Lauter, *et al.* (eds), *The Heath Anthology*, vol. 2, pp. 819–21, for a very helpful concise account of this historical context.

23. Cherríe Moraga, 'Art in America con Acento', in Roberta Fernández (ed.), *In Other Words*, p. 301. Future page references are given in the text.

CHAPTER 5

Westerns and Westward Expansion

The discussion of twentieth-century interpretations of the conquest of the West begins with Owen Wister's *The Virginian* and the fiction of Zane Grey, and then turns to the figure of John Ford and his cinematic creation of a modern myth of America, which has formed the basis of the genre. Responses to Ford's work in later Westerns, specifically 'spaghetti Westerns', shows the continuing impact of exceptionalist thinking on popular representational forms.

Mythologising the West

Perhaps the single best-known statement about the significance of the West for American cultural identity is the so-called Turner Thesis: Frederick Jackson Turner's address to the annual meeting of the State Historical Society of Wisconsin, 'The Significance of the Frontier in American History' (1894). In this statement, Turner defines the West not as a geographical place or region but as a process, a process that arises from and defines a unique American character. He begins by observing that in the 1890 census, the frontier has ceased to exist: 'Up to and including 1880 the country had a frontier of settlement, but at present the unsettled area has been so broken into by isolated bodies of settlement that there can hardly be said to be a frontier line.'[1] For Turner, this was a great historic moment. The continual recession of unsettled agricultural land as American settlement reached westward offered him an explanation for American development:

> The peculiarity of American institutions is, the fact that they have been compelled to adapt themselves to the changes of an expanding people – to the changes involved in crossing a continent, in winning a wilderness, and in developing at each area of this progress out of

the primitive economic and political conditions of the frontier into the complexity of city life (p. 3).

It was not so much the advance along a single westward line as the return to the primitive and a new development on an advancing frontier line that Turner found significant. It was from the experience of perennial rebirth, fluidity of social institutions, continual development and proximity to 'the simplicity of primitive society' that there arose the forces that dominate the American national character. So, for Turner, it was not the civilisation of the Atlantic states but the Great West that best described the American nation. The relevance of Turner's opinions to the mythology of America is not difficult to see. The process of self-transformation from corrupted European to perfected American has been central to New World mythology since the seventeenth century, as has the idea of discovering perfection through a return to primitive simplicity. Turner's thesis offers historical justification for a concept of the West that is informed by the imperialist assumptions of the ideology of Manifest Destiny.

This ideology and Turner's conception of the frontier as a meeting of savagery and civilisation find expression in that ever-popular twentieth-century form: the Western. It will be useful to consider, before discussing individual novels and films in detail, the characteristic features of the Western as a genre and what these characteristics contribute to the developing mythology of America's historical mission. In the previous chapter, I mentioned that the Wild West depicted by artists like Charles Russell and Frederick Remington was disappearing even as they sought to record it. The controlling irony of the Western is rooted in the nostalgic, elegiac conditions of its creation. The Western is a product of the twentieth century – the first Western was Owen Wister's *The Virginian* (1902) – and this century's desire to construct for itself a noble if doomed past. As James Folsom notes, the Western hero is often treated ironically: he cannot live in the world he has helped to create and even destroys the lawless environment that made him a hero. For example, in Jack Schaefer's movie *Shane* (1949) any relationship between the individual world of the hero and the social world of the novel can only coincide when society is as raw and adolescent as the hero.[2] Shane the gun-slinger defeats the villains who disrupt the 'sod-busters'' mission to transform the open range into small farms; but then he must move on. The violence that is a necessary part of his character can be used to redeem the frontier but also banishes him from the civilised society he makes possible. The contradictory relationship between violence and civilisation is expressed with wry humour by Paul Newman, playing Judge Roy Bean, in the 1972 movie *The Life and Times of Judge Roy Bean*:

> This is going to be a new place, a good place to live. I am the new judge. There will be law. There will be order, civilisation, progress and peace. Above all, peace. I don't care who I have to kill to get it.[3]

The formula presented in the Western is based on a story of individual heroism, where the individual is superior to the laws and institutions of the twentieth century, represented by the civilised East. In this way, the Western denies the consolidation of power and bureaucracy that took place within United States culture in the early part of the century. The values celebrated in the Western include: territorial expansion, liberty, democratic levelling, national identity, the work ethic, racial (white) superiority, and violence (when used with restraint). The hero is often to be admired for his ability to control his anger, his capacity for violence, his own self. The Western hero is the primary vehicle for these values. The extent to which he represents the idealised American, living out the extreme significance of America's exceptional destiny is apparent in his indebtedness to frontier heroes like Daniel Boone and Cooper's Leatherstocking. The hero is noble by nature rather than birth; he works, fights and kills according to a code of fair play, not by cunning and duplicity. So his moral superiority is revealed by his fairness in contrast to the scheming villains and the fundamental orderliness of the universe is revealed in the ultimate victory of fair play. The standard Western plot dramatises a fight for justice: against cattle rustlers or horse thieves, gunfighting bullies and outlaws, covetous bankers and empire builders like the railroad and cattle barons. The Western hero enjoys a special relationship with nature; there is a sympathetic relationship between hero and wilderness. The landscape is something to read and for those who are literate, nature is legible. Easterners cannot read this symbolic language and so are not authentically American, in the fashion of the Westerner. This conception of the Western hero is exemplified by the hero of Owen Wister's *The Virginian*. In that novel, Wister consciously created a new style for representing American experience. The novel begins with a statement to the reader setting out the new style of fiction Wister has written. This is not a historical romance, he argues, yet it has elements of romance and, yes, it is historical. But the Wyoming of his narrative exists only in memory:

> It is a vanished world. No journeys, save those which memory can take, will bring you to it now. The mountains are there, far and shining, and the sunlight, and the infinite earth, and the air that seems forever the true fountain of youth, – but where is the buffalo, and the wild antelope, and where the horseman with his pasturing thousands? So like its old self does the sage-brush seem when revisited, that you wait for the horseman to appear.
> But he will never come again. He rides in his historic yesterday.[4]

One of the devices Wister uses to make the transition from 'now' to 'then' is the figure of the narrator, a naive Easterner (a 'tenderfoot') who spends his summers hunting in Wyoming and who gradually comes to understand the difference and the ethos of the West. As he gains in understanding, so do we, and as he increases in admiration for the Virginian, so do we. The Virginian (and he is called by no other name) is responsible for the narrator's transformation into a new kind of American who is independent, noble of spirit, and committed to a code of values that include honour, justice and courage. Moral superiority is matched by his superior ability. When first the narrator notices the Virginian, he attracts attention by the very ease with which he ropes a wild pony; when the Virginian first meets his future bride, the Eastern schoolmarm Molly, he rescues her from a stream in full flood; his special knowledge of the landscape enables him to read the signs of life in this wilderness and to track down the rustlers who provide much of the novel's adventure. The Virginian takes his bride into the mountains for their honeymoon. These are mountains made safe for the civilising influences of femininity by the Virginian and his like, who have, in the preceding action, cleared out the villains. These same mountains are represented as the spiritual home of men like the Virginian, and his honeymoon in the wilderness is a testament to his final triumph over human and natural adversaries:

> So many visits to this island [in the mountain stream] had he made, and counted so many hours of revery spent in its haunting sweetness, that the spot had come to seem his own. It belonged to no man, for it was deep in the unsurveyed and virgin wilderness; neither had he

ever made his camp here with any man nor shared with any the intimate delight which the place gave him (p. 418).

This place belongs to the Virginian by moral right and spiritual kinship, if not by the laws of private property. Wister's hero, like the Western hero generally, possesses self-discipline, knowledge, skill, ingenuity, judgement, perseverance: qualities that uniquely fit his ability to cope with the special demands of America's geography, first, and the moral and spiritual demands of the nation, as well. Wister, in the essay 'The Evolution of the Cow-Puncher' sees the Western cowboy as the descendant of the Anglo-Saxon knight-at-arms and his heroic attributes (courage, toughness) are part of the legacy of his race. 'In personal daring and in skill as to the horse, the knight and the cowboy are nothing but the same Saxon of different environments.'[5] So all Anglo-Saxon males have the potential to become heroic in the fashion of the cowboy and this Wister finds an explanation for the Anglo-Saxon empire spreading across the North American continent: in Jane Tompkins's words, Anglo-Saxon men are 'the archetypal colonial conquerors who are peculiarly able to adapt to immediate conditions and subdue the environment to their will'.[6] It is this will to domination that characterises the hero's relation to everything: land, animals, women, men, his own body.

Zane Grey's first novel, The Last of the Plainsmendeals with this idea of domination as one of the features that distinguishes the Western hero from the Eastern 'greenhorn'. In this novel, a naive young man from the East travels west to accompany Colonel 'Buffalo' Jones on a final frontier journey that becomes a hunt for mountain lions. Early in the novel, one of the men objects to Jones's fame as the killer and captor of so many wild animals: 'How could a man have the strength and nerve? And isn't it cruel to keep wild animals in captivity? Isn't it against God's word?'[7] To which Jones immediately replies with a biblical quotation: 'And God said, "Let us make man in our image, and give him dominion over the fish of the sea, the fowls of the air, over all the cattle, and over every creeping thing that creepeth upon the earth!" And to add emphasis, he repeats 'Dominion – over all the beasts of the field! … Dominion! That was God's word!' (p. 229). The process by which he tames these creatures is described in dramatic detail throughout the various adventures reported in the narrative. What most disturbs his companions, however, is the manner in which Jones trains his dogs to follow the scent of mountain lions and not their usual prey, such as deer and rabbits. Every time the dogs chase the wrong trail, Jones hurts them: he shoots at them, whips them, and does not apologise for his treatment of them but explains: 'they've all got to be hurt to make them understand' (p. 268). In the chapter that follows this explanation, we see the incompetence of the men to shoe a bad–tempered pack-horse. What his companions fail to do, Jones does as a matter of course; he hog-ties the beast and when Frank objects 'He's chokin'!', Jones replies, 'Likely he is. ... It'll do him good' (p. 270). The apparent cruelty and want of feeling in the plainsman are shown to be essential features of the common sense that allows him to survive where others would die.

The Western hero achieves dominion not only over the beasts of the wilderness, he must also gain control over himself and particularly over his physical body. Zane Grey represents in detail the suffering and deprivation the frontier huntsmen undergo in the quest for survival, first, and dominion over nature. In one of the interpolated tales, Jones tells of his pursuit of the musk-oxen in the frozen wastes of the Hudson River country. Unimaginable cold, hostile natives, rabid wolves, starvation all confront him. In response, he overcomes his fear, his hunger, his cold and with grim determination crosses the frozen landscape with his bounty. It is the confrontation with extreme situations and the ability to triumph by setting aside conventional responses that makes the Western hero so heroic. As Jane Tompkins perceptively notes, the hero's sacrifice is what finally makes him heroic:

> He is not completely callous, not totally inured to the brutality he witnesses and shares in against his will. For what distinguishes the hero from the villains in a Western is that *he still feels* despite all the horror he has seen and all the horror he has perpetrated. In fact, that is how we know he is tough in the way a hero has to be, for his face shows that he has had to harden himself against his own feelings. His heart is not dead; it is battered and bruised inside the casing of his own chest .. It is his sacrifice, bound and smoking on the altar of his principles, the thing without which what he did would have no weight at all.[8]

The best proof that the hero remains spiritually alive is given in his acute perception of the significance of the landscape. The Western hero survives because of his knowledge of the land, his ability to read the landscape as a scout, and his fundamental appreciation of the land on its own terms. In *The Last of the Plainsmen*, the sight of sunset over the

Grand Canyon causes the narrator to exclaim in wonder: 'How infinite all this is', to which Buffalo Jones replies, 'To me it is very simple ... The world is strange. But this cañon – why, we can see it all! I can't make out why people fuss over it. I only feel peace. It's only bold and beautiful, serene and silent' (p. 336). The narrator then reflects:

> With the words of this quiet old plainsman, my sentimental passion shrank to the true appreciation of the scene. Self passed out to the recurring, soft strains of cliff song. I had been revelling in a species of indulgence, imagining I was a great lover of nature, building poetical illusions over storm-beaten peaks. The truth, told by one who had lived fifty years in the solitudes, among the rugged mountains, under the dark trees, and by the sides of the lonely streams, was the simple interpretation of a spirit in harmony with the bold, the beautiful, the serene, the silent (p. 337).

The plainsman, the Western hero, is perfectly in harmony with his surroundings and has of them a more profound appreciation, based on knowledge and understanding rather than sentiment and shallow feeling. Here, then, is the primitive simplicity to which Frederick Jackson Turner alludes; here is the return to an uncorrupted state of being that is integral to the conception of America's exceptional destiny and the exceptional Americans who will bring it about.

It is almost impossible to overestimate the importance of the landscape within the Western genre. The Western is most specific of genres in terms of historical period and geographical locale. In fact, the relationship of the characters to the landscape in which they live is as important as the way in which they relate to each other. West in the Western is the south-west, the desert states of Arizona, Utah, Nevada, New Mexico, Texas, Colorado, Montana, Wyoming, the Dakotas, and parts of California. The stark majesty of this region issues a challenge to the body and mind of the hero. He is able to dominate the living creatures of the wilderness but the landscape and mute nature is what the hero strives to emulate, to be as monumental, as threatening, as powerful and enduring, bleak and merciless as the desert. The harshness and austerity of the landscape selects a certain character type as heroic. Nature shows what is necessary in a man and the landscape then tests and proves who possesses those qualities.[9]

Westerns like Zane Grey's *Riders of the Purple Sage* base important elements of the narrative plot upon the hero's special knowledge of the landscape he inhabits. The theme of cattle rustling is one of the mechanisms by which the Mormon elders persecute the heiress, Jane Witherspoon, as they attempt to bully her into marrying Tull. The Mormons arrange that Oldring and his gang rustle Jane's herd and cause a stampede among the remaining cattle, they arrange for her hands to desert her and her servants to spy on her. But this secret scheming is uncovered when Venters, Jane's chief hand who has been run out by the Mormon men, discovers the secret canyon in which the stolen cattle are kept. It is Venters who, in this novel, reveals the almost mystical affinity experienced between the cowboy hero and the landscape. The valley that is his own secret retreat, and which bears the traces of ancient cliff-dwellers, is named by Venters 'Surprise Valley', in recognition of its Edenic nature, which is still completely hidden amid the wilderness. Venters's first experience of the valley is represented in a mystical, spiritual, vocabulary:

> Venters turned out of the gorge, and suddenly paused stock-still, astounded at the scene before him. The curve of the great stone bridge had caught the sunrise, and through the magnificent arch burst a glorious stream of gold that shone with a long slant down into the center of Surprise Valley. ... Even in his hurry and concern Venters could not but feel its majesty, and the thought came to him that the cliff-dwellers must have regarded it as an object of worship.[10]

The landscape is emphatically not empty, not a blank sheet – but only the Western hero knows how to read its messages and signs in order to survive. In this setting the hero is competent and he knows it. Venters does not fear stealing cattle from Oldring, even though Oldring's cattle are guarded by armed rustlers; he is confident of his ability to move through the landscape undetected. This confidence in his ability to survive in the wilderness is in contrast, however, with the Mormon town where safety and social order are ostensibly to be found. Venters is saved from death only by the sudden appearance of the gun-slinger Lassiter and to preserve his safety he retreats to 'the sage', as he calls it. Town represents all that Venters – and Lassiter and Jane too, eventually – must renounce. The Mormon town is synonymous with violence, oppression, persecution and tyranny and the church there is completely corrupt, particularly in comparison with the spiritual significance of the plains and mountains and sky. The nobility of Jane Witherspoon and the implacable sense of justice possessed by Lassiter lead them eventually to take refuge in Venters's Surprise Valley. The extreme of evil represented by Tull and the other Mormon men is such that it becomes impossible for Jane to reconcile the demands of her society with the natural code of justice that Lassiter, the Mormon-hater, represents. Jane and Lassiter escape pursuit by the Mormon posse by sealing themselves in Surprise Valley. As Lassiter rolls the huge boulder, 'Balancing Rock' down the canyon and into Deception Pass he destroys their Mormon pursuers but also seals their fate. His action triggers a massive landslide that entraps them in the valley.

Despite their flight from civilisation, Jane represents in typical Western fashion the female as a civilising influence. The Western heroine derives from nineteenth-century sentimental fiction and represents the values of Christian love and forgiveness, self-effacement, obedience to authority, and the sanctity of the family. These values are used by the Mormon elders to pressure Jane into marriage with the novel's prime villain, Tull. Her duty to her people and her God, her respect for her dead father's wishes, her desire to do what is expected of her and to avoid controversy all are used to manipulate her into an unwanted marriage. But Jane's personal vanity and her commitment to the idea of romantic love prevent her from agreeing to become just like the miserable Mormon women of her community. Her personal beauty, gentle demeanour and strong will first entrance Venters, who is persuaded by Jane to lay aside his guns and pursue a peaceful Christian lifestyle. More dramatically, after Jane has disarmed Venters, she turns her attention and civilising influence to the gun-slinger Lassiter, who has a reputation as a Mormon-hater and Mormon-killer. Lassiter comes to Cottonwoods to avenge the death of his sister, Milly Earn, who was enticed from her home and her husband by an unnamed Mormon man. When her attempts to return home were defeated and her child was taken from her in punishment, Milly died and it is this death that Lassiter would avenge. Instead, he falls in love with Milly's best friend, Jane Witherspoon. When he overhears Jane explain to Bishop Dyer that she has tried to charm Lassiter so that he will renounce his hatred of their religion and give up his revenge, Lassiter realises what has happened to him:

> For years I've been a lonely man set on one thing. I came here an' met you. An' now I'm not the man I was. The change was gradual, an' I took no notice of it. I understand now that never-satisfied longin' to see you, listen to you, watch you, feel you near me. It's plain now

why you were never out of my thoughts. I've had no thoughts but of you. I've lived and breathed for you. An' now when I know what it means – what you've done – I'm burnin' up with hell's fire! (p. 109).

The civilising influence Jane exerts over Lassiter, transforming him from a gun-slinger and killer, can find no expression within the civilisation of the novel. Only in the wilderness can they find surroundings that are in harmony with the values they hold.

The West in Western Movies

Riders of the Purple Sage embodies all of the classic elements of Western symbolism, listed by Irwin Blacker as: 'the hero and the villain, the clear-cut differences between good and evil, the shoot-down, the six gun [Colt revolver], the Stetson hat, the horse, the code of honor, the unkissed heroine'.[11] All these elements are based in fact, except for the figure of the heroine and the morality expressed by the genre. The moral code of the Western arose from the image of the West as a place for new beginnings, a new kind of democracy, where only a man's personality counted and only the strong survived (on the Oregon Trail, the dead averaged 17 per mile). The hero was then associated with the concept of the noble savage, as in Owen Wister's *The Virginian* and Zane Grey's *Riders of the Purple Sage*, where the cowboy hero becomes the noble savage. His only desire is for freedom, not for property; it is the villain who is marked by his greed for land, water, money, a woman: all of which he may not legitimately claim.

One of the most powerful contributions made by the Western to the ideology of American exceptionalism was the ability to distinguish between legitimate and illegitimate claims to such things as power, land, water, women. Kim Newman suggests this as he points to the single most powerful ideological aspect of movie Westerns:

While couched in terms of the coming of civilisation, the rise of law and order or the establishment of community values, the Western is essentially about conquest. Cavalries conquer the Indians, pioneers conquer the wilderness, lawmen conquer outlaws and individuals conquer their circumstances. But with each conquest, another stretch of territory, whether geographical or philosophical, comes under the hegemony of the United States of America.[12]

The expansion of the United States, so necessary for the survival of America's great model democracy that is its exceptional destiny, is given legitimacy by the mythology of conquest represented in Westerns. John Ford's Westerns develop a complex mythology of American exceptionalism and American domination of the continent, by right and by force. His movies, more than any other director's, sanction the dispossession of native peoples and the destruction of the existing cultures of the south-west in the name of American destiny.

In *Stagecoach* (1939, United Artists) Ford pits the individual against the alien and hostile environment of Utah's Monument Valley. The individual characters gathered in the stagecoach represent a variety of human personalities that are tested as they face extreme stress: they are threatened by the weather, by Indian attack, by the poor communications of the frontier. There is the military wife, Lucy Malory, travelling to meet her husband; the Southern gambler, Hatfield; the drunken doctor, Boon; the salesman, Peacock; the corrupt banker, Henry Gatewood; the showgirl, Dallas; and, joining the stage after it has left town, the Ringo Kid. Most of these characters are running away from civilisation, taking refuge in the wilderness of the frontier. But in the course of their journey they are tested, as the doctor's skill is tested when he is called upon to deliver Lucy Malory's baby. It is Ringo who emerges as the hero in true Western fashion. He is able to read the Apache war signals and when, during the chase scene, the horses need direction, he climbs precariously along the harness to guide the leaders by riding one of them. Consequently, Ringo assumes a moral authority among the passengers that is disproportionate to his status as an outlaw and misfit. By the standards of civilised, Eastern, society he is nothing but in the West he is tested and proved a genuine American hero. The microcosm of American society that finally triumphs in *Stagecoach* defeats the Apaches and wins the right to proceed westward by virtue of superior force and moral kinship with the land. In the shoot-out that accompanies the chase, the camera lingers on the difference between the Apache's arrows and the guns of the passengers. These Indians, then, are doomed to defeat in the face of technological superiority and also the superior knowledge of men like Ringo who can read the landscape with which the Indians are closely associated. The Indians are part of the natural world that must come under the dominion of Western heroes such as Ringo.

It was in the cavalry trilogy: *Fort Apache* (1948, RKO Radio Pictures), *She Wore a Yellow Ribbon* (1949, RKO Radio Pictures), and *Rio Grande*

(1950, Republic) that John Ford set out his mythology of America, based upon the legitimate conquest of the south-west by pioneering Americans, symbolised by the US Cavalry. *Fort Apache* is perhaps the most complex of the three movies, setting into play as it does tensions between East and West, savagery and civilisation, officers and troops, and so on. The story concerns the arrival of Colonel Owen Thursday (Henry Fonda) and his daughter Philadelphia (Shirley Temple) at the remote Arizona outpost of Fort Apache, where he is to assume command. Thursday deeply resents what he perceives to be his exile from civilised society. As he travels on the stagecoach with his daughter, he exclaims that he would rather be in Europe than in this wilderness, 'What a country!' he says with contempt, 'Forty miles from waterhole to waterhole.' Colonel Thursday does not possess the Western character we have come to identify from the values expressed by Western heroes. In fact, he represents the diametric opposite: the Yankee who refuses to recognise anything of worth in the West and who clings to Eastern values no matter how irrelevant they have become in the context of frontier life. The negativity of the values represented by Thursday is emphasised when he finally arrives at Fort Apache and discovers that a dance is in progress. After being introduced to his officers, Thursday asks Captain York (John Wayne) what occasion is marked by the party, since it is obviously not in honour of his arrival. After explaining that the telegraph wires have been down for two days following an Apache raid, and so no news of his imminent arrival was received, York also explains that he has interrupted a birthday party – a party in honour of General George Washington. The superior patriotism of the community at the fort is clear in this confrontation. The further distinction between Thursday's conception of military priority and those of the officers familiar with frontier conditions becomes clear during the officers' briefing the following morning. There, Thursday expresses a pedantic adherence to army regulations, particularly in regards to the military dress code, and this attitude of inflexibility is extended to his attitude towards what the cavalry must achieve on the south-western frontier and how they should achieve it. He is not shy of expressing his profound disappointment at his latest commission and in particular he regrets the lack of opportunities for glory represented by this border outpost; he regrets that he is not with the officers fighting what he considers to be worthy Indian foe – the Cheyenne and the Sioux – but instead has found himself fighting off the 'gnat stings and flea bites of a few cowardly digger

Indians', as he puts it. In outraged response, Captain York points out that the Apache are the most feared tribe among all Indians, but his view is dismissed by Thursday, only Captain Collingwood's warning that 'this is not the country for glory' registers with the self-regarding Colonel.

In parallel with the military theme is the romantic relationship that develops between the Colonel's daughter and Lieutenant Michael O'Rourke, the son of the company Sergeant-Major and newly arrived from West Point. Philadelphia, inevitably, finds herself caught between her disapproving father and her lover. Colonel Thursday disapproves of the match because he believes Philadelphia could 'do better' back East. He points, brutally, to the great gap in social class that separates the son of a non-commissioned officer from someone like himself, and he sets at naught Sergeant-Major O'Rourke's civil war service which earned him the Congressional Medal of Honor and made possible his son's West Point education. Thursday reveals in full the vanity, pride and supercilious attitude that motivate him in his encounter with Lt O'Rourke's parents. Ironically, Phil shares more in common with the O'Rourkes than with her own father. Out riding with Michael, she exclaims over the beauty of the harsh landscape, she accommodates herself immediately to conditions on the frontier post and willingly joins the community of soldiers' wives. The values of honesty, integrity, honour and plain-dealing win out both in the romantic sub-plot and the main military plot. The girl is won not by an individual but the Western personality and lifestyle. This is an important aspect of John Ford's mythologising effort: the winning of the heroine validates particular values and legitimises the actions of those who express these values. In Fort Apache it is opposing views of the Apache that are in tension.

Colonel Thursday is warned repeatedly of the power and strength of the Apache nation, yet he refuses to believe that Indians can be anything other than savages. Early in the movie, the troopers sent to repair the telegraph line are found dead, having been roasted alive over the burning remains of their wagon. Thursday orders a detail of four men accompanied by one officer to retrieve the bodies; Captain York advises that the whole platoon is needed, armed with sixty rounds of carbine ammunition – Thursday allows them thirty, dismissing York's objection with, 'I'm not asking for advice.' Thursday cannot conceive that the bodies may be used as a trap by the Apache to kill those who come to claim them; Thursday cites famous battles from military history and stratagems described at the Academy and concludes 'I do not hold with the "trap" as a military weapon.' To him, the Indian is incapable of thinking in such sophisticated military terms. Yet a trap is precisely what those four troopers and their officer, Lt O'Rourke, encounter when they try to load onto a wagon the bodies of their comrades. Gradually Thursday learns the true relationship between the Apache, their leader Cochise, and white civilisation. He visits the reservation agent and finds a dissolute and corrupt man, Meacham, who is selling whisky and guns but withholding meat and blankets from the Indians whose society has been degraded and nearly destroyed. Consequently, the Indians have followed Cochise off the reservation, thus breaking a treaty they consider already broken by the US government, across into Mexico where they cannot be pursued by the US military.

This story of the Apache's plight means little to Colonel Thursday, except that long-awaited opportunity to grasp at glory for himself. Captain York explains to him that Cochise cannot be brought back by force but that if one man whom he trusted promised to ensure a decent life for his people then Cochise could be persuaded to return the Apache to the reservation. York and interpreter are dispatched, unarmed, to arrange negotiations and York returns, dramatically interrupting the NCO's dance, to report that Cochise has returned to United States' soil, to negotiate peace. Thursday then issues a set of orders that contradicts the promises just made by York to Cochise. When York exclaims in disgust that his promises are rendered no more than a trick, Thursday replies of course it was a trick, to get the Indians back on American soil, arguing that there can be no honour between an American officer and a savage. In this fashion, Thursday earns the contempt of all his men but especially Captain York, who has been personally compromised by the Colonel's lack of integrity.

The Colonel's personal weakness and his lack of Western knowledge combine in the culminating encounter between the Indians and the cavalry. York offers his interpretation of the Indians' strategy, that they are concealed behind the rocky outcrops that line the canyon while squaws and children stir up dust near the encampment beyond to deceive the soldiers. York's views are again dismissed. Thursday adheres strictly to the manners of a West Point officer in his brief encounter with Cochise; he refuses the ritual introductions expected by the Indians, he refuses to listen to the Indians' grievances and when they lay down Meacham's removal as a condition for their return to the reservation,

Thursday explodes. He will not be dictated to nor threatened by an Indian; he orders Cochise to the reservation on pain of military attack. All the men know that Cochise is the aggrieved party and that he has been shamefully treated by Thursday. However, their own sense of honour demands that they follow his orders. In the face of York's violent objections, he orders a charge into the canyon in massed columns of four. The charge becomes a suicide mission, just as York warned. Thursday is among the first shot, and is left staggering, disoriented, without horse or dignity. When York rides down to offer his horse to the Colonel, he is also asked for his sabre so he can rejoin his command: 'Your command is wiped out, sir', he is told, yet he gathers what troops he can and they are then indeed wiped out.

The perspective of the movie alters in the next frame, and we see Colonel York answering the questions of Eastern newspapermen about General Thursday. We find that he has gained his glory, though he has lost his life, and that 'Thursday's Charge' is celebrated in a painting displayed in Washington DC that shows the cavalry facing an enemy also mounted in columns of four. York passes over the massive historical inaccuracies of this account and, in response to the question whether Thursday was a great soldier, he replies 'No one died more gallantly.' But he becomes much more interested when one of the reporters remarks that it is only the heroes, the Thursdays, that are remembered. 'You're wrong there, because they haven't died ... [they] keep on living so long as the regiment lives. ... [The] faces and names change but they are the regiment, the regular army. Now and fifty years from now.'

The same opposition between false Eastern values and the glory represented by the cavalry is represented in the second movie of the trilogy, *She Wore a Yellow Ribbon* (1949). The movie concludes with a seemingly endless parade of cavalrymen and a voice over that proclaims:

So here they are, the dog-faced soldiers, the regulars, the fifty cents a day professionals riding the outposts of the nation ... they are all the same, men in dirty shirt blue and only a page in the history book to mark their passing. But wherever they rode and whatever they fought for, that place became the United States.

In John Ford's representation of American history, the cavalry is the agent of national destiny. Manifest Destiny, the exceptional destiny that describes and is evidence of America's status as God's chosen people, is realised through the sacrifices and heroic actions of the US cavalry.

This mythic account of the nation's history is not assumed but in movies like *She Wore a Yellow Ribbon* and *Rio Grande* the heroism of the cavalry is proved to an unwilling woman. *She Wore a Yellow Ribbon* is set in the context of war between the Indians and the US cavalry, and begins with an elegy for Custer and a reminder that if another massacre were to follow no stagecoach would dare to cross the plains. Thus the work of the cavalry is identified closely with the expansion of the United States. This heroic mission to subdue the Indian tribes is disrupted by the influence of women and one in particular: Olivia Dandridge, niece of the commanding officer, who is 'not army enough' to face winter on the frontier and requires a military escort to meet the stage. Sparring for her attentions are two troopers, Parnell and Colehill. Olivia is drawn to Parnell because of his privileged Eastern background and she has persuaded him to leave the cavalry and join her in New York. However, she is irresistibly attracted to Colehill, in part through his mentor and commanding officer Nathan Brittles (John Wayne). Both Olivia and Parnell discover in the course of the action that conditions on the frontier demand the honourable sacrifices that the cavalry makes. Parnell witnesses the torture and murder of an illegal arms trader and his colleagues by a group of Indians drunk on the rot-gut whisky they have just been given. This sight convinces him, as he tells Brittles, that it would be wrong to leave the regiment. Similarly, after experiencing Indian attack and the perils of the frontier, Olivia ceases to be 'not army enough' for Colehill's choice of life and claims him as her beau.

In *Rio Grande* Colonel York (John Wayne) tells his estranged wife Kathleen (Maureen O'Hara) that duty is important to him because 'I've seen things that made my duty seem important.' After the wagon train evacuating women and children, while the regiment goes on a winter mission across the Rio Grande, is attacked by Indians and the children are taken hostage, Kathleen begins to change her mind. The children are rescued from certain torture and death by her son Jefferson York and his friends Travis Tyree and Daniel 'Sandy' Boone, and Kathleen begins to appreciate the values upheld by her husband as they are expressed by her adored son. Her intention in following him to the remote outpost where he had been stationed was to buy him out of the cavalry. However, his sense of honour, like that of his father, will not allow him, as it will not allow his father, to sign the release papers. Kathleen's view is warped by the experience of the Civil War when her husband, Kirby York, was ordered to burn her family's plantation. To her, a man who could obey such orders can have no real sense of honour. Added to that is the absence of glory in the life York chooses to lead in the cavalry. As he tells his son, 'Put out of your mind any romantic ideas that it's a way of glory. It's a life of suffering and of hardship, an uncompromising devotion to your oath and your duty.' In the West, Kathleen comes to understand just what that devotion to duty means, just as she realises the point of the personal sacrifices that are made, routinely, by the men of the American military. As she is persuaded of the special character and exceptional historical mission of these men, so are we carried along on a tide of exceptionalist rhetoric and nationalist sentiment. Sentiment is John Ford's most powerful means of conveying the values, the mythology, of his America. In the cavalry trilogy, the setting is the period of the Indian Wars, where pioneering emigrants and the cavalry that opens their way represent the Manifest Destiny of the West. The cost of this expansion is the displacement of the Indian population and the violent ending of the Indian way of life. John Ford represents this destruction as lamentable but inevitable. Not that the Indians should be dispossessed of their lands but how this process should proceed is at issue in his movies. The Western, as a genre, can be both anti- and pro-Indian (pro-Indian films include *Soldier Blue* and *Little Big Man*) but racial conflict is rarely seen as a moral issue, it is more a historical inevitability. Sexual violence towards women is a constant threat in Westerns; pro-Indian films often feature the rape of native women by cavalrymen as symptomatic of American cruelty and injustice; the captive children of *Rio Grande* suggest a similar threat but as the victims of Indian violence.

Sexual violence towards women is also related to the idea of 'legitimate property' explored in Westerns. The expansion of the United States into Indian and Mexican lands may be represented as a historical inevitability yet it must also be legitimised by coming into the possession of an appropriate American landholder. In John Ford's *The Searchers* (1956, Warner Brothers) the issue of who should possess the land is intimately related to who should possess the women. For women are the icons of civilisation, of the American society that is being brought into existence on the frontier. In Westerns women, and pioneer women especially, are generally associated with the civilising influence of Christianity, with religion and spiritual power rather than worldly power. Consequently, women are either ineffectual or else try actively to disrupt the hero's mission. But his violent heroism is defined in opposition to the values of harmony and reconciliation. Women and children legitimise violence as the hero goes about the business of making the world safe for women. The rejection of the church is a common motif in Westerns: an example would be the interruption of the massacred pioneers' funeral and, later, Laurie's wedding in *The Searchers*. In this movie, John Wayne plays the anti-hero, Ethan Edwards; an Indian-hating renegade who returns to his brother's frontier homestead after an unexplained absence of some years. His status as an outsider is established from the outset in his relationship with his brother's wife, Martha. It is Martha's figure, framed in the doorway, that first points to the distant horseman who is Ethan. Her suppressed joy and Ethan's restrained manner towards her suggests that there is some history between these two. This is confirmed later when she fetches Ethan's coat and, unconscious that she can be seen, caresses it lovingly. What is suggested here is that Martha has had to choose between the brothers and she has chosen a settled farming life because Ethan is not the sort of man to settle down. His unexplained absence is linked to such a romantic complication by Martha's guilty expression when Ethan is asked by his brother why he has stayed away for so long. During his absence, Ethan has fought for the Confederate army and he refuses to admit their defeat; he refuses the heroism that is symbolised by the medal he gives away to the child Debbie, claiming that it is just a bauble. In this way, his character is defined as that of a rebel, a renegade, a man of questionable loyalties though of unquestionable courage.

The morning after his arrival, word arrives with a group of Texas Rangers that Indians have killed a number of cattle on a nearby ranch. While the men are pursuing the culprits, Ethan suddenly recognises the signs of what he calls 'a murder raid': the Indians have lured the men away from the homestead so they may massacre the women and children remaining. This is, in fact, the case. All are murdered, except the girls Lucy and Debbie, who have been taken captive. Ethan, who has already revealed himself to be an Indian-hater by his hostile attitude towards the Edwards's adopted son Martin, who has some Indian blood, leads the pursuit. Lucy's body is found, though it is not shown and her beau Brad is prevented by Ethan from seeing her. The suggestion is, of course, that she has been tortured and raped. The pursuit then is for the captive Debbie and Ethan insists that he go on alone. He reluctantly accepts Martin as his companion, accepting Martin's reasoning that he wants to avenge his two families, adopted and natural, that have been massacred. Months pass, as the search widens, and finally they discover that she is held by a Comanche chief named Scar. The motive of the movie's plot then shifts, from a predominantly quest narrative to a suspense narrative based on the question: what will Ethan do when he finds Debbie? Other white children who have undergone the experience of captivity are shown to have been made mad by the trauma, or they have assimilated to Indian ways. In Ethan's view, a white woman is better off dead rather than the wife of a Comanche. And it becomes apparent to Martin that Ethan intends to kill Debbie when he finds her, and that he must stop him. For Ethan, there can be no such thing as a legitimate marriage between a white woman and an Indian. This attitude is linked to ideas about who can legitimately make claim to the land as well. There is a comic sub-theme of miscegenation, when Martin inadvertently buys a wife from an Indian trader. 'Look', as they call her, simply follows Martin as he heads off down the trail and refuses to leave him. Ethan, once he has recovered from his hilarity, explains to Martin that he now has a wife. Certainly, Look serves Martin just as the white women serve their husbands; Look's behaviour mirrors that of Martha in the opening scenes. She leaves, suddenly in the night, scared off by the prospect of an encounter with Scar and when she reappears she is dead, killed with the rest of an Indian village by the cavalry. Where the dead body of a white woman is never shown, Look's is. This has the dual effect of arousing sympathy for this character but it also makes her a less serious character than the white women who are represented. The comic pseudo-marriage between Martin and Look can never be taken seriously at any point, because we know that Martin has an attachment to Laurie Jorgensen, daughter of one of the frontier families. At first, Laurie undertakes to wait for Martin but as the months pass and he shows no sign of completing or abandoning his pursuit of Debbie she accepts another marriage proposal. It takes Ethan and Martin five years to locate Debbie and when they find her she has become Indian by nurture. Ethan still believes that she has been con-taminated by her Indian upbringing and particularly by her Indian marriage, which to him is no marriage at all. However, he cannot finally kill her and so he brings her home. The discovery of Debbie and her illegitimate marriage is juxtaposed with the great slapstick scene of the movie. Ethan and Martin return to interrupt Laurie's wedding. Just before she is to take her vows, they enter and a fight ensues. The question of whom Laurie should marry is, like Ford's earlier exploration of this theme, divided between the self-sacrificing hero and the domesticated rival, the true Westerner who blazes a trail into the wilderness and the settler who follows to establish an extension of American society. This is the difficulty of the Western: the hero makes possible but is not part of the expansion of civilisation. There is no place in civilised society for the values held by Ethan, who places in question the very distinction between savagery and civilisation. Ethan remains the outlaw, the misfit, thus allowing Martin to marry Laurie and so vindicate the status of the Western hero. Martin moves from a false and illegitimate marriage to Look, to a proper marriage with Laurie; Debbie moves from an illegitimate marriage with Scar to her rightful place in white society. What these shifting relationships mean for the theme of territorial expansion, for that is what is at issue between the Comanche and the white settlers, is that Indians cannot make a legitimate claim to what has become white land just as they cannot claim white women. The pioneers assert their ownership of the land not only by cultivating and settling it but by establishing on it a society that perpetuates itself through the ritual of marriage. Thus, the ideology of American exceptionalism informs all the details of a movie like *The Searchers*, as it informs John Ford's entire conception of American mythology.

Spaghetti Westerns, such as the classic movies made by Sergio Leone throughout the 1960s: *A Fistful of Dollars* (1964), *For a Few Dollars More* (1965), *The Good, the Bad, and the Ugly* (1966), and *Once Upon a Time in the West* (1967), offer a pastiche but also an extension of the ideas, themes and motifs developed in classic Westerns like John Ford's. *Once Upon a Time in the West* begins with a prolonged meditation upon the lonely grandeur of the Western landscape, the landscape of the south-west that John Ford had elevated to mythical status. Shots such as the cowboy framed in the doorway, and illuminated by the harsh sunlight behind him, as we look from the relative comfort offered inside the building, are deliberate stylistic quotations taken from John Ford's films, in this case *The Searchers*. In Sergio Leone's movie, the incursion of civilisation into the wilderness is represented by the railroad, which, as Kim Newman points out, 'itself is not exactly tainted, but it serves to shake up the west to such a degree that the heroes have to make a stand against the evil that creeps in whenever there is the chance for wide-open speculation'.[13] *Once Upon a Time in the West* is based on the villain's fore-knowledge of the railroad's path and the soaring value that will be placed on land needed by the railroad. So Morton and Frank set out to buy, through whatever means, all the land in question. They terrorise and murder the farming communities that lie in their way, in a style of Western that is significantly more violent than the classic Ford Westerns. Westerns such as this for the first time graphically depict the impact and exit wounds inflicted by bullets, and are therefore considerably more bloody than earlier Westerns. There is also a blackness, a pessimism of tone, in such films. The Western, as a genre, celebrates the triumph of American capital and progress but in *Once Upon a Time in the West* the railroad also represents an influx of predatory and unscrupulous 'business' men. The outlaw hero, Harmonica (Charles Bronson), is driven to commit violent crimes by the murderous behaviour of Morton and Frank. Other types of Western place the hero in necessary opposition to corrupt and unscrupulous cattle barons, and violent, bloody cattle wars (like the Lincoln County wars) are the consequence. As Kim Newman observes, East meets West geographically in the railroad but the opposites meet ideologically in these characters.[14] Death is a central theme in all Westerns – present even in the iconic place names like Deadwood and Tombstone. How death is faced, whether with honour and courage or with cringing cowardice, is at issue. For the threat of death provides the ultimate test of an individual's capacity for heroism, the values he lives by, and the mission that motivates him. Jane Tompkins goes so far as to describe the Western as 'a narrative of male violence'.[15] She argues that the Western embodies a twentieth-century rejection of Christianity and all organised religion: in the Western, the struggle is not to conquer sin but to prove one's courage in the face of annihilation. When it is life itself at stake, all else seems trivial: social ritual, everyday actions, class ceremony and distinction. This sacrifice of the conventions of normal life is what constitutes Western heroism. The Christian God, Christian forgiveness and mercy do not work against the godless elements that confront the Western hero. These elements are destroyed by violence, not Christian humility. This perception accounts for the blackness that characterises spaghetti Westerns, which, in their pastiche of the genre, emphasise the generic features of Westerns at the expense of individual traits in particular movies. The necessary violence that is vindicated by the American mission and justified by the individual American citizens who are served by their nation's Manifest Destiny demands the sacrifice of gentle emotions and sentiments.

The Western emerged out of the mythology of America: exceptionalism and its peculiar nineteenth-century embodiment in the doctrine of Manifest Destiny. The Western began with James Fenimore Cooper's frontier scouts and gradually the cowboy was identified as the Western hero. With Owen Wister, the Western formula acquired its characteristic elements: the frontier setting, reflected in geography and costume, the historical context offered by the frontier where civilisation and savagery meet, generating what John Cawelti calls, 'striking antitheses without raising basic questions about American society or life in general. In the Western formula savagery is implicitly understood to be on the way out' and so the story is resolved with 'a reaffirmation of the values of modern society'.[16] In this way, the Western past can be made continuous with the civilization of the present and the continuity of the American mission therefore remains undisrupted in history. Cawelti goes on to argue:

> Twentieth-century America is perhaps the most ideologically pacifistic nation in history. Its political and social values are antimilitaristic, its legal ideals reject personal violence and it sees itself as a nation dedicated to world peace and domestic harmony through law and order. Yet this same nation supports one of the largest military establishments in history, its rate of violent crime is enormously high and it possesses the technological capacity to destroy the world. Perhaps one source of the cowboy hero's appeal is the way in which he resolves this ambiguity by giving a sense of moral significance and order to violence.[17]

The conflict between progress and the cost of progress, of course, places in question the entire ideology of progress: America's inherited commitment to the concept of divine providence and the mythology of the nation's special historical mission ensured that progress was seen as a benevolent process. But for those who did not succeed or progress? Failure is not accounted for by the mythology of American exceptionalism – conformity or elimination (as was intended for the Indians) are the only alternatives. So Cawelti concludes,

> America in the twentieth century has had to confront a number of profound and disturbing ambiguities about violence which stem from

conflicting historical traditions and realities. The popular nineteenth century image of America as a redeemer nation, a new peace-loving Christian democracy, innocent of the hatred and violence of the past and with a mission to bring peace, prosperity and democracy to the world was a compelling cultural self-image. Yet the vision contrasted profoundly with the reality of an inordinately high level of individual and social aggression, beginning with the revolution which created the new nation and continuing through domestic and foreign wars of moralistic conquest and the violent subjection of black people and Indians. To preserve the self-image it has been necessary to disguise the aggressive impulse of these historical realities under the mask of moral purity and social redemption through violence. Thus, there has always been an observable similarity between the pattern of justifying rhetoric used to defend American military policy and the Western drama.[18]

How contemporary writers, living in the contemporary America to which Cawelti alludes, deal with the enduring mythology of American exceptionalism is the issue to which I now turn.

Notes

1. Frederick Jackson Turner, 'The Significance of the Frontier in American History' (1894), in Clyde A. Milner II, Anne M. Butler and David Rich Lewis (eds), *Major Problems in the History of the American West* (Boston and New York: Houghton Mifflin Co., 1997), p. 2.
2. James Folsom, 'Introduction', *The Western: A Collection of Critical Essays* (Englewood Cliffs, NJ: Prentice-Hall, 1979), p. 9.
3. Quoted in Kim Newman, *Wild West Movies: How the West was Found, Won, Lost, Lied About, Filmed and Forgotten* (London: Bloomsbury, 1990), epigram.
4. Owen Wister, *The Virginian* (1902, rpt Lincoln and London: University of Nebraska Press, 1992), p. xix. Future page references are given in the text.
5. Owen Wister, 'The Evolution of the Cow-Puncher', quoted by Jane Tompkins, *West of Everything: The Inner Life of Westerns* (New York and Oxford: Oxford University Press, 1992), p. 145.
6. Tompkins, ibid, p. 146.
7. Zane Grey, *The Last of the Plainsmen* (1908), rpt in *Riders of the Purple Sage, The Last of the Plainsmen, and Lone Star Ranger* (London: Chancellor Press, 1992), p. 229. Future page references are given in the text.
8. Tompkins, *West of Everything*, p. 219.
9. See Tompkins, ibid., p. 73 for a discussion of the prescriptive power of the Western landscape.
10. Zane Grey, *Riders of the Purple Sage* (1912, rpt New York and London: Penguin Books, 1990), p. 93. Future page references are given in the text.
11. Irwin R. Blacker, *The Old West in Fiction* (New York: Ivan Obolensky, 1961), p. iii.

12. Newman, *Wild West Movies*, p. 1.
13. Ibid., p. 36.
14. Ibid., p. 37.
15. Tompkins, *West of Everything*, p. 28.
16. John G. Cawelti, *The Six-Gun Mystique* (Bowling Green, OH: Bowling Green University Popular Press, 1973), see the discussion on pp. 35–8.
17. Ibid., pp. 60–1.
18. Ibid., p. 84.

CHAPTER 6

Contemporary Interpretations of Exceptionalism

Continuing the theme of Westerns, this chapter begins with an account of Larry McMurtry's post-modern deconstruction of the myth of the West and the exceptionalist assumptions upon which it is based. I move then to Thomas Pynchon's deconstruction of American exceptionalism in *The Crying of Lot 49*, *Mason & Dixon* and the post-modern classic *Gravity's Rainbow*, and Toni Morrison's extended response to exceptionalism in her revision of America's historical narrative in *Beloved* and *Jazz*. To underline the power and longevity of exceptionalism as a key element in American cultural identity, I conclude with a discussion of exceptionalism and the representation of the Vietnam conflict in contemporary fiction and film.

Deconstructing the Myth of America

As we saw in the preceding chapter, the mythology of the West is both highly charged and highly contradictory. The West in American mythology is a fiction created by individuals who struggled to make the West something more than mere fiction but in the process often destroyed the very qualities they sought to enshrine. In his contemporary Western novels, Larry McMurtry takes a self-consciously nostalgic approach to the mythology of the West. Novels like *Lonesome Dove* (1985), *Streets of Laredo* (1993), *Dead Man's Walk* (1995), *Buffalo Girls* (1990), and *Anything for Billy* (1988) focus upon the central irony of all Western fictions: the West was 'tamed' by men who were drawn to the West in the first place because it was untamed, wild, beyond the strictures of civilised life. By taming the wilderness they brought civilisation and the destruction of what they had themselves valued. This contradiction is poignantly represented by the characters of *Buffalo Girls*, who join Buffalo Bill's Wild West Show because that is the only place where they can discover the kind of life that has escaped them in the 'real' West. Calamity Jane, Annie Oakley, Sitting Bull – all escape a West that has become meaningless for them by joining the travelling show. There, among the imagery of Manifest Destiny and the rhetoric of national identity they can find refuge from a reality that is devoid of the meaning it claims. One of the most pathetic characters is the trapper, Jim Ragg, who travels the West compulsively, with his partner Bartle, searching for the beaver that they themselves have long since destroyed. Ironically it is in London Zoo, during the show's European tour, that Jim finds the long sought-after object of his desires:

> A little fog still drifted across the surface of the pond when he heard the beaver slap the water; it was a sound he had first heard on the Platte as a boy of sixteen; it was the sound that had called him on, deeper and deeper into the West, to the Missouri and then the Yellowstone, all the way to the dangerous Bitterroot; then it became a sound he heard less and less often as the beaver vanished from the Bitterroot and the Tongue, from the golden Madison valley, from Wyoming, from Colorado; the last time he heard the beaver's slap was high in the Medicine Bow forest more than ten years before. He had listened for it in vain ever since – but here it was, at last! [1]

Once he has rediscovered the beaver, Jim refuses to leave London. What is important to him above all else is the symbolism, the iconography, of the West as a pristine landscape not yet corrupted and decimated by the incursions of civilised life. Whether he finds this representation of the West in the city of London or in the make-believe of the Wild West Show is irrelevant and unimportant in comparison to his need to find and keep it. Though Jim is, finally, compelled to rejoin the troupe and their return to America, he dies during the voyage and does not again confront the landscape to whose barrenness he has contributed.

The most articulate spokesman for this view of the West as riddled with contradictions is Augustus McCrae, ex-Texas Ranger and cattleman who travels with his partner Woodrow Call on an epic cattle drive from Texas to Montana, in McMurtry's Pulitzer Prize winning novel, *Lonesome Dove*. The cattle drive is a motif common to many Westerns but the motive McMurtry attributes to his characters is quite distinctive. Call wants to travel to Montana territory because Texas has become too civilised for him. Call wants to rediscover, once more before he dies, the excitement and danger of life on the frontier. This motivation remains unknown to most of the characters, who believe they are simply seeking better cattle country, but Gus McCrae, who shares Call's intuition, is able to see through to the fundamentals of the Western ethos. In his view, Rangers like he and Call did their job of taming the wilderness just too well and too effectively. Ironically, their reward has been the multiplication of towns and settlements, such as they always sought to avoid, and the shrinking of the frontier wilderness in which they feel at home. Gus's response to the suggestion that they go to Montana is the bleak opinion that Montana will turn out to be just the same as Texas.

> 'If we go the [lawyers and bankers] won't be far behind,' Augustus said. 'The first ones that get there will hire you to go hang all the horsethieves and bring in whichever Indians have got the most fight left, and you'll do it and the place will be civilized. Then you won't know what to do with yourself, no more than you have these last ten years.' [2]

Gus's interpretation of what the West has become is borne out in the scenes that follow as they cross the continent (not from East to West as in classic narratives of westward progress, instead they cut across south to north, from Mexico to Canada). The Indians they encounter are starving, demoralised and decimated by disease, hunger and the United States Army. The land is ruled by the rule of law though lynching is not uncommon; the villains – murderers and rustlers, mostly – are sufficiently few so that they are recognised on sight and all the characters we encounter on the drive know these criminals by name. The West has become a closed and shrinking world, turning inwards upon itself. The greatest threat of all comes from the land itself, which violently resists all efforts at transformation, whether these are efforts to civilise or mythologise the landscape. And the heroism of this epic journey is likewise found in an unexpected place. The historical figures that do appear in McMurtry's fiction – for instance, Billy the Kid in *Anything for Billy*, Judge Roy Bean, John Wesley Hardin and Charles Goodnight in *Streets of Laredo* – are all painfully ordinary and completely devoid of heroic characteristics, except for an unusual taste for violence. In *Lonesome Dove* it is Call himself who emerges as the exemplar of the Western code of honour, the ethos and lifestyle that he seeks nostalgically but cannot recognise in himself. Despite his deeply flawed personality, Call develops the stature of a hero in his unquestioning commitment to realising his dead partner's dying wish. Despite the enormous physical and geographical difficulties, Call returns Gus's body to Texas for burial. In his absolute adherence to the code of honour that demands he keep his word Call reveals his own inheritance of the Western ethos. Call then is not only motivated by nostalgia for the frontier lifestyle he has lost, but he also becomes the object of the narrative's nostalgic re-creation of the ideals that have been sacrificed to the pursuit of progress and the march of civilisation.

Larry McMurtry deconstructs the mythology of the West by pointing to the extent to which the patriotic rhetoric of exceptionalism was (and is) divorced from the reality of Western life and history. The mythical version of frontier history may satisfy deep longings within the national psyche but, at the same time, it creates a desire for a lifestyle that never existed except within the closed realm of exceptionalist discourse. In the earlier novel, *Horseman Pass By* (1961), the adolescent narrator Lonnie seeks an adult example of the romantic Western lifestyle about which he has been told so much. He visits the local cinema to see a Gene Autry Western, *Streets of Laredo*, only to find the conventional Hollywood icons of cowboy life ridiculed by the ranch hand, Lonzo, who accompanies him: ' "Look at that silver mounted saddle", he said snickering. "You couldn't lift that bastard on a horse with a goddamn crane".' [3] Jesse claims to have seen Gene Autry at a rodeo once but, as Lonnie discovers, even the rodeo offers little opportunity to witness the real Western ethos. The annual rodeo offers Lonnie an opportunity to locate, among these cowboys, the romanticism he fails to find on his own home ranch. But Jesse tries to tell Lonnie the truth about rodeo cowboys:

> 'That's no life,' he said. 'You boys think stayin' in one place is tiresome, just wait till you see that goddamn road comin' at you ever monin'. And still comin' late that evenin' and sometimes way into the night. I run that road for ten years and never caught up with nothin' (p. 94).

And so Lonnie finds at the rodeo only the pathetic spectacle of those who share his elusive pursuit of a myth, and their recourse to alcohol, casual sex and violence to disguise their deep disappointment. On the last night of the rodeo Lonnie recognises the real condition of his life and those around him:

'All of them wanted more and seemed to end up with less; they wanted excitement and ended up stomped by a bull or smashed against a highway; ... and anyway, whatever it was they wanted, that was what they ended up doing without' (p. 145).

McMurtry's treatment of the wasted lives and disappointed hopes sacrificed to the mythology of America's exceptional national destiny is characterised by an elegiac tone, a wistfulness that mourns the loss of a vision that was heroic despite its lack of reality. But in Toni Morrison's revision of American history, her project to reinscribe race as a fundamental element determining the shape of the national destiny, she offers a damning indictment of the destructive capability of this very vision. Morrison emphasises the racial aspect of American exceptionalism: the visible saints, God's chosen people, are invariably white, untouched by the curse of Ham or any other sign of imperfection. To be perfected, in exceptionalist terms, is to be Europeanised; to be European is to be Caucasian and it is certainly not to be black. The racial aspect of exceptionalism became problematic only after the original ecclesiastical and spiritual mission of American exceptionalism was replaced with a political mission to promote and protect the institution of democracy as a model for all national governments. Even then, it was the abolitionist focus upon America's actual departure from the idealism of the national mythology that introduced race as a troubling element. In slave narratives and other abolitionist forms, slavery and racism were identified as corrupting America's approach to the condition of national perfection; slavery proved how far fallen were God's chosen people. Toni Morrison does not rehearse these ideas over in her writing; rather, she goes beyond to expose the history that is obscured by an exclusive focus on a narrative of American history that is motivated solely by the mythology of exceptionalism. In *Playing in the Dark: Whiteness and the Literary Imagination* (1992) she is concerned to explore the importance of the theme of race, twinned with that of colour, in the canonical texts of the American literary tradition.[4] She recontextualises American literature so that classic 'white' works are seen afresh within the historical moment of their production and reception, uncensored by exceptionalist expectations. She explains, 'Living in a racially articulated and predicated world, I could not be alone in reacting to this aspect of the American cultural and historical condition. I began to see how the literature I revered, the literature I loathed, behaved in its encounter with racial ideology. American literature could not help being shaped by that encounter.'[5] Not only American literature but American history also is shaped by the racial encounter. As Morrison subsequently re-marked about the Clarence Thomas–Anita Hill hearing: 'as is almost always the case, the site of the exorcism of critical national issues was situated in the miasma of black life and inscribed on the bodies of black people'.[6] The relationship between racism and exceptionalism is one of these 'critical national issues'.

Beloved (1987) and Jazz (1992) belong to a grand historical narrative Morrison intended to publish as a single book. Her publishers insisted that the first part should appear on its own; the final novel of what became a trilogy has yet to appear. In these novels Morrison records American history as African–American history, using three key events each separated from one another by some half-century as the structural framework. Beloved is set during the final years of slavery, seen in retrospect from the post-Civil War period; Jazz, as the title indicates is set in the 1920s, a time of mass migration North from the Jim Crow laws and post-Reconstruction South. These historical events determine the characters' pasts and the novel traces their journeys in reverse, to explore the various strategies by which they have tried to come to terms with freedom, with personal responsibility, with the need to find a place for themselves and a home in America.

These individuals, Joe Trace and his wife Violet, live in the immediate aftermath of slavery, when the emancipation of black bodies demanded a corresponding emancipation of black minds: to accept and take owner-ship of one's own self by becoming the agent of your own destiny, responsible for the choices and actions that make that destiny – this is the immensely difficult historical burden of Morrison's characters. 'People think the past is something you can romanticise and which threatens you. I think of it as something that walks along with you. I know I can't change the future but I can change the past. Insight and knowledge change the past. It is the past, not the future, which is infinite. Our past was appropriated. I am one of the people who has had to re-appropriate it.'[7] What this re-appropriation means for individuals acting in history is the subject of Morrison's fiction. Sethe, in Beloved, like Morrison's other characters, faces the difficult transition from slave to individual human being. Rather than see her children returned to slavery she tries to kill them; she is then left to struggle with the moral implications of her action. She struggles alone. There is no successful model of black family life for Sethe to follow: her own mother is a shadowy figure whose offspring were almost exclusively the result of rape; her mother-in-law Baby Suggs had all her children but one taken from her. All the people around her are destroyed by their encounter with white supremacy and the fact of white power over black lives, what Baby Suggs comes to call 'the Misery'. So when Paul D. accuses her for what she has done, she cannot understand: ' "You got two feet, Sethe, not four", he said'.[8] But seeing herself from the racist perspective of the slave system, in which she has been educated to think of herself as more closely related to beasts than to humans, Sethe cannot see that she must take responsibility for what she has chosen to do. She has no sense of personal sovereignty. What she learns in the course of the narrative is that she is her own 'best thing', she takes possession of herself. And by telling her story, Morrison takes possession of the history Sethe represents. The novel ends with a series of paragraphs, each describing how Beloved and her story were forgotten, punctuated by the phrase, 'It was not a story to pass on.' But Morrison has passed on this story, for it and the history it represents must be remembered as part of the American historical experience. To forget is to censor, to fashion a partial narrative that leads inevitably to the destiny inscribed by exceptionalism and which excludes from its remit African Americans, poor whites, and all those who do not fall within the category of God's elect. Morrison's work challenges the assumptions and exclusions of American exceptionalism by reinstating the history that exceptionalism would forget.

Thomas Pynchon also uses the mythology of exceptionalism to offer a critique of American culture. Pynchon focuses upon the exploitation of cultural mythology to perpetuate internal class divisions and to further America's imperialistic ambitions. The primary discovery made by the protagonist of *The Crying of Lot 49* (1966) is that the Republic she has known, that she has been taught to know, does not begin to encompass all that is the United States. Oedipa Maas is named executrix of the will of a property mogul, Pierce Inverarity, and so this ordinary Californian housewife must inventory his estate and then dispose of it in accordance with his will. What she uncovers are the signs of a secret organisation, the Tristero, dedicated to the dispossessed and disinherited. Tristero appears to communicate via an organisation called W.A.S.T.E.: 'We Await Silent Tristero's Empire', whose symbol is a muted posthorn, indicative of their ambition to disrupt orthodox channels of communication. In the course of Oedipa's quest to bring Inverarity's estate into a condition of meaning, she encounters proliferating signs, everywhere she turns. Out of this proliferation emerges a history of the Tristero, reaching back to the European Middle Ages, a history of violent disruption and internecine conflict. More disturbing for Oedipa than this is the growing awareness that an underclass of the dispossessed exists in her own society, hidden from her complacent middle-class view by the official rhetoric of the Republic. During an all-night descent into the twilight world of San Francisco, 'the infected city',[9] she uncovers some of the fugitives that cluster beneath Tristero's banner: a society of failed suicides; the Inamorati Anonymous, dedicated to overcoming love; street children and street gangs; Jesús Arrabal, a Mexican anarchist; blacks working graveyard shifts; AC–DC, the Alameda County Death Cult:

> Oedipa played the voyeur and listener. Among her other encounters were a facially-deformed welder, who cherished his ugliness; a child roaming the night who missed the death before birth as certain outcasts do the deal lulling blankness of the community; a Negro woman with an intricately-marbled scar along the baby-fat of one cheek who kept going through rituals of miscarriage each for a different reason, deliberately as others might the ritual of birth ...; an aging nightwatchman, nibbling at a bar of Ivory Soap, who had trained his virtuoso stomach to accept lotions, air-fresheners, fabrics, tobaccoes and waxes in a hopeless attempt to assimilate it all, all the promise, productivity, betrayal, ulcers, before it was too late (p. 91).

Each alienation is 'decorated' with the sign of the posthorn. And out of this experience, Oedipa begins to realise the extent to which her own life has been circumscribed by the formless 'magic' represented in Remedios Varo's painting of the girls trapped in a tower who embroider a tapestry that is the world. Oedipa sees herself reflected in those figures and she realises 'that what keeps her where she is is magic, anonymous and malignant, visited on her from outside and for no reason at all' (p. 11). By the end of her quest, Oedipa knows that it is not true that there is no reason; what keeps her trapped inside her self-made world is the same force that keeps the outcasts and derelicts of San Francisco out of the official life of the United States. She tells the anonymous inamorato, 'I use the US Mail because I was never taught any different.' ... 'But I'm not your enemy. I don't want to be' (p. 82). Inverarity's legacy to Oedipa is this new understanding of what America means; a nation that still adheres to a mythology of visible sainthood, which means that a class of the unredeemed must be defined in order to distinguish God's chosen few. A member of the redeemed, the elect herself, Oedipa has never known those who are sacrificed, dispossessed, disinherited, to make her privilege possible. But Inverarity has given her that knowledge. At the end of the novel, alone, desperate, Oedipa wanders down a railroad track and, in the dark, becomes disoriented: she cannot find the mountains, cannot find the sea. What she does find is a sense of the limitlessness of the land upon which she stands, in the absence of the divisions that are imposed by society. And she asks how it could have happened that in the New World, in a land of infinite possibility, all should be reduced to binary choices: elect or preterite, citizen or exile.

Pynchon takes up that same question in *Gravity's Rainbow* (1973), as he explores the mythology of American exceptionalism operating now in the European theatre, in the final days of World War Two. It is the threat of fascism from which American troops must save the Old World. That 'cittie upon a hill', the model society that is so central to American exceptionalism, is now represented by the Capitol, symbol of the democratic institutions perfected in America as a model for all the nations of the world. But in *Gravity's Rainbow* the manner in which the Old World is to be saved from itself is by a global extension of American power and influence. Very significant to the historical theme of the novel is the demise of European imperialist ambitions, the end of nineteenth-century colonial rule, and in its place the rise of global capitalism directed by American interests. Pynchon questions the origins of American cultural imperialism, and finds that imperialist assumptions are inscribed in the very ideology of mission that brought Puritan colonists to Massachusetts Bay.

The character of William Slothrop, first American ancestor of the hero Tyrone Slothrop, is a dissenter, heretic, fugitive from what Pynchon calls 'the Winthrop machine'. He is the spokesman for the preterite, the unredeemed who define by opposition the class of the elect; they are 'the "second Sheep" without whom there'd be no elect'.[10] William argues for the holiness of the pigs he escorts to slaughter, the preterite pigs that define by their mortality the election of those who may transcend death, the pigs who are 'possessed ... by trust for men, which the men kept betraying ... possessed by innocence they couldn't lose ... by faith in William as another variety of pig, at home with the Earth, sharing the same gift of life' (p. 647). This attitude of acceptance, of simply being at home in the world, represents in the narrative an alternative to the 'grim rationalization of the World' that is the means by which American imperialism spreads and perpetuates itself. Variously referred to as 'Them' or 'The Firm', these neo-colonial interests seek to replace natural diversity and disorder with stable, rational and controllable systems of meaning. But the more 'They' try to control, the more eludes Their grasp and so, ironically, the more They become caught up in the very category of the chaotic, the un-controllable, the worthless (the preterite) that They seek to destroy. Like the native peoples and landscape of the New World, who were faced with a grim choice between assimilation and destruction, the nations of the world are now subject to the choice inscribed in excep-tionalist ideology: submission to Their control or destruction. Exceptionalism allows no other possibility. William Slothrop suggests an alternative: 'the fork in the road America never took, the singular point she jumped the wrong way from' (p. 647). William manages to escape the control of the colonial authorities by settling in the wilderness, at a distance from Boston. There, he is free of the demands of colonial rhetoric, the mythology of the Great Migration as a divinely-appointed errand, the imperative to assert control over the New World. So the narrator asks, 'Suppose the Slothropite heresy had had the time to consolidate and prosper? Might there have been fewer crimes in the name of Jesus [representing the interests of the elect] and more mercy in the name of Judas Iscariot? It seems to Tyrone Slothrop that there might be a route back' (pp. 647–8). That quest for a way back, out of the complications of America's historical mission and exceptionalist rhetoric, engages all the characters of *Gravity's Rainbow*. The same issue occupies the thoughts of Charles Mason and Jeremiah Dixon, the eponymous heroes of Pynchon's latest novel, *Mason & Dixon* (1997).

Pynchon's narrative follows the efforts of Mason and Dixon to survey a line between Pennsylvania and Maryland. In accomplishing this, they are in effect mapping the identity of the new nation. Though they think of themselves as scientists (Mason is passed over for the position of Astronomer Royal by Nevil Maskelyne, Clive of India's brother-in-law, in rather suspicious circumstances), they come to recognise that their mission has served the interests of commerce, decadence, savagery and, ultimately, death. They have made the New World conform to the Old, with all its corruption. The surveying of the line, or Visto as they call it, imposes upon the American wilderness a European worldview, a European metaphysic, that is deadly. They encounter literal instances where the settlement they are helping to extend into the interior has resulted in the massacre of Indian women and children. Upon a visit to Baltimore Dixon becomes involved in a street fight with a brutal slave-trader and later remarks that if their commission serves the interests of trade, then they have also served the interests of the trade in human flesh. 'Having acknowledg'd at the Warpath the Justice of the Indians' Desires ... Mason and Dixon understand as well that the Line is exactly what Capt. Zhang and a number of others have been styling it all along – a conduit for Evil.' [11] Zhang describes the Visto as terrible *Feng-Shui*, a conduit of bad energy, less a boundary than an assault on nature that will be answered. He is eluding pursuit by a malevolent Jesuit, Father Zarpazo, 'the Wolf of Jesus', who is sworn to destroy all who deny Jesus's mediating function: 'If access to God need not be by way of Jesus, what is to become of Jesuits?' (p. 543), Zhang explains. Zarpazo is a villain in the mould of Captain Blicero (*Gravity's Rainbow*) and Brock Vond (*Vineland*), fanatics who relentlessly seek to destroy what they cannot control. They are the arch-colonists, though Blicero and Vond operate in a post-colonial world. Like Zarpazo, they are Lords of the Zero, 'sworn to Zero Degrees, Zero Minutes, Zero Seconds, or perfect North' (p. 544): the region of death. This commitment to the control of death is identified as characteristic of the colonial ideology that Mason and Dixon unwittingly serve. The narrator speculates:

Does Brittania, when she sleeps, dream? Is America her dream? – in which all that cannot pass in the metropolitan Wakefulness is allow'd Expression away in the restless Slumber of these Provinces, and on West-ward, wherever 'tis not yet mapp'd, nor written down, nor ever, by the majority of Mankind, seen, – serving as a very Rubbish-Tip for subjunctive Hopes, for all that *may yet be true*, – Earthly Paradise, Fountain of Youth, Realms of Prester John, Christ's Kingdom, ever behind the sunset, safe till the next Territory to the West be seen and recorded, measur'd and tied in, back into the Net-Work of Points already known, that slowly triangulates its Way into the Continent, changing all from subjunctive to declarative, reducing Possibilities to Simplicities that serve the ends of Governments, – winning away from the realm of the Sacred, its Borderlands one by one, and assuming them unto the bare mortal World that is our home, and our Despair (p. 345).

In this lengthy passage, Pynchon's narrator describes the wilderness as the ideological dumping-ground of Western colonialism, where all the corruption and decadence and savagery of the metropolis can be safely stowed, together with the hopes and dreams and aspirations of those who dare to speculate about the future. But the pathology of colonialism is such that the wilderness, the unknown, must always, inevitably, be brought into relation with metropolitan authority and control. And this is what is happening in the America described by *Mason & Dixon* (subjunctive is becoming declarative, possibilities are becoming simplicities) and it is what has happened in the America occupied by Tyrone Slothrop, Oedipa Maas, and the characters of *Vineland*. The unknown gives way to the political as the desired ends of government take control. This debasement of America's promise is represented as an inevitable consequence of the mythology of American exceptionalism, imported from Tudor narratives of cultural supremacy, and carrying with it the seed of corruption that the colonists sought so strenuously to escape.

Resurrecting the Myth: Representing the Vietnam Conflict

In an important essay, 'American Paramilitary Culture and the Reconstitution of the Vietnam War', James William Gibson questions the mythical place of war in American culture and extends the application of exceptionalist thinking from the Manifest Destiny that informed nineteenth-century expansionist conflicts to the Vietnam War. Citing Richard Slotkin's work on the ritual violence of representations of the frontier, Gibson argues:

> The Indian wars formed a fundamental American myth: to justify taking away Indian lands, first colonists and later 'American' explorers and settlers developed a national mythology in which 'American' technological and logistic superiority in warfare became culturally transmitted as signs of cultural-moral superiority. European and 'American' 'civilisation' morally deserved to defeat Indian 'savagery'. Might made right and each victory recharged the culture and justified expansion – what Slotkin calls 'regeneration through violence'.[12]

Gibson extends this analysis from nineteenth-century expansionist activities to the Vietnam conflict. He claims that the '[p]rimary American mythology survived the closing of the frontier and the final subordination of the Indians by changing to incorporate new enemies at the very same time US economic and political interests wanted an overseas empire'. Here he cites the conflict with Cuba, the battle of San Juan Hill, Theodore Roosevelt and the 'Rough Riders', who were named for the cowboys and Indians of Buffalo Bill Cody's Wild West Show, some of whom enlisted in the First Cavalry under a special deal with Cody.[13] Hollywood was 'purged' of communism in 1947 and through the 1950s produced the Westerns and war movies that were perceived to be safe and to promote a coherent view of American warfare: Americans fight on the morally correct side; Americans are more skilled than their opponents (so might meets right); no–one is innocent and any civilian casualties are caused by the bad guys; war does not appear dangerous and the principal heroes usually do not die; war is portrayed as a process of male bonding and a necessary rite of passage to manhood.[14] The connection between Vietnam movies, Westerns and the enduring legacy of American exceptionalism is underlined by Alf Louvre and Jeffrey Walsh in their introduction to a collection of essays about the cultural rhetoric employed by film representations of the Vietnam War: *Tell Me Lies About Vietnam: Cultural Battles for the Meaning of the War*. They describe films like *Little Big Man*, *The Wild Bunch*, *Chato's Land*, *Ulzana's Raid* and *Soldier Blue* as exemplifying 'the tortured accommodations the western was ... forced to make' after Vietnam. They go on, 'Such movies reverse previous generic formulations and expectations by including scenes of massacres, rapes, mutilations and pillage carried out by white frontiersmen: hence the Indian population substitutes mythically for the Vietnamese devastated by Rolling Thunder. America is forced to confront its own genocidal past.'[15] Beyond the horror of genocide, America confronts the controlling ideology of exceptionalism which has justified these acts of violence. The conception of an exceptional historical mission is extended, in representations of Vietnam, beyond the continental United States and beyond the nationalistic grasp of Manifest Destiny to encompass foreign policy and a role in global politics as well. Once again, America is required to save the world from itself. Not, as in the seventeenth century, from misguided religious institutions, but now from corrupt political institutions that are inconsistent with the

democratic capitalism that America is destined to exemplify and disseminate.

Westerns and Vietnam do share in common the mythology of American exceptionalism; that is why Westerns made such powerful vehicles
for the exploration of issues that Hollywood could not confront directly.
David E. James observes that '[w]ith the singular exception of *The Green
Berets* (John Wayne, 1968), Hollywood was able to approach Vietnam
only in more or less vague allegorical displacements that often took the
form of conspicuous aberrations of other genres: *The Dirty Do*ʒ*en*
(Robert Aldrich, 1967), *The Wild Bunch* (Sam Peckinpah, 1969), and
M*A*S*H (Robert Altman, 1969)'.[16] James identifies four phases in the
production of Hollywood movies about Vietnam:

1. From the beginning of the American presence until the late seventies, when there were no significant films except *The Green Berets*.

2. The late seventies, through the inauguration of the revisionist history announced by President Reagan's designation of the invasion
   as 'a noble cause' ...

3. The early to mid eighties, when the ascendancy of the revisionist
   reading was reinforced by the MIA issue. In this period, the tradition
   of films about more or less deranged veterans ... gave way to films
   in which the veteran became a vengeful superhero victoriously
   refighting the war, often to rescue the MIAs ...

4. The late eighties when, partially as a reaction against the Stallone
   films' meretricious absurdities, more complex representations established what was taken as a new standard of realism – *Platoon* and
   the films that followed it.[17]

It is with this concept of revisionist history, and the movie representations of it, that I am concerned because the revision of America's
involvement in the south-east Asian conflict draws directly upon exceptionalist rhetoric as a powerful source of authority and justification. In
the revised version of the Vietnamese conflict, American democracy
was under an imperative to rescue the nations of the Indo-Chinese
Peninsula from the threat of communism, in keeping with America's
historical mission. Defeat in south-east Asia, within the context of exceptionalism and the assumptions that control the representation of the
American military, could only be explained in terms like 'self-imposed
restraint', which is used to great effect in the Rambo movies. In *First*

Blood, Rambo represents the veteran as victim – of public indifference, government incompetence, military mediocrity, the violence of Vietnam; he confesses to Colonel Trautman that he thought they had fought well enough to win but 'Somebody wouldn't let us win.' In *Rambo: First Blood, Part II*, he represents the veteran as avenging warrior. What this means is that the cultural narrative of the lone gunfighter or superhero, who acts outside the law to eliminate a threat that cannot be defeated from within the constraints of society, allows for an explanation of military defeat as the consequence of a corrupt or cowardly political structure that will not allow the military to take the action necessary to win. In *Rambo: First Blood, Part II*, Rambo tells the representative of this cowardly government, his mentor Colonel Trautman, 'I did as you asked. I did what I had to but you wouldn't let me win.' In Hollywood Vietnam films, then, there appears a new kind of paramilitary hero, described by Gibson, who is empowered to act autonomously, who wins back for America an American victory. Robert McKeever calls the Rambo movies the '[q]uintessential reflection of this reactionary current', especially *Rambo: First Blood, Part II* where the 'real' enemy is defined as international communism – the Russians who are controlling the Vietnamese – and the real source of blame for military defeat is the political bureaucracy back home.[18] Rambo asks Colonel Trautman 'Do we get to win this time?' and he is answered 'This time it's up to you.' The actions Rambo needs to take in order to win are extreme, as he says, 'to win a war, you gotta become war'. Adi Wimmer has recognised that in the Rambo movies war is everywhere: Rambo describes returning to the States only to find another war going on, 'a quiet war. A war against the soldiers returning. That's the kind of war you can't win. That's my problem.' In Vietnam the guards are dressed in a fashion reminiscent of Japanese soldiers and their Russian commanders echo images of German soldiers; this characterisation is replaying World War Two and the John Wayne movie iconography of that war.[19]

Wimmer goes on to give a perceptive account of the messianism implicit in the film's imagery. Rambo functions as a redemptive figure: 'He takes the sins of the fatherland upon him (like Jesus, through suffering on the cross), and then redeems America by searching out and destroying even greater sins and sinners.'[20] In this way, he is able to erase and then rewrite the history of American involvement in the conflict in south-east Asia. Rambo derives his power to achieve this rhetorical transformation by virtue of his inheritance, which is the pioneer spirit of such cultural ancestors as Cooper's Leatherstocking. Rambo represents the noble savage in contrast to the decadent, technocrat Murdock; he cuts himself free from the complications of American technological excess and uses tactics to escape Vietnam that are reminiscent of Indian strategy: he comes to possess the new frontier of the Asian wilderness apart from American decadence. Just as Leatherstocking must move ever westward, away from the corruptions of the civilisation he serves, to find purification in the untouched wilderness, so Rambo renews the myth of America by conquering a new frontier. Redemption, national and personal, through war is what is portrayed so powerfully in these Rambo movies. Rambo is promised no restraints that might prevent his military success, though he is betrayed by the commanding CIA officer, and forced to become the unrestrained warrior hero of myth. His Vietnamese opponents are portrayed as criminals, as sexually perverted, and as operating outside the boundaries of civilised moral conduct; the warrior is a pure fighting machine, what James William Gibson calls 'a unified biological and mechanical weapons system'; the warrior operates alone or in small groups of brother warriors; the warrior's sexuality is fatal to his women lovers, who are less important than fellow warriors (especially the enemy counterpart he pursues).[21] Rambo the hero figure draws on traditional frontier iconography: long hair, headband, naked torso, preference for knife and bow-and-arrow over sophisticated weaponry, but Rambo differs from the traditional Western hero in that he sets out to win at all costs and abandons any code of honour that might disbar the use of some extreme forms of violence.[22]

The question then must be asked, why is it the mythology of exceptionalism that is invoked to revise and redeem the history of American involvement in Vietnam? Why not a new mythology? Robert McKeever argues that what has occurred in the 1980s is a 'retreat into pre-Vietnam ideologies', because the power of the cultural myths challenged by defeat in Vietnam was such that to change the myths would be to destroy them and the interpretations of the past and the vision of the future that are embodied by those myths and which unite the entire American people. McKeever expands: 'to change national myths is not simply a question of reinterpreting history but rather amounts to a demand that the nation do no less than reinvent itself, in terms of values, culture and behaviour as well as in terms of history .. [S]ince the tension between the

Vietnam experience and controlling national myths could not be borne indefinitely, entailing as it is a paralysis of will and action, the time soon came when Vietnam, rather than the national myths, had to be reinvented.'[23] McKeever quotes Henry Steele Commager's view that American foreign policy has historically been determined by, first, the myth of American uniqueness and, second, by the myth of American political, social and moral (and, after World War Two, military) superiority. These myths encompassed American isolationism and also Manifest Destiny or American imperialism. 'Crucial here was the well-established theme of Old World corruption and New World innocence, and this, combined with America's pre-Columbian historical and geographical isolation, created the myth that the United States was destined to be a new, different and superior society that would act as a model for the future social development of all nations.'[24] McKeever sees American foreign policy of this period as deeply affected by the ideology of exceptionalism; he argues that it precipitated the Manichean vision of American versus Soviet morality and the bi-polar view of international relations that became known as the Cold War. Vietnam, then, was a test of the authenticity of American cultural mythology. The hero, the fictional carrier of the myth, is placed in a crisis in Vietnam films, where the context no longer provides the structure of values that support and justify his actions. Therefore he either cannot act or else acts outside a justifying moral and social context. Michael Cimino's *The Deer Hunter* and Karel Reisz's *Dog Soldiers* (*Who'll Stop the Rain* in the US) illustrate heroic individualism defeated by uncontrollable forces.[25]

The attitude expressed by the Reagan administration demonstrates the 'self-imposed restraint' interpretation of the defeat in Vietnam: 'Reagan's foreign policy is underpinned not merely by the belief that the Vietnam War was both honourable and winnable but, more importantly, by the conviction that the setback in Vietnam was caused not by flaws in traditional American ideology and mythically based foreign policies but rather by the partial abandonment of that ideology by influential sectors of the American public.'[26] What remain unthreatened in the revised version of America's involvement in the conflict are the cultural myths of innocence and moral superiority; America may no longer be invincible but Americans are still God's chosen people. And what threatens American invincibility is lack of faith; lack of patriotic faith in the American mission defeats American purpose. After successfully liberating five POWs from a Vietnamese prison camp, he is asked what he wants: Rambo says, 'I want what they want, and what every other guy who came over here and spilt his guts and gave everything he has wants – for our country to love us as much as we love it.' The MIAs he has rescued have been denied by their government, by their country and yet they still display courage, heroism and patriotism. In the figure of Marshall Murdock, Washington bureaucrat and CIA plant, Rambo confronts the personification of governmental betrayal. Murdock ostensibly uses his technical skill to supervise Rambo's mission but once it becomes obvious that the MIAs his government has denied for so long are alive and are imprisoned by the Vietnamese, then Murdock attempts to sabotage the mission so that his government's lies will not be challenged. Murdock operates with a corrupt sense of patriotism, much like those Eastern 'greenhorns' who lack a genuine Western commitment to the values of home and country. Like Colonel Owen Thursday in John Ford's *Fort Apache*, who gives his own authority priority over that of George Washington, and who lacks the simple patriotism of the frontiersfolk, Murdock fails to understand true patriotism and so becomes one of the enemy.

The parallel between the conflict in Vietnam and John Ford's movie is picked up in Michael Herr's *Dispatches* (1978), where Colonel Thursday is described as 'obsessed, brave like a maniac, not very bright, a West Point aristo wounded in his career and his pride, posted out to some Arizona shithole with only marginal consolation: he's a professional and this is a war, the only war we've got.' [27] But when he ignores John Wayne's advice, he and half his command get wiped out; Herr concludes, 'More a war movie than a Western, Nam paradigm, Vietnam, not a movie' (p. 44). Much of the rhetoric of Michael Herr's narrative *Dispatches* divides the ordinary combat soldiers (the grunts) from the military bureaucracy, which is shown to be, in important respects, more dangerous than the Vietcong. This opposition between the country's guilt (represented by American brutality) versus the innocence of the grunts (who represent American suffering) dramatises a critical loss of innocence: 'the first casualty of war is innocence', Olive Stone's movie *Platoon* claimed. And in *Dispatches* Herr describes the face of one of the Marines, 'all the youth sucked out of the eyes ... [l]ife had made him old, he'd live it out old' (p. 21). Herr himself, the reporter-narrator-voyeur, undergoes a shift of perspective from the naiveté of his first impressions, when he realises that the grunts will not tell their stories to anyone as ignorant as he (p. 14), to a growing identification with the grunts as he is just as terrorised by Vietnam as they are.

Vietnam exposed the limits of American power and the moral ambivalence of advanced technology and so does not fit the style of earlier stories of successful wars: '*The Green Berets* doesn't count', says Herr in an aside, 'That wasn't really about Vietnam, it was about Santa Monica' (p. 153). John Wayne's movie offers an easy understanding of the war, representative of the attitude that 'the United States got involved in the Vietnam War, commitments and interests aside, simply because we thought it would be easy' (p. 81). But the Vietcong expose the limits of American military power and put into question the values, 'commitments and interests', that support the attitude of military invincibility. The voice that speaks to these values is that of the military command and Herr offers a sustained satire of the 'command psyche' and its jargon:

> The spokesmen spoke in words that had no currency left as words, sentences with no hope of meaning in the sane world, and if much of it was sharply queried by the press, all of it got quoted ... The most repulsive, transparent gropes for sanctity in the midst of the killing received serious treatment in the papers and on the air ... that Pacification, for example, was hardly anything more than a swollen, computerized tit being forced upon an already violated population, a costly, valueless programme that worked only in press conferences (p. 173).

He condemns conventional styles of reporting that work in complicity with military command to evade the reality of the moral outrage that is the war. Herr's style fuses this jargon with grunt talk, black slang, pop lyrics, the vocabulary of the youth and drug cultures. This language is rich in images that oppose the official image of the war, and demonstrates Herr's allegiance to a sixties revolutionary or counter-cultural consciousness. And it is this allegiance that relates to his sympathy for the resistance culture of the combat troops, represented by Mayhew and Day Tripper at Khe San, and the charismatic figures, Tim Page and Sean Flynn. What these individuals have in common is a sceptical attitude towards easy distinctions between sanity and madness. Combat troops live 'too close to their bones' and, in any case, in a war zone the unpredictable is the norm. Gradually, through the narrative, the distinction between sanity and insanity is broken down: 'going crazy was part of the tour'. But the most dangerous form of insanity is the insanity of military command, which is taken to be sane, normal, rational. The officers Herr encounters are all mad on the glamour of destruction and the imminence of death on an unprecedented scale. One example out of a myriad: Herr tells, 'Once I met a colonel who had a plan to shorten the war by dropping piranha into the paddies of the North. He was talking fish but his dreamy eyes were full of mega-death' (p. 55).

Ultimately, however, the opposition between troops and command that Herr describes collapses as the American experience of Vietnam comes to represent a paradigm of American culture and its competing value systems. This is represented graphically by the collage created by the gunner, Davies, in his unofficial Vietnamese home:

> It included glimpses of burning monks, stacked Viet Cong dead, wounded Marines screaming and weeping, Cardinal Spellman waving from a chopper, Ronald Reagan, his face halved and separated by a stalk of cannabis; pictures of John Lennon peering through wire-rimmed glasses, Mick Jagger, Jimi Hendrix, Dylan, Eldridge Cleaver, Rap Brown; coffins draped with American flags whose stars were replaced by swastikas and dollar signs; odd parts clipped from *Playboy* pictures, newspaper headlines (FARMERS BUTCHER HOGS TO PROTEST PORK PRICE DIP), photo captions (*President Jokes with Newsmen*), beautiful girls holding flowers, showers of peace symbols; Ky standing at attention and saluting, a small mushroom cloud forming where his genitalia should have been; a map of the western United States with the shape of Vietnam reversed and fitted over California and one large, long figure that began at the bottom with shiny leather boots and rouged knees and ascended in a microskirt, bare breasts, graceful shoulders and a long neck, topped by the burned, blackened face of a dead Vietnamese woman (p. 144).

This striking collage, described to achieve maximum dramatic effect, summarises the military versus public conflict of values that informs the Rambo movies. The peace movement, the counter-culture, Flower Power, takes on a grotesque aspect in Vietnam, as icons of an alien culture. The issue of patriotism emerges again here: underpinning the insanity of military command is an unquestioning belief in the doctrine of Manifest Destiny, a profound commitment to the inevitability of American expansion and an uncompromising vision of America as the redeemer nation committed to extending the domain of freedom and America's control over it. The theme of Manifest Destiny is underlined in *Dispatches* by a network of references to Indians; the Vietnamese conflict becomes a game of 'Cowboys and Indians', in one captain's words (p. 55) and, as I remarked above, the conflict between officers and grunts is made to echo the conflict between Owen Thursday (Henry Fonda) and Kirby York (John Wayne), models of the Easterner versus the Westerner. The imposition of exceptionalist mythology, rather than its discovery, is revealed by that image in Davies's collage of 'a map of the western United States with the shape of Vietnam reversed and fitted over California' (p. 144). Exceptionalism provides a cognitive map, a structure, by which to bring the chaos of Vietnam into some kind of pattern, order, logic. And Herr does this, using the terminology of seventeenth-century Puritan exceptionalism to describe his own confrontation with the howling wilderness. He writes of the Vietnamese jungle: 'The Puritan belief that Satan dwelt in Nature could have been born here' (p. 80); this observation formalises his earlier perception:

> Forget the Cong, the *trees* would kill you, the elephant grass grew up homicidal, the ground you were walking over possessed malignant intelligence, your whole environment was a bath. Even so, ... it was a privilege just to be able to feel afraid (p. 59).

The environment that is Vietnam is, in this way, translated into the terms of American cultural mythology. The Vietnamese landscape becomes comprehensible if seen to require a kind of redemption that can only come from God's chosen people, those whose historical mission it is to save other nations from their own folly. Exceptionalism has always offered a mythological refuge from the chaos of history and the uncertainty of life. In the process, American history has been made a site of contention where the struggle to control and dominate the terms of national destiny, on the one hand, has involved, on the other hand, a struggle for cultural survival: by appropriation, annexation, conquest and invasion, the Anglo-Saxon United States has spun the thread of exceptionalism across a continent and through four centuries of cultural development. Exceptionalism *was* the legacy of the Old World for the New, but exceptionalism *is now* the legacy of the United States for us all.

Notes

1. Larry McMurtry, *Buffalo Girls* (1990, rpt New York: Simon & Schuster, 1991), p. 169.
2. Larry McMurtry, *Lonesome Dove* (1985, rpt London: Pan Books, 1990), pp. 83–4.

3. Larry McMurtry, *Horseman Pass By* (1961, rpt London: Pan Books, 1961), p. 35. Future page references are given in the text.

4. See Toni Morrison, *Playing in the Dark: Whiteness and the Literary Imagination* (Cambridge, MA and London: Harvard University Press, 1992), and 'Unspeakable Things Unspoken: The Afro-American Presence in American Literature', *Michigan Quarterly Review* 28 (Winter 1989), pp. 1–34.

5. Toni Morrison, 'The Mind of the Masters', *New Statesman and Society*, 24 April 1992, p. 34.

6. Toni Morrison, 'Introduction: Friday on the Potomac', *Race-ing Justice, En-Gendering Power: Essays on Anita Hill, Clarence Thomas and the Construction of Social Reality* (London: Chatto & Windus, 1993), p. x.

7. Toni Morrison quoted by Christopher Bigsby, 'Jazz Queen', *The Independent on Sunday*, 26 April 1992, p. 29.

8. Toni Morrison, *Beloved* (New York: Signet, 1987), p. 202. Future page references are given in the text.

9. Thomas Pynchon, *The Crying of Lot 49* (1966, rpt New York: Bantam, 1978), p. 86. Future page references are given in the text.

10. Thomas Pynchon, *Gravity's Rainbow* (1973, rpt New York: Bantam, 1984), p. 647. Future page references are given in the text.

11. Thomas Pynchon, *Mason & Dixon* (London: Jonathan Cape, 1997), p. 701. Future page references are given in the text.

12. James William Gibson, 'American Paramilitary Culture and the Reconstitution of the Vietnam War', Jeffrey Walsh and James Aulich (eds), *Vietnam Images: War and Representation* (Basingstoke: Macmillan, 1989), p. 14.

13. Ibid., p. 15.

14. Ibid., p. 18.

15. 'Introduction', Walsh and Aulich, op. cit., p. 5.

16. David E. James, 'Rock and Roll in Representations of the Invasion of Vietnam', *Representations* 29 (Winter 1990), p. 79.

17. Ibid., p. 87.

18. Robert McKeever, 'American Myths and the Impact of the Vietnam War: Revisionism in Foreign Policy and Popular Cinema of the 1980s', in Walsh and Aulich (eds), *Vietnam Images*, p. 52.

19. Adi Wimmer, 'Rambo: American Adam, Anarchist and Archetypal Frontier Hero', in Walsh and Aulich (eds), *Vietnam Images* pp. 187–8.

20. Ibid., p. 189.

21. Gibson, 'American Paramilitary Culture and the Reconstitution of the Vietnam War', in Walsh and Aulich (eds), *Vietnam Images*, pp. 24–25.

22. Ibid., see the discussion, pp. 53–54.

23. McKeever, 'American Myths and the Impact of the Vietnam War', Walsh and Aulich (eds), *Vietnam Images*, p. 44.

24. Ibid., pp. 44–5.

25. Ibid., pp. 47–8.

26. Ibid., p. 51.

27. Michael Herr, *Dispatches* (1968, rpt London: Picador, 1979), p. 44. Future page references are given in the text.

El Plan Espiritual de Aztlán

In the spirit of a new people that is conscious not only of its proud historical heritage but also of the brutal 'gringo' invasion of our territories, *we*, the Chicano inhabitants and civilisers of the northern land of Aztlán from whence came our forefathers, reclaiming the land of their birth and consecrating the determination of our people of the sun, *declare* that the call of our blood is our power, our responsibility, and our inevitable destiny.

We are free and sovereign to determine those tasks which are justly called for by our house, our land, the sweat of our brows, and by our hearts. Aztlán belongs to those who plant the seeds, water the fields, and gather the crops and not to the foreign Europeans. We do not recognise capricious frontiers on the bronze continents.

Brotherhood unites us, and love for our brothers makes us a people whose time has come and who struggles against the foreigner 'gabacho' who exploits our riches and destroys our culture. With our heart in our hands and our hands in the soil, we declare the independence of our mestizo nation. We are a bronze people with a bronze culture. Before the world, before all of North America, before all our brothers in the bronze continent, we are a nation, we are a union of free pueblos, we are *Aztlán*.

Programme

El Plan Espiritual de Aztlán sets the theme that the Chicanos (La Raza de Bronze) must use their nationalism as the key or common denominator for mass mobilisation and organisation. Once we are committed to the idea and philosophy of El Plan de Aztlán, we can only conclude that social, economic, cultural and political independence is the only road to total liberation from oppression, exploitation, and racism. Our struggle then must be for the control of our barrios, campos, pueblos, lands, our economy, our culture, and our political life. El Plan commits all levels of Chicano society – the barrio, the campo, the ranchero, the writer, the teacher, the worker, the professional – to La Causa.

Nationalism

Nationalism as the key to organisation transcends all religious, political, class, and economic factions or boundaries. Nationalism is the common denominator that all members of La Raza can agree upon.

Organisational Goals

1. UNITY in the thinking of our people concerning the barrios, the pueblo, the campo, the land, the poor, the middle class, the professional – all committed to the liberation of La Raza.

2. ECONOMY: economic control of our lives and our communities can only come about by driving the exploiter out of our communities, our pueblos, and our lands and by controlling and developing our own talents, sweat, and resources. Cultural background and values which ignore materialism and embrace humanism will contribute to the act of co-operative buying and the distribution of resources and production to sustain an economic base for healthy growth and development. Lands rightfully ours will be fought for and defended. Land and realty ownership will be acquired by the community for the people's welfare. Economic ties of responsibility must be secured by nationalism and the Chicano defence units.

3. EDUCATION must be relative to our people, i.e., history, culture, bilingual education, contributions, etc. Community control of our schools, our teachers, our administrators, our counsellors, and our programmes.

4. INSTITUTIONS shall serve our people by providing the service necessary for a full life and their welfare on the basis of restitution, not handouts or beggars' crumbs. Restitution for past economic slavery, political exploitation, ethnic and cultural psychological destruction and denial of civil and human rights. Institutions in our community which do not serve the people have no place in the community. The institutions belong to the people.

5. SELF-DEFENCE of the community must rely on the combined strength of the people. The front–line defence will come from the barrios, the campos, the pueblos, and the ranchitos. Their involvement as protectors of their people will be given respect and dignity. They in turn offer their responsibility and their lives for their people. Those who place themselves in the front ranks for their people do so out of love and carnalismo. Those institutions which are fattened by our brothers to provide employment and political pork barrels for the gringo do so only as acts of liberation and for La Causa. For the very young there will no longer be acts of juvenile delinquency, but revolutionary acts.

6. CULTURAL values of our people strengthen our identity and the moral backbone of the movement. Our culture unites and educates the family of La Raza towards liberation with one heart and one mind. We must insure that our writers, poets, musicians and artists produce literature and art that is appealing to our people and relates to our revolutionary culture. Our cultural values of life, family and home will serve as a powerful weapon to defeat the gringo dollar value system and encourage the process of love and brotherhood.

7. POLITICAL LIBERATION can only come through independent action on our part, since the two-party system is the same animal with two heads that feed from the same trough. Where we are a majority, we will control; where we are a minority, we will represent a pressure group; nationally, we will represent one party: La Familia de la Raza!

Action

1. Awareness and distribution of El Plan Espiritual de Aztlán. Presented at every meeting, demonstration, confrontation, courthouse, institution, administration, church, school, tree, building, car, and every place of human existence.

2. September 16, on the birthdate of Mexican Independence, a national walk-out by all Chicanos of all colleges and schools to be sustained until the complete revision of the educational system: its policy makers, administration, its curriculum, and its personnel to meet the needs of our community.

3. Self-defence against the occupying forces of the oppressors at every school, every available man, woman, and child.

4. Community nationalisation and organisation of all Chicanos: El Plan Espiritual de Aztlán.

5. Economic programme to drive the exploiter out of our community and a welding together of our people's combined resources to control their own production through co–operative effort.

6. Creation of an independent local, regional, and national political party.

A nation autonomous and free – culturally, socially, economically, and politically – will make its own decisions on the usage of our lands, the taxation of our goods, the utilisation of our bodies for war, the determination of justice (reward and punishment), and the profit of our sweat.

El Plan de Aztlán is the plan of liberation!

Note: El Plan Espiritual de Aztlán was written at the First Chicano National Conference in Denver, Colorado, in 1969.

Source: *Documents of the Chicano Struggle* (1971).

Bibliography

Adair, Gilbert, *Hollywood's Vietnam* (London: Proteus, 1981).

Alter, Robert and Frank Kermode (eds), *The Literary Guide to the Bible* (Cambridge, MA: The Belknap Press of Harvard University Press, 1987).

Anaya, Rudolfo, *Bless Me, Ultima* (Berkeley: Tonatiuh-Quinto Sol Publications, 1972).

Anaya, Rudolfo and Francisco Lomelí (eds), *Aztlán: Essays on the Chicano Homeland* (Albuquerque: University of New Mexico Press, 1989).

Antelyes, Peter, *Tales of Adventurous Enterprise: Washington Irving and the Poetics of Westward Expansion* (New York: Columbia University Press, 1990).

Anzaldúa, Gloria, *Borderlands/La Frontera: The New Mestiza* (San Francisco: Aunt Lute, 1987).

Apess, William, *On Our Own Ground: The Complete Writings of William Apess*, ed. Barry O'Connell (Amherst, MA: University of Massachusetts Press, 1992).

Arvin, Newton, *Hawthorne* (1929, rpt New York: Russell & Russell, 1961).

Baym, Nina, Wayne Franklin, Ronald Gottesman, Laurence B. Holland, David Kalstoe, Arnold Krupat, Francis Murphy, Hershel Parker, William H. Pritchard and Patricia B. Wallace (eds), *The Norton Anthology of American Literature*, 4th edn, 2 vols (New York and London: W. W. Norton & Co., 1994).

Beidler, Philip D., *American Literature and the Experience of Vietnam* (Athens, GA: University of Georgia Press, 1982).

Beidler, Philip D., *Re-Writing America: Vietnam Authors in their Generation* (Athens, GA: University of Georgia Press, 1991).

Bell, Ian F. A., 'The Hard Currency of Words: Emerson's Fiscal Metaphor in *Nature*', *English Literary History* LII. 3 (Fall, 1985), pp. 733–53.

Bercovitch, Sacvan (ed.), *Typology and Early American Literature* (Amherst: University of Massachusetts Press, 1972).

Bercovitch, Sacvan (ed.), *The American Puritan Imagination: Essays in Revaluation* (Cambridge: Cambridge University Press, 1974).

Bercovitch Sacvan, *The Puritan Origins of the American Self* (New Haven and London: Yale University Press, 1975).

Bercovitch, Sacvan, *The American Jeremiad* (Madison and London: University of Wisconsin Press, 1978).

Bercovitch, Sacvan (ed.), *Reconstructing American Literary History*, Harvard English Studies 13 (Cambridge, MA and London: Harvard University Press, 1986).

Bercovitch, Sacvan and Myra Jehlen (eds), *Ideology and Classic American Literature* (Cambridge: Cambridge University Press, 1986).

Berg, Rick and John Carlos Rowe (eds), *Cultural Critique* 3 (Spring 1985), special issue, 'American Representations of Vietnam'.

Bigsby, Christopher, 'Jazz Queen', *The Independent on Sunday*, 26 April 1992, p. 29.

Blacker, Irwin, *The Old West in Fiction* (New York: Ivan Obolensky, 1961).

Boorstin, Daniel J., *The Americans: The Colonial Experience* (1958, rpt New York: Random House, 1968).

Brumm, Ursula, *American Thought and Religious Typology*, trans. John Hoalglund (New Brunswick: Rutgers University Press, 1970).

Buell, Lawrence, *Literary Transcendentalism: Style and Vision in the American Renaissance* (Ithaca and London: Cornell University Press, 1973).

Buell, Lawrence, *New England Literary Culture: From Revolution Through Renaissance* (Cambridge: Cambridge University Press, 1986).

Burr, George Lincoln (ed.), *Narratives of the Witchcraft Cases, 1648–1706*, Original Narratives of Early American History (1914, rpt New York: Barnes & Noble, 1963).

Caldwell, Patricia, *The Puritan Conversion Narrative: The Beginnings of American Expression* (Cambridge: Cambridge University Press, 1983).

Castillo, Ana, *My Father Was a Toltec and Selected Poems, 1973–1988* (New York and London: W. W. Norton, 1995).

Castillo, Ana, *Massacre of the Dreamers: Essays on Chicanisma* (New York: Plume, 1995).

Cawelti, John G., *The Six-Gun Mystique* (Bowling Green, OH: Bowling Green State University Popular Press, 1973).

Clark, Thomas D. and John D. W. Guice, *Frontiers in Conflict: The Old Southwest, 1795–1830* (Albuquerque: University of New Mexico Press, 1989).

Conner, Seymour V. and Odie B. Faulk, *North America Divided: The Mexican War, 1846–1848* (New York: Oxford University Press, 1971).

Cooper, James Fenimore, *The Pioneers* (1823, rpt New York: Signet, 1980).

Cooper, James Fenimore, *The Last of the Mohicans*, ed. John McWilliams (1826, rpt Oxford and New York: Oxford University Press, 1990).

Cotton, John, *Gods Mercie Mixed with His Justice or His Peoples Deliverance in Times of Danger*, ed. Everett Emerson (1958, rpt New York: Scholars' Facsimiles and Reprints, 1977).

Cotton, John, *The New England Way*. A Library of American Puritan Writings: The Seventeenth Century, vol. 12 (New York: AMS Press, n.d.).

Cotton, John, *The Way of Faith*. A Library of American Puritan Writings: The Seventeenth Century, vol. 13 (New York: AMS Press, n.d.).

Daly, Robert, *God's Altar: The World and the Flesh in Puritan Poetry* (Berkeley, Los Angeles and London: University of California Press, 1978).

Davis, Charles T. and Henry Louis Gates, Jr. (eds), *The Slave's Narrative* (Oxford and New York: Oxford University Press, 1985).

Davis, William T. (ed.), *Bradford's History of Plymouth Plantation, 1606–1646*. Original Narratives of Early American History (1908, rpt New York: Barnes & Noble, 1970).

Dekker, George, *The American Historical Romance* (Cambridge: Cambridge University Press, 1987).

Deloria, Vine, Jr, *Custer Died for Your Sins: An Indian Manifesto* (1969, rpt Norman, OK: University of Oklahoma Press, 1988).

Dittmar, Linda and Gene Michaud (eds), *From Hanoi to Hollywood: The Vietnam War in American Film* (New Brunswick, NJ: Rutgers University Press, 1990).

Douglass, Frederick, *Narrative of the Life of Frederick Douglass, An American Slave*, ed. Christopher Bigsby (1845, rpt London: J. M. Dent, 1992).

Eastman, Charles Alexander (Ohiyesa), *From the Deep Woods to Civilization*, introduction by Raymond Wilson (1916, rpt Lincoln and London: University of Nebraska Press, 1977).

Eastman, Charles Alexander (Ohiyesa), *The Soul of the Indian: An Interpretation* (1911, rpt Lincoln and London: University of Nebraska Press, 1980).

Emerson, Everett (ed.), *Letters from New England: The Massachusetts Bay Company, 1629–1638* (Amherst: University of Massachusetts Press, 1976).

Emerson, Ralph Waldo, *The Collected Works of Ralph Waldo Emerson*, vols 2 & 3, ed. Joseph Slater, Alfred R. Ferguson and Jean Ferguson Carr (Cambridge, MA and London: The Belknap Press of Harvard University Press, 1979, 1983).

Emerson, Ralph Waldo, *The Journals and Miscellaneous Notebooks of Ralph Waldo Emerson*, ed. Merton M. Sealts, Jr (Cambridge, MA: The Belknap Press of Harvard University Press).

Every, Dale Van, *Disinherited: The Lost Birthright of the American Indians* (New York: Morrow, 1966).

Fehrenbach, T. R., *Lone Star: A History of Texas and the Texans* (New York: Macmillan, 1968).

Feidelson, Charles, Jr, *Symbolism and American Literature* (Chicago: University of Chicago Press, 1953).

Fender, Stephen, *American Literature in Context, I: 1620–1830* (London: Methuen, 1983).

Fernández, Roberta (ed.), *In Other Words: Literature by Latinas of the United States* (Houston, TX: Arte Público, 1994).

Folsom, James, *The Western: A Collection of Critical Essays* (Englewood Cliffs, NJ: Prentice-Hall, 1979).

Foreman, Grant, *The Five Civilized Tribes* (Norman: University of Oklahoma Press, 1934).

Foster, Stephen, *Their Solitary Way: The Puritan Social Ethic in the First Century of Settlement in New England* (New Haven and London: Yale University Press, 1971).

Fritz, Henry E., *The Movement for Indian Assimilation, 1860–1890* (Philadelphia: University of Pennsylvania Press, 1963).

Gilmore, Michael T., *The Middle Way: Puritanism and Ideology in American Romantic Fiction* (New Brunswick: Rutgers University Press, 1977).

Grey, Zane, *Riders of the Purple Sage, The Last of the Plainsmen, and Lone Star Ranger* (London: Chancellor Press, 1992).

Grey, Zane, *Riders of the Purple Sage* (1912, rpt New York and London: Penguin Books, 1990).

Gura, Philip F., *The Wisdom of Words: Language, Theology, and Literature in the New England Renaissance* (Middletown, Conn.: Wesleyan University Press, 1981).

Gura, Philip F., *A Glimpse of Sion's Glory: Puritan Radicalism in New England, 1620–1660* (Middletown, CT: Wesleyan University Press, 1984).

Hagan, W. T., *American Indians* (Chicago: University of Chicago Press, 1961).

Hamilton, Holman, *Prologue to Conflict: The Crisis and Compromise of 1850* (Lexington: University of Kentucky Press, 1954).

Hawthorne, Nathaniel, *The Centenary Edition of the Works of Nathaniel Hawthorne*, ed. William Charvat, *et al.* (Columbus, Ohio: Ohio State University Press, 1962).

Hawthorne, Nathaniel, *The Scarlet Letter*, Sculley Bradley (eds) (New York: W. W. Norton, 1978).

Heimert, Alan and Andrew Delbanco (eds), *The Puritans in America: A Narrative Anthology* (Cambridge, MA and London: Harvard University Press, 1985).

Hellman, J., *American Myth and the Legacy of Vietnam* (New York: Columbia University Press, 1986).

Herr, Michael, *Dispatches* (1968, rpt London: Picador, 1979).

Herzog, T. C., '*Going After Cacciato*: The Soldier-Author-Character Seeking Control', *Critique*, 24.2 (Winter 1983), pp. 88–96.

Hietala, Thomas, *Manifest Design: Anxious Aggrandizement in Late Jacksonian America* (Ithaca, NY: Cornell University Press, 1985).

Hill, Christopher, *The World Turned Upside Down: Radical Ideas During the English Revolution* (London: Temple Smith, 1973).

Holsti, Ole R. and James N. Rosenau, *The American Leadership in World Affairs: Vietnam and the Breakdown of Consensus* (Boston, MA: Allen & Unwin, 1984).

Hosmer, James Kendall (ed.), *Winthrop's Journal, History of New England,' 1630–1649*. Original Narratives of Early American History, 2 vols (1908, rpt New York: Barnes & Noble, 1959).

Hoxie, Fred E., *A Final Promise: The Campaign to Assimilate the Indians, 1880–1920* (Lincoln: University of Nebraska Press, 1984).

Hughes, John T., *Doniphan's Expedition: An Account of the Conquest of New Mexico* (1914, rpt Chicago: Rio Grande, 1962).

Jacobs, Harriet, *Incidents in the Life of a Slave Girl, Written by Herself*, Jean Fagan Yellin (ed.) (Cambridge, MA and London: Harvard University Press, 1987).

James, David E., 'Rock and Roll in Representations of the Invasion of Vietnam', *Representations* 29 (Winter 1990), pp. 78–98.

Jeffords, Susan, *The Remasculinisation of America: Gender and the Vietnam War* (Bloomington and Indianapolis: Indiana University Press, 1989).

Jensen, Merrill, *The New Nation: A History of the United States during the Confederation* (New York: Knopf, 1950).

Jewett, Robert and John Lawrence, *The American Monomyth* (Garden City, NY: Anchor/Doubleday, 1977).

Jones, Richard F. (ed.), *The Seventeenth Century: Studies in the History of English Thought and Literature From Bacon to Pope* (Stanford, CA: Stanford University Press, 1951).

Kermode, Frank, *Shakespeare, Spenser, Donne: Renaissance Essays* (London: Routledge & Kegan Paul, 1971).

Kibbey, Ann, *The Interpretation of Material Shapes in Puritanism: A Study of Rhetoric, Prejudice, and Violence* (Cambridge: Cambridge University Press, 1986).

Kolodny, Annette, *The Land Before Her: Fantasy and Experience of the American Frontiers, 1630–1860* (Chapel Hill and London: University of North Carolina Press, 1984).

Lamar, Howard R. (ed.), *Reader's Encyclopaedia of the American West* (New York: Crowell, 1977).

Larsen, Laurence, *The Urban West at the End of the Frontier* (Lawrence: Regents Press of Kansas, 1978).

Lauter, Paul (eds), *The Heath Anthology of American Literature*, 2nd edn, 2 vols (Lexington, MA and Toronto: D. W. Heath & Co., 1994).

Lewis, L. B. *The Tainted War: Culture and Identity in Vietnam War Narratives* (Westport, CT: Greenwood Press, 1985).

Lincoln, Charles H. (ed.), *Narratives of the Indian Wars, 1675–1699*. Original Narratives of Early American History (1913, rpt New York: Barnes & Noble, 1941).

Louvre, Alf and Jeffrey Walsh (eds), *Tell Me Lies About Vietnam: Cultural Battles for the Meaning of the War* (Milton Keynes and Philadelphia: Open University Press, 1988).

Lowance, Mason I. Jr, *The Language of Canaan: Metaphor and Symbol in New England from the Puritans to the Transcendentalists* (Cambridge, MA and London: Harvard University Press, 1980).

McMurtry, Larry, *Buffalo Girls* (1990, rpt New York: Simon & Schuster, 1991).

McMurtry, Larry, *Horseman Pass By* (1961, rpt London: Pan Books, 1961).

McMurtry, Larry, *Lonesome Dove* (1985, rpt London: Pan Books, 1990).

McNickle, D'Arcy, *Native American Tribalism: Indian Survivals and Renewals* (New York, Oxford and London: Oxford University Press for the Institute for Race Relations, 1973).

McNickle, D'Arcy, *Wind from an Enemy Sky* (1978, rpt Albuquerque: University of New Mexico Press, 1995).

Madsen, Deborah L., *The Postmodernist Allegories of Thomas Pynchon* (Leicester and London: Leicester University Press, 1991).

Madsen, Deborah L., *Allegory in America*. Studies in Literature and Religion (Basingstoke: Macmillan, 1996).

Malone, Michael and Richard W. Etulain, *The American West: A Twentieth Century History* (Lincoln: University of Nebraska Press, 1989).

Martí, José, *Our America: Writings on Latin America and the Cuban Struggle for Independence*, trans. Elinor Randall with Juan de Onis and Roslyn Held Foner, ed. Philip S. Foner (New York and London: Monthly Review Press, 1977).

Mather, Cotton, *Days of Humiliation: Times of Affliction and Disaster, Nine Sermons For Restoring Favor With An Angry God (1696–1727)*, ed. George Harrison Orians (Gainsville, Florida: Scholars' Facsimiles and Reprints, 1970).

Mather, Cotton, *Magnalia Christi Americana*, 2 vols (New York: Russell & Russell, 1967).

Mather, Cotton, *The Wonders of the Invisible World* (London: John Russell, 1862).

Mather, Increase, *Doctrine*. A Library of American Puritan Writings: The Seventeenth Century, vol. 21 (New York: AMS Press, n.d.).

Mather, Increase, *Jeremiads*. A Library of American Puritan Writings: The Seventeenth Century, vol. 20 (New York: AMS Press, n.d.).

Matthiessen, F. O., *American Renaissance: Art and Expression in the Age of Emerson and Whitman* (1941, rpt London, Oxford and New York: Oxford University Press, 1968).

Melville, Herman, *The Letters of Herman Melville*, ed. Merrell R. Davis and William H. Gilman (eds) (1960, rpt New Haven and London: Yale University Press, 1965).

Melville, Herman, *Moby-Dick; or The Whale* ed. Harold Bearer (1851, rpt Harmondsworth: Penguin, 1982).

Michaels, Walter Benn and Donald E. Pease (eds), *The American Renaissance Reconsidered*. Selected Papers from the English Institute, 1982–3 (Baltimore and London: The Johns Hopkins University Press, 1985).

Middlekauff, Robert, *The Mathers: Three Generations of Puritan Intellectuals, 1592–1728* (New York: Oxford University Press, 1971).

Miller, Perry, *Errand into the Wilderness* (1956, rpt Cambridge, MA: The Belknap Press of Harvard University Press, 1964).

Miller, Perry, *Nature's Nation* (Cambridge, MA: The Belknap Press of Harvard University Press, 1967).

Miller, Perry, *The New England Mind: The Seventeenth Century* (New York: Macmillan, 1939).

Miller, Perry, *The New England Mind: From Colony to Province* (Cambridge: MA, Harvard University Press, 1953).

Miller, Perry and Thomas H. Johnson (eds), *The Puritans: A Sourcebook of Their Writings*, 2 vols (1938, rev. edn; New York, Evanston and London: Harper & Row, 1963).

Milner, Clyde A., II, Anne M. Butler and David Rich Lewis (eds), *Major Problems in the History of the American West*, 2nd edn (Boston and New York: Houghton Mifflin Co., 1997).

Miner, Earl (ed.), *Literary Uses of Typology from the Late Middle Ages to the Present* (Princeton: Princeton University Press, 1977).

Morgan, Dale L. *Jedediah Smith and the Opening of the West* (Indianapolis: Bobbs-Merrill, 1953).

Morgan, Edmund S., *Roger Williams: The Church and the State* (New York: Harcourt, Brace & World, Yale University Press, 1967).

Morrison, Toni, *Beloved* (New York: Signet, 1987).

Morrison, Toni, 'Unspeakable Things Unspoken: The Afro-American Presence in American Literature', *Michigan Quarterly Review* 28 (Winter 1989), pp. 1–34.

Morrison, Toni, *Playing in the Dark: Whiteness and the Literary Imagination* (Cambridge, MA and London: Harvard University Press, 1992).

Morrison, Toni, 'The Mind of the Masters', *New Statesman and Society*, 24 April 1992.

Morrison, Toni, *Race-ing Justice, En-Gendering Power: Essays on Anita Hill, Clarence Thomas and the Construction of Social Reality* (London: Chatto & Windus, 1993).

Murdock, Kenneth B., *Literature and Theology in Colonial New England* (1949, rpt New York and Evanston: Harper & Row, 1963).

Murdock, Kenneth B. (ed.), *Selections from Cotton Mather* (New York: Harcourt, Brace & Co., 1926).

Newman, Kim, *Wild West Movies: How the West was Found, Won, Lost, Lied About, Filmed and Forgotten* (London: Bloomsbury, 1990).

Niebuhr, Richard, *The Kingdom of God in America* (1937, rpt New York: Harper Torchbooks, 1959).

Olsen, V. Norskov, *John Foxe and the Elizabethan Church* (Berkeley, Los Angeles and London: University of California Press, 1973).

Payne, Darwin, *Owen Wister: Chronicles of the West, Gentleman of the East* (Dallas: Southern Methodist University Press, 1985).

Pearce, Roy Harvey, *Savagism and Civilization: A Study of the Indian and the American Mind* (1953, rev. edn Berkeley, Los Angeles and London: University of California Press, 1988).

Plumstead, A. W. (ed.), *The Wall and the Garden: Selected Massachusetts Election Sermons, 1670–1775* (Minneapolis: University of Minnesota Press, 1968).

Puccini, Giacomo, *La Fanciulla del West* (1910, London: Decca, 1989)

Pynchon, Thomas, *The Crying of Lot 49* (1966, rpt New York: Bantam, 1978).

Pynchon, Thomas, *Gravity's Rainbow* (1973, rpt New York: Bantam, 1984).

Pynchon, Thomas, *Mason & Dixon* (London: Jonathan Cape, 1997).

Raymond, M. W., 'Imagined Responses to Vietnam: Tim O'Brien's *Going After Cacciato*', *Critique*, 24.2 (Winter 1983), pp. 97–104.

Rebolledo, Tey Diana, *Women Singing in the Snow: A Cultural Analysis of Chicana Literature* (Tucson, AZ and London: University of Arizona Press, 1995).

Reinitz, Richard (ed.), *Tensions in American Puritanism* (New York: John Wiley & Sons, 1970).

Reynolds, David S., *Faith in Fiction: The Emergence of Religious Literature in America* (Cambridge, MA and London: Harvard University Press, 1981).

Richardson, Rupert N., *et al.*, *Texas: The Lone Star State* (New York: Prentice-Hall, 1943).

Rivera, Tomás, *… y no se lo tragó la tierra/… And the Earth Did Not Devour Him*, trans. Evangelina Vigil-Piñón (1987, rpt Houston: Arte Público, 1992).

Ruiz de Burton, María Amparo, *Who Would Have Thought It?*, eds. Rosaura Sánchez and Beatrice Pita, Recovering the US Hispanic Literary Heritage Project (1872, rpt Houston: Arte Público Press, 1995).

Sekora, John and Darwin T. Turner (eds), *The Art of Slave Narrative: Original Essays in Criticism and Theory* (Western Illinois University, 1982).

Silko, Leslie Marmon, *Almanac of the Dead* (New York: Viking Penguin, 1991).

Singletary, Otis A., *The Mexican War* (Chicago: University of Chicago Press, 1960).

Slotkin, Richard, *Regeneration Through Violence: The Mythology of the American Frontier, 1600–1860* (Middletown, CT: Wesleyan University Press, 1973).

Smith, Henry Nash, *Virgin Land: The American West as Symbol and Myth* (New York: Vintage, 1950).

Smith, Valerie, *Self-Discovery and Authority in Afro-American Narrative* (Cambridge, MA and London: Harvard University Press, 1987).

Standing Bear, Luther, *The Land of the Spotted Eagle*, foreword by Richard N. Ellis (1933, rpt Lincoln and London: University of Nebraska Press, 1978).

Standing Bear, Luther, *My People the Sioux*, ed. E. A. Brininstool, introduction by Richard N. Ellis (1928, rpt Lincoln and London: University of Nebraska Press, 1975).

Steckmesser, Kent Ladd, *Western Outlaws: The 'Good Badman' in Fact, Film and Folklore* (Claremont, CA: Regina Books, n.d.).

Stout, Harry S., *The New England Soul: Preaching and Religious Culture in Colonial New England* (New York: Oxford University Press, 1986).

Sweet, William Warren, *The Story of Religion in America* (New York: Harper & Brothers, 1950).

Taylor, Graham D., *The New Deal and American Indian Tribalism: The Administration of the Indian Reorganization Act, 1935–1945* (Lincoln: University of Nebraska Press, 1980).

Taylor, Joshua C. with a contribution by John G. Cawelti, *America as Art* (Washington, DC: Smithsonian Institution Press for the National Collection of Fine Arts, 1976).

Tillam, Thomas, 'Upon the First Sight of New England' (1638), ed. Harold Jantz. *Proceedings of the American Antiquarian Society*, vol. 53, p. 331.

Tompkins, Jane, *West of Everything: The Inner Life of Westerns* (New York and Oxford: Oxford University Press, 1992).

Toulouse, Teresa, *The Art of Prophesying: New England Sermons and the Shaping of Belief* (Athens and London: University of Georgia Press, 1987).

Truettner, William H. (ed.), *The West as America: Reinterpreting Images of the Frontier, 1820–1920* (Washington and London: Smithsonian Institution Press for the National Museum of American Art, 1991).

Utley, Robert M., *The Last Days of the Sioux Nation* (New Haven: Yale University Press, 1963).

Utley, Robert M., *Cavalier in Buckskin: George Armstrong Custer and the Western Military Frontier* (Norman: University of Oklahoma Press, 1988).

Vaughn, Alden T. and Edward W. Clark (eds), *Puritans Among the Indians: Accounts of Captivity and Redemption, 1676–1724* (Cambridge, MA and London: The Belknap Press of Harvard University Press, 1981).

Vizenor, Gerald, *Bearheart: The Heirship Chronicles* (1978, rpt Minneapolis: University of Minnesota Press, 1990).

Walsh, Jeffrey and James Aulich (eds), *Vietnam Images: War and Representation* (Basingstoke: Macmillan, 1989).

Washington, Mary Helen, *Invented Lives: Narratives of Black Women, 1860–1960* (1987, rpt London: Virago, 1989).

Watkins, Owen C., *The Puritan Experience* (London: Routledge & Kegan Paul, 1972).

Welch, James, *Fools Crow* (New York: Viking Penguin, 1986).

Whitman, Walt, *Leaves of Grass and Selected Prose*, ed. John A. Kouwenhoven (New York: Modern Library, 1950).

Williams, Roger, *The Complete Writings of Roger Williams*, ed. Perry Miller (New York: Russell & Russell, 1963).

Winthrop, John, 'Reasons to Be Considered for … the Intended Plantation in New

England' (1629), *Proceedings of the Massachusetts Historical Society* vol. 8 (1864–65), pp. 420–5.

Winthrop, John, *Winthrop's Journal: History of New England, 1630–1649*, ed. James Kendall Hosmer. Original Narratives of Early American History (1908, rpt New York: Barnes & Noble, 1959).

Winthrop, John, *The Winthrop Papers* (Boston: Massachusetts Historical Society, 1931).

Wister, Owen, *The Virginian* (1902, rpt Lincoln and London: University of Nebraska Press, 1992).

Young, Alexander (ed.), *Chronicles of the Pilgrim Fathers of the Colony of Plymouth, 1602–1625* (1841, rpt New York: Da Capo Press, 1971).

Zamora, Bernice, *Releasing Serpents* (Tempe, AZ: Bilingual Press/Editorial Bilingüe, 1994).

Ziff, Larzer (ed.), *John Cotton on the Churches of New England* (Cambridge, MA: The Belknap Press of Harvard University Press, 1968).

Ziff, Larzer (ed.), *The Literature of America: The Colonial Period* (New York: McGraw-Hill, 1970).

Ziff, Larzer, *Puritanism in America: New Culture in a New World* (New York: Viking Press, London, Oxford University Press, 1973).

Index